Praise for *Cyber Security Engineering*

"This book presents a wealth of extremely useful material and makes it available from a single source."

—*Nadya Bartol, Vice President of Industry Affairs and Cybersecurity Strategist, Utilities Technology Council*

"Drawing from more than 20 years of applied research and use, CSE serves as both a comprehensive reference and a practical guide for developing assured, secure systems and software—addressing the full lifecycle; manager and practitioner perspectives; and people, process, and technology dimensions."

—*Julia Allen, Principal Researcher, Software Engineering Institute*

Cyber Security Engineering

The SEI Series in Software Engineering

Software Engineering Institute of Carnegie Mellon University and Addison-Wesley

 Software Engineering Institute | **Carnegie Mellon University**

Visit **informit.com/sei** for a complete list of available publications.

The SEI Series in Software Engineering is a collaborative undertaking of the Carnegie Mellon Software Engineering Institute (SEI) and Addison-Wesley to develop and publish books on software engineering and related topics. The common goal of the SEI and Addison-Wesley is to provide the most current information on these topics in a form that is easily usable by practitioners and students.

Titles in the series describe frameworks, tools, methods, and technologies designed to help organizations, teams, and individuals improve their technical or management capabilities. Some books describe processes and practices for developing higher-quality software, acquiring programs for complex systems, or delivering services more effectively. Other books focus on software and system architecture and product-line development. Still others, from the SEI's CERT Program, describe technologies and practices needed to manage software and network security risk. These and all titles in the series address critical problems in software engineering for which practical solutions are available.

Make sure to connect with us!
informit.com/socialconnect

 | |
Addison
Wesley

ALWAYS LEARNING

PEARSON

Cyber Security Engineering

A Practical Approach for Systems and Software Assurance

Nancy R. Mead
Carol C. Woody

✦ Addison-Wesley

Boston • Columbus • Indianapolis • New York • San Francisco
Amsterdam • Cape Town • Dubai • London • Madrid • Milan • Munich
Paris • Montreal • Toronto • Delhi • Mexico City • São Paulo • Sydney
Hong Kong • Seoul • Singapore • Taipei • Tokyo

Carnegie Mellon
Software Engineering Institute

The SEI Series in Software Engineering

For my husband Woody—he was my mentor,
sounding board, and best friend

—Nancy

With thanks to my husband Robert for his constant
love and support and in memory of my parents who
taught me the value of hard work and the constant
pursuit of knowledge

—Carol

Contents at a Glance

Register your copy of *Cyber Security Engineering* at informit.com for convenient access to downloads, updates, and corrections as they become available. To start the registration process, go to informit.com/register and log in or create an account. Enter the product ISBN 9780134189802 and click Submit. Once the process is complete, you will find any available bonus content under "Registered Products."

Contents

Acknowledgments

We are pleased to acknowledge the encouragement and support of many people who were involved in the book development process. Rich Pethia and Bill Wilson, the leaders of the CERT Division at the Software Engineering Institute (SEI), encouraged us to write the book and provided support to make it possible. Our SEI technical editors edited and formatted the entire manuscript and provided many valuable suggestions for improvement, as well as helping with packaging questions. Sandy Shrum and Barbara White helped with the early drafts. Hollen Barmer worked across the Christmas holidays to edit the draft. Matthew Penna was tremendously helpful in editing and formatting the final draft for submission. Pennie Walters, one of our editors, and Sheila Rosenthal, our head librarian, helped with obtaining needed permissions to use previously published materials.

Much of the work is based on material published with other authors. We greatly appreciated the opportunity to collaborate with these authors, and their names are listed in the individual chapters that they contributed to, directly or indirectly. In addition, we would like to acknowledge the contributions of Mark Ardis and Andrew Kornecki to Chapter 4, and Gary McGraw to Chapter 5.

Julia Allen of the SEI provided internal review, prior to the initial submission to the publisher. Her review led to a number of revisions and improvements to the book. We also appreciate the inputs and thoughtful comments of the Addison-Wesley reviewers: Nadya Bartol and Ian Bryant. Nadya reminded us of the many standards available in this area, and Ian provided an international perspective.

We would like to recognize the encouragement and support of our contacts at Addison-Wesley. These include Kim Boedigheimer, publishing partner; Lori Lyons, project editor; and Dhayanidhi, production manager. We also appreciate the efforts of the Addison-Wesley and SEI artists and designers who assisted with the cover design, layout, and figures.

About the Authors

Dr. Nancy R. Mead is a Fellow and Principal Researcher at the Software Engineering Institute (SEI). She is also an Adjunct Professor of Software Engineering at Carnegie Mellon University. She is currently involved in the study of security requirements engineering and the development of software assurance curricula. She served as director of software engineering education for the SEI from 1991 to 1994. Her research interests are in the areas of software security, software requirements engineering, and software architectures.

Prior to joining the SEI, Dr. Mead was a senior technical staff member at IBM Federal Systems, where she spent most of her career in the development and management of large real-time systems. She also worked in IBM's software engineering technology area and managed IBM Federal Systems' software engineering education department. She has developed and taught numerous courses on software engineering topics, both at universities and in professional education courses, and she has served on many advisory boards and committees.

Dr. Mead has authored more than 150 publications and invited presentations. She is a Fellow of the Institute of Electrical and Electronic Engineers, Inc. (IEEE) and the IEEE Computer Society, and is a Distinguished Educator of the Association for Computing Machinery. She received the 2015 Distinguished Education Award from the IEEE Computer Society Technical Council on Software Engineering. The Nancy Mead Award for Excellence in Software Engineering Education is named for her and has been awarded since 2010, with Professor Mary Shaw as the first recipient.

Dr. Mead received her PhD in mathematics from the Polytechnic Institute of New York, and received a BA and an MS in mathematics from New York University.

Dr. Carol C. Woody has been a senior member of the technical staff at the Software Engineering Institute since 2001. Currently she is the manager of the Cyber Security Engineering team, which focuses on building capabilities in defining, acquiring, developing, measuring, managing, and sustaining secure software for highly complex networked systems as well as systems of systems.

Dr. Woody leads engagements with industry and the federal government to improve the trustworthiness and reliability of the software products and capabilities we build, buy, implement, and use. She has helped organizations identify effective security risk management solutions, develop approaches to improve their ability to identify security and survivability requirements, and field software and systems with greater assurance. For example, she worked with the Department of Homeland Security (DHS) on defining security guidelines for its implementation of wireless emergency alerting so originators such as the National Weather Service and commercial mobile service providers such as Verizon and AT&T could ensure that the emergency alerts delivered to your cell phones are trustworthy. Her publications define capabilities for measuring, managing, and sustaining cyber security for highly complex networked systems and systems of systems. In addition, she has developed and delivered training to transition assurance capabilities to the current and future workforce.

Dr. Woody has held roles in consulting, strategic planning, and project management. She has successfully implemented technology solutions for banking, mining, clothing and tank manufacturing, court and land records management, financial management, human resources management, and social welfare administration, using such diverse capabilities as data mining, artificial intelligence, document image capture, and electronic workflow.

Dr. Woody is a senior member of the Institute of Electrical and Electronic Engineers, Inc. Computer Society and a senior member of the Association for Computing Machinery. She holds a BS in mathematics from the College of William & Mary, an MBA with distinction from The Babcock School at Wake Forest University, and a PhD in information systems from NOVA Southeastern University.

Foreword

Why, Why, Why…???

- Why this topic matters and why this book?
- Why me and why these authors?
- Why should you read and use this book?

Information Technology (IT) matters. The security of IT matters. IT is ubiquitous. We depend on it working as intended every minute of every day. All too often, IT is designed and built for a pristine, uncontested environment. But this is not the real world—the world in which we live, work, and play. The real world is not a scientific "clean room." Competitive adversaries will take advantage of known flaws in IT and even insert their own weaknesses to exploit later. We need to do a better job of building security into the IT we develop. We also need to do a better job of managing security risks in the IT we buy and use. This book will help all of us to "build security in" and make better decisions about risks in IT and the enterprises it enables.

The world is in the throes of a technological revolution. At first, it primarily focused on mechanical systems. Later, it expanded to electro-mechanical systems. Now, it's mostly electronic (or digital) systems. Microelectronic hardware (HW) and software (SW) are embedded within devices that are being networked together to maximize system effectiveness and efficiency. We have nearly completed the first two phases of this revolution. But we are still in the middle of the third, digital phase, in which people and the tools they use are becoming more and more dependent on information and digital systems.

While IT itself is fairly mature, IT security is not. A single, agreed-upon methodology for securing IT systems simply doesn't exist. This book takes the realistic approach of sampling and presenting a variety of perspectives on how to best "build IT security in." It establishes a common language to use in designing IT systems and making risk tradeoffs throughout their lifecycles. Everyone agrees that it is difficult to manage what we can't measure. To develop consistent, repeatable, transferable information that leads to trust in and confident use of secure IT, we first must agree on how to measure IT security. This book identifies methods to close that confidence gap throughout the IT lifecycle. Using its suggested measurement techniques can transform IT security from an art into a science.

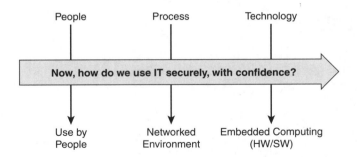

With more than 42 years of experience in improving organizational processes—including leveraging the skills of people to use the tools and technologies at their disposal—I have most recently (2009-present) worked in the Office of the Department of Defense, Chief Information Officer for Cybersecurity (DoD-CIO/Cybersecurity). I lead security efforts for IT and the science of IT security, or as this book describes it, "Cyber Security Engineering." I met Nancy Mead and Carol Woody early in this most recent endeavor. They have continuously provided expertise and leadership to improve the academic discipline contributing to this "Practical Approach for Systems and Software Assurance" and advancing the science and discipline for all of us to use.

Thank you, Nancy and Carol, for your continuing research in this challenging area. Thanks also for your ongoing collaboration with like-minded cyber security professionals such as Warren Axelrod, Dan Shoemaker, and other subject matter experts who have contributed to this book's content.

—Donald R. Davidson, Jr.
Deputy Director for Cybersecurity (CS)
Implementation and CS/Acquisition
Integration in the Office of the DoD-CIO for Cybersecurity (CS)

Preface

The Goals and Purpose for This Book

Security problems are on the front page of newspapers daily. A primary cause is that software is not designed and built to operate securely. Perfect security is not achievable for software that must also be usable and maintainable and fast and cheap, but realistic security choices do not happen by accident. They must be engineered. Software is in every field and all those involved in its construction and use must learn how to choose wisely.

Security has traditionally been dealt with in operational, production environments as a reactive process focused on compliance mandates and response to incidents. Engineering requires structuring the capability to proactively plan and design for security during development and acquisition. Determining what security actions to take based on budget and schedule is not effective.

The book is primarily a reference and tutorial to expose readers to the range of capabilities available for building more secure systems and software. It could be used as an accompanying text in an advanced academic course or in a continuing education setting. Although it contains best practices and research results, it is not a "cookbook" which is designed to provide predictable repeatable outcomes.

After reading this book, the reader will be prepared to:

- Define and structure metrics to manage cyber security engineering

- Identify and evaluate existing competencies and capabilities for cyber security engineering

- Identify competency and capability gaps for cyber security engineering

- Define and prioritize cyber security engineering needs

- Explore a range of options for addressing cyber security engineering needs

- Plan for improvements in cyber security engineering performance

The book will begin with an introduction to seven principles of software assurance followed by chapters addressing the key areas of cyber security engineering. The principles presented in this book provide a structure for prioritizing the wide range of possible actions, helping to establish why some actions should be a priority and how to justify the investments required to take them. Existing security materials focus heavily on the actions to be taken (best practices) with little explanation of why they are needed and how one can recognize if actions are being performed effectively. This book is structured using a group of assurance principles that form a foundation of why actions are needed and how to go about addressing them.

Audience for This Book

The audience for this book is broad, and includes systems and software engineering, quality engineering, reliability and security managers and practitioners. The book targets an interdisciplinary audience including acquisition, software and systems engineering, and operations, since all of them have a vested interest in ensuring that systems and software operate securely.

Some basic background in software engineering or the software and acquisition life cycles is needed. The reader should also understand the importance of cyber security and the difficulties of engineering, developing, and acquiring secure software. Although not a requirement, it would help if they have read other books in the SEI Software Engineering or Software Security Series.

Organization and Content

This book provides material for multiple audiences. Not everyone may want to read all of the material, so we offer the following guide to the chapters.

Chapter 1 lays the groundwork for why a lifecycle approach to cyber security engineering is critical for ensuring system and software security. All audiences should read this material.

Chapter 2 focuses on ways to define and prioritize cyber security engineering needs. Threat and risk analysis are key capabilities, and this chapter provides material about specific methods and practices needed by those performing cyber security engineering to determine and prioritize needs. Both practitioners and students wishing to develop skills in this area can benefit from reading this material.

Chapters 3 and 4 focus on the critical competencies and capabilities needed organizationally, programmatically, and technically to perform cyber security engineering for systems and software. This material can benefit project staff and managers who want to learn how to evaluate existing capabilities and establish resource needs. Technical leaders and practitioners can find out how cyber security engineering competencies figure into a longer-term career strategy.

Chapter 5 provides examples of gap analysis, from both organizational and engineering perspectives. Such analysis identifies the gaps in competencies and capabilities needed to successfully perform cyber security engineering.

Chapter 6 provides information about metrics for cyber security. Those who manage, monitor, and perform software and system engineering can benefit from this material.

Chapter 7 presents options for addressing cyber security needs gathered from standards, best practices, and highly regarded sources. Both practitioners and students of cyber security engineering should become familiar with this content.

Chapter 8 provides a summary of current cyber security engineering capabilities and suggests ways to evaluate and improve cyber security engineering practice. This material is of particular interest to cyber security practitioners and those who manage these resources.

Additional Content

The book's companion website for Cyber Security Engineering is:

www.cert.org/cybersecurity-engineering/

In addition, for purchasers of this book, we are providing free access to our online course: **Software Assurance for Executives**. This course provides an excellent overview of software assurance topics for busy managers and executives. To obtain access to Software Assurance for Executives, please send an email to:

stepfwd-support@cert.org

RE: SwA Executive Course

Chapter 1

Cyber Security Engineering: Lifecycle Assurance of Systems and Software

with Warren Axelrod and Dan Shoemaker

In This Chapter

- 1.1 Introduction
- 1.2 What Do We Mean by Lifecycle Assurance?
- 1.3 Introducing Principles for Software Assurance
- 1.4 Addressing Lifecycle Assurance
- 1.5 Case Studies Used in This Book

1.1 Introduction

Everything we do these days involves system and software technology: Cars, planes, banks, restaurants, stores, telephones, appliances, and entertainment rely extensively on technology. The operational security of these software-intensive systems depends on the practices and techniques used during their design and development. Many decisions made during acquisition and development have an impact on the options for security once systems are deployed. Quality is important, but simply reducing software defects is not sufficient for effective operational security. Lifecycle processes must consider the security-related risks inherent in the operational environments where systems are deployed. Increased consideration of operational security risk earlier in the acquisition and development processes provides an opportunity to tune decisions to address security risk and reduce the total cost of operational security. This book provides key operational management approaches, methodologies, and practices for assuring a greater level of software and system security throughout the development and acquisition lifecycle.

This book contains recommendations to guide software professionals in creating a comprehensive lifecycle process for system and software security. That process allows organizations to incorporate widely accepted and well-defined assurance approaches into their own specific methods for ensuring operational security of their software and system assets. It's worth pointing out that the material in this book is applicable to many different types of systems. Although many of our recommendations originated from our work in information systems security, the recommendations are equally applicable to systems used to support critical infrastructure, such as industrial control systems and SCADA (supervisory control and data acquisition) systems. The same can be said for other hardware/software systems that are not primarily information systems but exist to support other missions.

This book also provides a learning tool for those not familiar with the means and methods needed in acquisition and development to address operational security. Today's tools and existing products allow almost anyone to create a software-based system that meets its functional requirements, but critical skills and practices are needed to ensure secure deployment results.

The exponential increase in cybercrime is a perfect example of how rapidly change is happening in cyberspace and why operational security is a critical need. In the 1990s, computer crime was usually nothing more than simple trespasses. Twenty-five years later, computer crime has become a vast criminal enterprise, with profits estimated at $1 trillion annually. And one of the primary contributors to this astonishing success is the vulnerability of America's software to exploitation through defects. How pervasive is the problem of vulnerability? Veracode, a major software security firm, found that "58 percent of all software applications across supplier types [failed] to meet acceptable levels of security in 2010" [Veracode 2012].

Increased system complexity, pervasive interconnectivity, and widely distributed access have increased the challenges for building and acquiring operationally secure capabilities. Therefore, the aim of this book is to show you how to create and ensure persistent operational assurance practice across all of the typical activities that take place across the system and software lifecycle.

1.2 What Do We Mean by Lifecycle Assurance?

The accelerating pace of attacks and the apparent tendency toward more vulnerabilities seem to suggest that the gap between attacks and data protection is widening as our ability to deal with them seems to diminish. Much of the information protection in place today is based on principles established by Saltzer and Schroeder in "The Protection of Information in Computer Systems," which appeared in *Communications of the ACM* in 1974. They defined security as "techniques that control who may use or modify the computer or the information contained in it" and described three main categories of concern: confidentiality, integrity, and availability (CIA) [Saltzer 1974].

As security problems expanded to include malware, viruses, Structured Query Language (SQL) injections, cross-site scripting, and other mechanisms, those problems changed the structure of software and how it performs. Focusing just on information protection proved vastly insufficient. Also, the role of software in systems expanded such that software now controls the majority of functionality, making the impact of a security failure more critical. Those working with deployed systems refer to this enhanced security need as *cyber security assurance*, and those in the areas of acquisition and development typically reference *software assurance*. Many definitions of each have appeared, including these:

- "The level of confidence we have that a system behaves as expected and the security risks associated with the business use of the software are acceptable" [Woody 2014]

- "The level of confidence that software is free from vulnerabilities, either intentionally designed into the software or accidentally inserted at any time during its lifecycle, and that the software functions in the intended manner"[1]

- "Software Assurance: Implementing software with a level of confidence that the software functions as intended and is free of vulnerabilities, either intentionally or unintentionally designed or inserted as part of the software, throughout the lifecycle" [Woody 2014]

---

1. U.S. Department of Transportation Federal Aviation Administration Order 1370.109 http://www.faa .gov/documentLibrary/media/Order/1370.109.pdf

However, the most recent set of definitions of software assurance from the Committee on National Security Systems [CNSS 2015] takes a different tack, using DoD and NASA definitions:

- "The level of confidence that software functions as intended and is free of vulnerabilities, either intentionally or unintentionally designed or inserted as part of the software throughout the lifecycle" [DoD 2012]

- "The planned and systematic set of activities that ensure that software lifecycle processes and products conform to requirements, standards, and procedures" [NASA 2004]

Finally, the ISO standards provide comprehensive coverage of the various topics, although the topics appear in various places in the standards, and not necessarily in a concise definition [ISO/IEC 2008a, 2008b, 2009, 2011, 2015].

As shown in Table 1.1, the various definitions of *software assurance* generally include the requirement that software functions as expected or intended. Referring to the definitions, it is usually more feasible to achieve an acceptable risk level (although what that risk level might be remains somewhat obscure) than to feel confident that software is free from vulnerabilities. But how do you know how many vulnerabilities actually remain? In practice, you might continue looking for errors, weaknesses, and vulnerabilities until diminishing returns make it apparent that further testing does not pay. However, it is not always obvious when you are at that point. This is especially the case when testing for cyber security vulnerabilities, since software is delivered into many different contexts and the variety of cyberattacks is virtually limitless.

Since we are increasingly seeing the integration and interoperation of security-critical and safety-critical systems, it makes sense to come up with an overarching definition of software assurance that covers both security and safety. In some ways, the different approaches suggested by the existing definitions result from risks related to modern systems of systems.

Further challenges to effective operational security[2] come from the increased use of commercial off-the-shelf (COTS) and open source software as components within a system. The resulting operational systems integrate software from many sources, and each piece of software is assembled as a discrete product.

Shepherding a software-intensive system through project development to deployment is just the beginning of the saga. Sustainment (maintaining a deployed system

---

2. These ideas are adapted from "Sustaining Software Intensive Systems—A Complex Security Challenge," by Carol Woody, which appears in *Cyber Security: Strengthening Corporate Resilience*, a 2007 booklet from Cutter.

Table 1.1 *Comparison of Software Assurance Definitions from Various Sources*

Definition of Software Assurance Refers to	Woody 2014	MITRE	CNSS 2009	CNSS April 2015		ISO/IEC 15408 Parts 1, 2, and 3	ISO/IEC 27034 Parts 1 and 2
				DoDI 5200.44	NASA-STD 8739.8		
Level of confidence	X	X	X	X		X	X
Functions as intended	X	X	X	X	X	X	X
Free from vulnerabilities		X	X	X		X	X
Intentionally or accidentally inserted		X	X	X		X	
Software lifecycle process		X	X	X		X	X
Acceptable business risks	X					X	X
Business use of software	X					X	X
Set of activities that conform to product requirements, standards, and procedures					X	X	X

over time as technology and operational needs change) is a confusing and multifaceted challenge: Each discrete piece of a software-intensive system is enhanced and repaired independently and reintegrated for operational use. As today's systems increasingly rely on COTS software, the issues surrounding sustainment grow more complex. Ignoring these issues can undermine the stability, security, and longevity of systems in production.

The myth linked to systems built using COTS products is that commercial products are mature, stable, and adhere to well-recognized industry standards. The reality indicates more of a Rube Goldberg mix of "glue code" that links the pieces and parts into a working structure. Changing any one of the components—a constant event since vendors provide security updates on their own schedules—can trigger a complete restructuring to return the pieces to a working whole. This same type of sustainment challenge for accommodating system updates appears for system components built to function as common services in an enterprise environment.

Systems cannot be constructed to eliminate security risk but must incorporate capabilities to recognize, resist, and recover from attacks. Initial acquisition and design must prepare the system for implementation and sustainment. As a result, assurance must be planned across the lifecycle to ensure effective operational security over time.

Within this book we use the following definition of software assurance developed to incorporate lifecycle assurance [Mead 2010a]:

Application of technologies and processes to achieve a required level of confidence that software systems and services function in the intended manner, are free from accidental or intentional vulnerabilities, provide security capabilities appropriate to the threat environment, and recover from intrusions and failures.

1.3 Introducing Principles for Software Assurance

In 1974, Saltzer and Schroeder proposed software design principles that focus on protection mechanisms to "guide the design and contribute to an implementation without security flaws" [Saltzer 1974]. Students still learn these principles in today's *macrocycle* classrooms [Saltzer 1974]:

- **Economy of mechanism**—Keep the design as simple and small as possible.
- **Fail-safe defaults**—Base access decisions on permission rather than exclusion.
- **Complete mediation**—Every access to every object must be checked for authority.

- **Open design**—The design should not be secret. The mechanisms should not depend on the ignorance of potential attackers but rather on the possession of specific, and more easily protected, keys or passwords.

- **Separation of privilege**—Where feasible, a protection mechanism that requires two keys to unlock it is more robust and flexible than one that allows access to the presenter of only a single key.

- **Least privilege**—Every program and every user of the system should operate using the least set of privileges necessary to complete the job.

- **Least common mechanism**—Minimize the amount of mechanism common to more than one user and depended on by all users.

- **Psychological acceptability**—It is essential that the human interface be designed for ease of use so that users routinely and automatically apply the protection mechanisms correctly.

Time has shown the value and utility in these principles, but new challenges surfaced soon after Saltzer and Schroeder proposed them. The Morris worm generated a massive denial of service by infecting more than 6,000 UNIX machines on November 2, 1988 [Wikipedia 2011a]. An advanced operating system, Multiple Virtual Storage (MVS), where memory sharing was now available to all programs under control of the OS, was released in March of the same year [Wikipedia 2011b]. As a result, the security of the operating system became of utmost importance. Although Saltzer and Schroeder's principles still apply to security within an individual piece of technology, they are no longer sufficient to address the complexity and sophistication of the environment within which that component must operate.

We propose a set of seven principles focused on addressing the challenges of acquiring, building, deploying, and sustaining systems to achieve a desired level of confidence for software assurance:

1. **Risk shall be properly understood in order to drive appropriate assurance decisions**—A perception of risk drives assurance decisions. Organizations without effective software assurance perceive risks based on successful attacks to software and systems and usually respond reactively. They may implement assurance choices such as policies, practices, tools, and restrictions based on their perception of the threat of a similar attack and the expected impact if that threat is realized. Organizations can incorrectly perceive risk when they do not understand their threats and impacts. Effective software assurance requires organizations to share risk knowledge among all stakeholders and technology participants. Too frequently, organizations consider risk information

highly sensitive do not share it; protecting the information in this way results in uninformed organizations making poor risk choices.

2. **Risk concerns shall be aligned across all stakeholders and all interconnected technology elements**—Highly connected systems like the Internet require aligning risk across all stakeholders and all interconnected technology elements; otherwise, critical threats are missed or ignored at different points in the interactions. It is not sufficient to consider only highly critical components when everything is highly interconnected. Interactions occur at many technology levels (e.g., network, security appliances, architecture, applications, data storage) and are supported by a wide range of roles. Protections can be applied at each of these points and may conflict if not well orchestrated. Because of interactions, effective assurance requires that all levels and roles consistently recognize and respond to risk.

3. **Dependencies shall not be trusted until proven trustworthy**—Because of the wide use of supply chains for software, assurance of an integrated product depends on other people's assurance decisions and the level of trust placed on these dependencies. The integrated software inherits all the assurance limitations of each interacting component. In addition, unless specific restrictions and controls are in place, every operational component, including infrastructure, security software, and other applications, depends on the assurance of every other component. There is a risk each time an organization must depend on others' assurance decisions. Organizations must decide how much trust they place in dependencies based on realistic assessments of the threats, impacts, and opportunities represented by various interactions. Dependencies are not static, and organizations must regularly review trust relationships to identify changes that warrant reconsideration. The following examples describe assurance losses resulting from dependencies:

   • Defects in standardized pieces of infrastructure (e.g., operating systems, development platforms, firewalls, and routers) can serve as widely available threat entry points for applications.

   • Using many standardized software tools to build technology establishes a dependency for the assurance of the resulting software product. Vulnerabilities can be introduced into software products by the tool builders.

4. **Attacks shall be expected**—A broad community of attackers with growing technology capabilities can compromise the confidentiality, integrity, and availability of an organization's technology assets. There are no perfect protections against attacks, and the attacker profile is constantly changing. Attackers use

technology, processes, standards, and practices to craft compromises (known as socio-technical responses). Some attacks take advantage of the ways we normally use technology, and others create exceptional situations to circumvent defenses.

5. **Assurance requires effective coordination among all technology participants**—The organization must apply protection broadly across its people, processes, and technology because attackers take advantage of all possible entry points. The organization must clearly establish authority and responsibility for assurance at an appropriate level in the organization to ensure that the organization effectively participates in software assurance. This assumes that all participants know about assurance, but that is not usually the case. Organizations must educate people on software assurance.

6. **Assurance shall be well planned and dynamic**—Assurance must represent a balance among governance, construction, and operation of software and systems and is highly sensitive to changes in each of these areas. Assurance requires an adaptive response to constant changes in applications, interconnections, operational usage, and threats. Assurance is not a once-and-done activity. It must continue beyond the initial operational implementation through operational sustainment. Assurance cannot be added later; it must be built to the level of acceptable assurance that organizations need. No one has resources to redesign systems every time the threats change, and adjusting assurance after a threat has become reality is impossible.

7. **A means to measure and audit overall assurance shall be built in**—Organizations cannot manage what they do not measure, and stakeholders and technology users do not address assurance unless they are held accountable for it. Assurance does not compete successfully with other competing needs unless results are monitored and measured. All elements of the socio-technical environment, including practices, processes, and procedures, must be tied together to evaluate operational assurance. Organizations with more successful assurance measures react and recover faster, learn from their reactive responses and those of others, and are more vigilant in anticipating and detecting attacks. Defects per lines of code is a common development measure that may be useful for code quality but is not sufficient evidence for overall assurance because it provides no perspective on how that code behaves in an operational context. Organizations must take focused and systemic measures to ensure that the components are engineered with sound security and that the interaction among components establishes effective assurance.

1.4 Addressing Lifecycle Assurance[3]

In general, we build and acquire operational systems through coordinated actions involving a set of predefined steps referred to as a *lifecycle*. Most organizations use a lifecycle model of some type, although these models vary from one organization to another. In this book, the approaches we describe relate to particular lifecycle activities, but we try to be independent of specific lifecycle models. Standards such as ISO 15288 and NIST SP 800-160 can provide guidance to those looking for additional background on suitable lifecycles in support of software assurance.

Organizations make or buy their technology to meet specified performance parameters but rarely consider the ways in which a new development or acquisition functions within its intended deployment environment and the unintended consequences that are possible. For example, security defects (also referred to as *vulnerabilities*) provide opportunities for attackers to gain access to confidential data, disrupt access to system capabilities, and make unauthorized changes to data and software. Organizations tend to view higher quality and greater security as increasing operational cost, but they fail to consider the total cost of ownership over the long term, which includes the cost of dealing with future compromises. The lack of a comprehensive strategy in approaching how a system or software product is constructed, operated, and maintained creates fertile ground for compromise.

Every component of the software system and its interfaces must be operated and sustained with organizational risk in mind. The planning and execution of the response is a strategic requirement, which brings the absolute requirement for comprehensive lifecycle protection processes into the discussion.

There is always uncertainty about a software system's behavior. At the start of development, we have very general knowledge of the operational and security challenges that might arise as well as the security behavior that we want when the system is deployed. A quality measure of the design and implementation is the confidence we have that the delivered system will behave as specified.

At the start of a development cycle, we have a limited basis for determining our confidence in the behavior of the delivered system; that is, we have a large gap between our initial level of confidence and the desired level of confidence. Over the development lifecycle, we need to reduce that confidence gap, as shown in Figure 1.1, to reach the desired level of confidence for the delivered system.

With existing software security practices, we can apply source-code static analysis and testing toward the end of the lifecycle. For the earlier lifecycle phases, we need to evaluate how the engineering decisions made during design affect the injection or

---

3. Material in this section comes from *Predicting Software Assurance Using Quality and Reliability Measures* [Woody 2014].

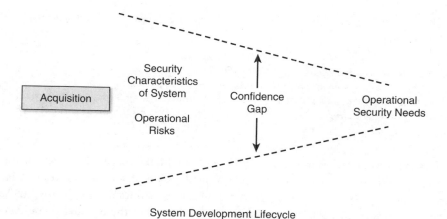

Figure 1.1 *Confidence Gap*

removal of defects. Reliability depends on identifying and mitigating potential faults. Software security failure modes, such as unverified input data, are exploitable conditions. A design review must confirm that the business risks linked to fault, vulnerability, and defect consequences are identified and mitigated by specific design features. Software-intensive systems are complex; it is not surprising that the analysis—even when an expert designer performs it—can be incomplete, can overlook a security problem, or can make simplifying but invalid development and operating assumptions.

Our confidence in the engineering of software must be based on more than opinion. If we claim the resulting system will be secure, our confidence in the claim depends on the quality of evidence provided to support the claim, on confirmation that the structure of the argument about the evidence is appropriate to meet the claim, and on the sufficiency of the evidence provided. If we claim that we have reduced vulnerabilities by verifying all inputs, then the results of extensive testing using invalid and valid data provide evidence to support the claim.

We refer to the combination of evidence and argument as an assurance case, which can be defined as follows:[4]

> *Assurance case is a documented body of evidence that provides a convincing and valid argument that a specified set of critical claims about a system's properties are adequately justified for a given application in a given environment.*
>
> *[Kelly 1998]*

---

4. Assurance cases were originally used to show that systems satisfied their safety-critical properties. For this use, they were (and are) called *safety cases*. The notation and approach used here has been used for over a decade in Europe to document why a system is sufficiently safe [Kelly 1998, 2004]. The application of the concept to reliability was documented in an SAE standard [SAE 2004]. We extend the concept to cover system security claims.

ISO/IEC 15026 provides the following alternative definition of an assurance case [ISO/IEC 2007]:

An assurance case includes a top-level claim for a property of a system or product (or set of claims), systematic argumentation regarding this claim, and the evidence and explicit assumptions that underlie this argumentation. Arguing through multiple levels of subordinate claims, this structured argumentation connects the top-level claim to the evidence and assumptions.

An analysis of an assurance case does not evaluate the process by which an engineering decision was made. Rather, it is a justification of a predicted result based on available information (evidence). An assurance case does not imply any kind of guarantee or certification. It is simply a way to document the rationale behind system design decisions.

Doubts play a significant role in justifying claims. During a review, an assurance case developer must justify through evidence that a set of claims has been met. A typical reviewer looks for reasons to doubt the claim. For example, a reviewer might do any of the following:

- **Doubt the claim**—There is information that contradicts the claim.
- **Doubt the argument**—For example, the static analysis does not apply to the claim that a specific vulnerability has been eliminated or the analysis does not consider the case in which the internal network has been compromised.
- **Doubt the evidence**—For example, the security testing or static analysis was done by inexperienced staff or the testing plan does not sufficiently consider recovery following a compromise.

Quality and reliability can be considered evidence to be incorporated into an argument about predicted software security. Standard and policy frameworks become an important part of this discussion because they are the software industry's accepted means of structuring and documenting best practice. Frameworks and policies encapsulate and then communicate a complete and coherently logical concept as well as methods of tailoring the approach for use by a particular aspect of "real-world" work. Frameworks for a defined area of work are created and endorsed by recognized entities such as the Software Engineering Institute (SEI), International Organization for Standardization (ISO), National Institute of Standards and Technology (NIST), Institute of Electrical and Electronics Engineers (IEEE), and Association for Computing Machinery (ACM).

Each framework typically focuses on a specific aspect of the lifecycle. The SEI has published several process models that center on communicating a particular approach to an issue or concern. Within the process domain, some SEI models focus on applying best practices to create a more effective software organization. Many widely accepted frameworks predate the emergence of critical operational security concerns and do not effectively address security.

1.5 Case Studies Used in This Book

Throughout the book we use three case studies to illustrate real problems that organizations and individuals face:

- **Wireless Emergency Alerts (WEA)**—A real system for issuing emergency alerts
- **Fly-By-Night Airlines**—A fictitious airline with realistic problems
- **GoFast Automotive**—A fictitious automobile manufacturer with realistic problems

Brief descriptions of each case study follow, and we recommend that you familiarize yourself with these case study descriptions to understand the context for the case study vignettes that appear.

1.5.1 Wireless Emergency Alerts Case Study[5]

The Wireless Emergency Alerts (WEA) service is a collaborative partnership that includes

- The cellular industry
- Federal Communications Commission (FCC)
- Federal Emergency Management Agency (FEMA)
- U.S. Department of Homeland Security (DHS) Science and Technology Directorate (S&T)

---

5. This case study was developed by Christopher Alberts and Audrey Dorofee to use in training materials for Security Engineering Risk Analysis (SERA).

The WEA service enables local, tribal, state, territorial, and federal public safety officials to send geographically targeted emergency text alerts to the public.

An *emergency alert* is a message sent by an authorized organization that provides details of an occurring or pending emergency situation to designated groups of people. Alerts are initiated by many diverse organizations—for example, AMBER alerts from law enforcement and weather alerts from the National Weather Service.

Wireless emergency alerts are text messages sent to mobile devices, such as cell phones and pagers. The process of issuing this type of alert begins with a request from an initiator (such as law enforcement or the National Weather Service) to submit an alert. The request is forwarded to an organization that is called an alert originator (AO). A team from the AO receives the initiator alert request and decides whether to issue the alert. If it decides to issue the alert, it then determines the distribution channels for the alert (for example, television, radio, roadside signs, wireless technologies).

If the team decides to issue a wireless emergency alert, an operator from the AO enters the *alert message* into an alert originating system (AOS), which then formats the message. The AOS forwards the alert message to FEMA systems, which validate and process it. After the FEMA systems process the alert message, they then forward it to cellular service providers (for example, AT&T, Verizon). Finally, the cellular service providers send a text message to recipients with capable devices in the targeted geographic area.

1.5.2 Fly-By-Night Airlines Case Study[6]

Fly-Florida Airlines was a small regional passenger airline serving Florida cities. In late 2013, it merged with two other regional airlines, becoming Fly-By-Night Airlines. It now serves airports throughout the southeastern United States and is headquartered in Orlando, Florida.

At a recent meeting of the executive board of Fly-By-Night Airlines, the board discussed ways to increase business and retain and expand the number of passengers by providing higher-quality service. Also, Fly-By-Night's chief financial officer shared with the board a report which showed that the company could save substantial labor costs by automating certain services. As a result of this discussion, the chief executive officer of Fly-By-Night decided that a web-based automated airline reservations system (ARS) for Fly-By-Night Airlines should be developed, along with a frequent flyer program.

---

6. This case study was developed by Tom Hilburn, professor emeritus, Embry-Riddle Aeronautical University.

With the web-based ARS, passengers can make reservations online. A reservation includes the passenger name, flight number, departure date and time, reservation type (first class, business, coach), a seat number, and the price of the ticket. (As designated by DOT Directive 1573, ticket prices may not change more than once in a 12-hour period.) After the system completes the reservation and verifies the credit card information, the customer can print tickets or use an e-ticket. Passengers can also use the ARS to cancel or change completed reservations and check frequent flyer mileage. In addition, anyone can check the status of a flight (on-time, delayed, canceled). An ARS system administrator can enter flight data and ticket information or get a report on reservations for an existing flight. Reports on reservations must be sent, on a daily basis, to the U.S. Department of Homeland Security.

1.5.3 GoFast Automotive Corporation Case Study

GoFast is one of the "big 4" automobile manufacturers in the United States. It produces cars, sedans, vans, SUVs, and pickup trucks. At times it also produces the Tiger sports car. The Tiger was first introduced in 1965 and saw a revival in 2010. Recently, GoFast has been a leader in incorporating self-driving car features and advanced electronics.

The Tiger dashboard is very appealing to those who are interested in high-tech features. It supports all the options that are available to the driver: front and rear window windshield wipers that can be synchronized, sensors that indicate when other cars are close, cameras that allow the driver to "see through" the blind spot, and front and rear cameras to assist in parking and backing up. Naturally, the Tiger has a sophisticated and proprietary entertainment system that gives GoFast a competitive edge compared to other sports car manufacturers.

Software supports many of the Tiger's systems and some of the systems in GoFast's other models. Software underlies many safety features (e.g., anti-lock braking), self-driving features, and entertainment and communication systems. GoFast develops much of its own software but also uses contractors.

In addition to its software development organization, GoFast has a specialized software security team that is responsible for activities such as security risk assessment, security requirements and architecture development, and security reviews throughout the software development process. The security team is also responsible for development and maintenance of corporate software security process documents and practices. The security team is permitted to test and perform "ethical hacking" of the completed software prior to release and to advise executive management on whether release should take place.

Chapter 2

Risk Analysis—Identifying and Prioritizing Needs

with Christopher Alberts and Audrey Dorofee

In This Chapter

- 2.1 Risk Management Concepts
- 2.2 Mission Risk
- 2.3 Mission Risk Analysis
- 2.4 Security Risk
- 2.5 Security Risk Analysis
- 2.6 Operational Risk Analysis—Comparing Planned to Actual
- 2.7 Summary

Risk management in systems acquisition and development has typically focused exclusively on cost and schedule concerns. Organizations fund desired features and functions selected for implementation based on cost estimates, budget availability, and perceived criticality of need. Organizations closely monitor changes in any of these three areas and make adjustments to planned delivery dates and features based on risk evaluation.

Risk is one of the assurance principles described in Chapter 1, "Cyber Security Engineering: Lifecycle Assurance of Systems and Software," and effective risk management of software assurance is a competency that is not consistently applied in acquisition and development projects. This competency considers what could go wrong and establishes how to reduce, mitigate, or avoid the undesirable results that would occur if the risk were realized. Most project participants focus on how to reach success and dismiss those raising the problems that may impede achieving the project's objectives. A successful project needs both perspectives working collaboratively side by side.

Risk can be connected to systems and software from many directions, and organizations must consider all of those connections to effectively manage risk. Acquisition and development are complex, and opportunities for things to go wrong abound. Effective risk analysis for assurance requires, at a minimum, consideration of the following types of risk:

- Development risk
- Acquisition risk
- Mission risk

Development and acquisition risks typically dominate risk management efforts and relate primarily to cost and schedule. These are actually short-term concerns, but they dominate the early stages of the lifecycle. In this chapter we explore ways to consider the software assurance aspects of all three types of risk.

2.1 Risk Management Concepts

For risk to exist in any circumstance, all of the following must be true [Alberts 2002]:

- The potential for loss exists.
- Uncertainty related to the eventual outcome is present.[1]
- Some choice or decision is required to deal with the uncertainty and potential for loss.

The essence of risk, no matter what the domain, can be succinctly captured by the following definition of risk: *Risk is the probability of suffering harm or loss.*[2]

---

1. Some researchers separate the concepts of certainty (the absence of doubt), risk (where the probabilities of alternative outcomes are known), and uncertainty (where the probabilities of possible outcomes are unknown). However, because uncertainty is a fundamental attribute of risk, we do not differentiate between decision making under risk and decision making under uncertainty.

2. This definition is derived from the definition used in *Introduction to the Security Engineering Risk Analysis (SERA) Framework* [Alberts 2014].

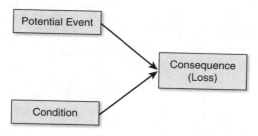

Figure 2.1 *Components of Risk*

Figure 2.1 illustrates the three components of risk:

- **Potential event**—An act, an occurrence, or a happening that alters current conditions and leads to a loss
- **Condition**—The current set of circumstances that leads to or enables risk
- **Consequence**—The loss that results when a potential event occurs; the loss is measured in relationship to the status quo (i.e., current state)

From the risk perspective, a condition is a passive element. It exposes an entity[3] (e.g., project, system) to the loss triggered by the occurrence of an event. However, by itself, a risk condition does not cause an entity to suffer a loss or experience an adverse consequence; it makes the entity vulnerable to the effects of an event [Alberts 2012a].

Consider the following scenario: A project team is developing a software system for a customer. The team has enough people with the right skills to perform its tasks and complete its next milestone on time and within budget (status quo). However, the team does not have redundancy among team members' skills and abilities (condition). If the team loses people with certain key skills (potential event), then it will not be able to complete its assigned tasks (consequence/loss). This puts the next milestone in jeopardy, which is a loss when measured in relationship to the status quo (on track to achieve the next milestone).

However, if none of the team members leaves or is reassigned (the event does not occur), then the project should suffer no adverse consequences. Here, the condition enables the event to produce an adverse consequence or loss.

When a risk occurs, an adverse consequence (a loss) is realized. This consequence ultimately changes the current set of conditions confronting the entity (project or system). In this example, a realized risk means that the project team has lost people

---

3. An *entity* is an object affected by risk. The entities of interest in this chapter are interactively complex, software-reliant systems. Examples include projects, programs, business processes, and networked technologies.

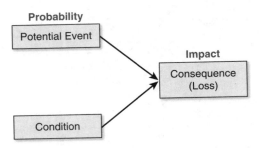

Figure 2.2 *Risk Measures and the Components of Risk (Simplified View)*

and no longer has enough people to complete its assigned tasks. The project now faces a problem that must be resolved. Put another way, the risk has become an issue/problem (a condition that directly results in a loss or adverse consequence).

Three measures are associated with a risk: probability, impact, and risk exposure.[4] The basic relationships between probability and impact and the components of risk are shown in Figure 2.2.[5] In this context, *probability* is defined as a measure of the likelihood that an event will occur, while *impact* is defined as a measure of the loss that occurs when a risk is realized. Risk exposure provides a measure of the magnitude of a risk based on current values of probability and impact.

Risk management is a systematic approach for minimizing exposure to potential losses. It provides a disciplined environment for the following:

- Continuously assessing what could go wrong (i.e., assessing risks)

- Determining which risks to address (i.e., setting mitigation priorities)

- Implementing actions to address high-priority risks through avoidance or mitigation

---

4. A fourth measure, time frame, is sometimes used to measure the length of time before a risk is realized or the length of time in which action can be taken to prevent a risk.

5. The relationships between probability and impact and the components of risk depicted in Figure 2.2 are based on the simplifying assumption that the loss resulting from the occurrence of an event is known with certainty. In many cases, a range of adverse outcomes might be possible. For example, consider a project team that is worried about the consequence of losing team members. The magnitude of the loss will depend on a number of factors, such as which team member leaves the project, whether anyone is available to take the team member's place, the skills and experience of potential replacements, and so forth. The consequence could be minor if an experienced person is available to step in and contribute right away. On the other hand, the consequence could be severe if no one is available to step in and contribute. A range of probable outcomes is thus possible. When multiple outcomes are possible, probabilities are associated with the potential outcomes. As a result, risk analysts must consider two probabilities—one associated with the potential event and another associated with the consequence. However, basic risk assessments assume that the loss is known with relative certainty (or they only focus on the most likely consequence), and only the probability associated with the event is considered.

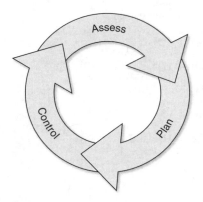

Figure 2.3 *Risk Management Activities*

Figure 2.3 illustrates the three core risk management activities:

- **Assess risk**—Assessment involves transforming concerns people have into distinct, tangible risks that are explicitly documented and analyzed.
- **Plan for controlling risk**—Planning involves determining an approach for addressing each risk and producing a plan for implementing the approach.
- **Control risk**—Controlling risk involves dealing with each risk by implementing its defined control plan and tracking the plan to completion.

When you consider the subactivities under the three main activities, the connection to the well-known "Plan, Do, Check, Act" (PDCA) model is apparent:

- Individuals and interactions over processes and tools
- Working software over comprehensive documentation
  - Attributes
- Responding to change over following a plan
  - Activity 2.1 Assess risk
  - 2.1.1 Identify risk
  - 2.1.2 Analyze risk
  - 2.1.3 Develop risk profile
  - Activity 2.2 Plan for risk control

- 2.2.1 Determine control approach

- 2.2.2 Develop control plan

- Activity 2.3 Control risk

- 2.3.1 Implement control plan

- 2.3.2 Track control plan

- 2.3.3 Make tracking decision

The mapping to PDCA is

- **Plan**—2.2.2 Develop control plan
- **Do**—2.3.1 Implement control plan
- **Check**—2.3.2 Track control plan
- **Act**—2.3.3 Make tracking decision

Everything before subactivity 2.2.2 (risk identification, risk analysis, risk prioritization/risk profile, and control approach) prepares risk management personnel to be able to implement the PDCA cycle. The same type of mapping could be done for the OODA (Observe, Orient, Decide, and Act) decision-making framework.

One of the fundamental conditions of risk is uncertainty regarding its occurrence. A risk, by definition, might or might not occur. With an issue, no uncertainty exists—the condition exists and is having a negative effect on performance.[6] Issues can also lead to (or contribute to) risks by

- Creating a circumstance that enables an event to trigger additional loss

- Making an existing event more likely to occur

- Aggravating the consequences of existing risks

Figure 2.4 illustrates the two components of an issue or a problem:

- **Condition**—The current set of circumstances that produces a loss or an adverse consequence

- **Consequence**—The loss that is triggered by an underlying condition that is present

---

6. Many of the same tools and techniques can be applied to both issue and risk management.

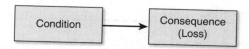

Figure 2.4 *Components of an Issue/Problem*

From the issue perspective, a condition directly causes an entity (e.g., project, system) to suffer a loss or experience an adverse consequence. Unlike a risk, an issue does not need an event to occur to produce a loss or an adverse consequence.

2.2 Mission Risk

From the mission perspective, *risk* is defined as the probability of mission failure (i.e., not achieving key objectives). *Mission risk* aggregates the effects of multiple conditions and events on a system's ability to achieve its mission.

Mission risk analysis is based on systems theory.[7] The underlying principle of systems theory is to analyze a system as a whole rather than decompose it into individual components and then analyze each component separately [Charette 1990]. In fact, some properties of a system are best analyzed by considering the entire system, including the following:

- Influences of environmental factors
- Feedback and nonlinearity among causal factors
- Systemic causes of failure (as opposed to proximate causes)
- Emergent properties

2.3 Mission Risk Analysis

The goal of mission risk analysis is to gauge the extent to which a system is in a position to achieve its mission and objective(s). This type of risk analysis provides a top-down view of how well a system is addressing risks.

The Mission Risk Diagnostic (MRD) [Alberts 2006] is one method that can be used to address this type of analysis. The first step in this type of risk analysis is to establish the objectives that must be achieved. The objectives define the desired

---

7. Because mission risk analysis is based on system theory, the term *systemic risk* can be used synonymously with *mission risk*. The term *mission risk* is used throughout this chapter.

Table 2.1 *Core Tasks of the MRD*

Task	Description
1. Identify the mission and objective(s).	This task establishes the focus of the analysis and the specific aspects of the system that are important to decision makers. One or more objectives are identified during this activity.
2. Identify drivers.	Here, a small set of critical factors (typically 10–25) that have a strong influence on whether the objective(s) will be achieved are established. These factors are called *drivers*.
3. Analyze drivers.	During driver analysis, the value of each driver is evaluated to determine how it is currently influencing performance. Next, the reasons underlying the evaluation of each driver (called the rationale) and any tangible evidence that supports the rationale are documented. Finally, a visual summary of the current values of all drivers relevant to the mission and objectives being assessed is documented.

outcome, or "picture of success," for a system. Next, systemic factors that have a strong influence on the outcome (i.e., whether the objectives will be achieved) are identified. These systemic factors, called *drivers* in this chapter, are important because they define a small set of factors that can be used to assess a system's performance and gauge whether the system is on track to achieve its key objectives. The drivers are then analyzed to enable decision makers to gauge the overall risk to the system's mission.

Table 2.1 presents a summary of the three core tasks that form the basis of the MRD. The MRD comprises 13 tasks that must be completed. (A description of all MRD tasks is provided in Section 5 of the *Mission Risk Diagnostic (MRD) Method Description* [Alberts 2006].)

We describe how to address each of these core tasks in the following sections.

2.3.1 Task 1: Identify the Mission and Objective(s)

The overarching goals when identifying the mission and objective(s) are to (1) define the fundamental purpose, or mission, of the system that is being examined and (2) establish the specific aspects of the mission that are important to decision makers. Once they have been established, the mission and objective(s) provide the foundation for conducting the assessment.

The mission statement is important because it defines the target, or focus, of the analysis effort. Each mission typically comprises multiple objectives. When assessing a system, analysts must select which specific objective(s) will be evaluated during the assessment. Selecting objectives refines the scope of the assessment to address the specific aspects of the mission that are important to decision makers.

While decision makers have a tacit understanding of their objectives, they often cannot precisely articulate or express the objectives in a way that addresses the criteria. If a program's objectives are not clearly articulated, decision makers may have trouble assessing whether the program is on track for success.

2.3.2 Task 2: Identify Drivers

The main goal of driver identification is to establish a set of systemic factors, called *drivers*, that has a strong influence on the eventual outcome or result to be used to measure performance in relation to a program's mission and objectives. Knowledge within the organization can be tapped to review and refine the prototype set of drivers provided in Table 2.2. Once the set of drivers is established, analysts can evaluate each driver in the set to gain insight into the likelihood of achieving the mission and objectives. To measure performance effectively, analysts must ensure that the set of drivers conveys sufficient information about the mission and objective(s) being assessed.

Each driver has two possible states: a success state and a failure state. The *success state* means that the program's processes are helping to guide the program toward a successful outcome (i.e., achieving the objective[s] being evaluated). In contrast, the failure state signifies that the program's processes are driving the program toward a failed outcome (i.e., not achieving the objective[s] being evaluated).

2.3.3. Task 3: Analyze Drivers

Analysis of a driver requires determining how it is currently acting (i.e., its current state) by examining the effects of conditions and potential events on that driver. The goal is to determine whether the driver is

- Almost certainly in its success state
- Most likely in its success state
- Equally likely to be in its success or failure states
- Most likely in its failure state
- Almost certainly in its failure state

This list can be used to define a qualitative scale for driver analysis.

Table 2.2 *Prototype Set of Driver Questions for Software Acquisition and Development Programs*

Driver Name	Driver Question
Program Objectives	Are program objectives (product, cost, schedule) realistic and achievable?
Plan	Is the plan for developing and deploying the system sufficient?
Process	Is the process being used to develop and deploy the system sufficient?
Task Execution	Are tasks and activities performed effectively and efficiently?
Coordination	Are activities within each team and across teams coordinated appropriately?
External Interfaces	Will work products from suppliers, partners, or collaborators meet the program's quality and timeliness requirements?
Information Management	Is the program's information managed appropriately?
Technology	Does the program team have the tools and technologies it needs to develop the system and transition it to operations?
Facilities and Equipment	Are facilities and equipment sufficient to support the program?
Organizational Conditions	Are enterprise, organizational, and political conditions facilitating completion of program activities?
Compliance	Does the program comply with all relevant policies, laws, and regulations?
Event Management	Does the program have sufficient capacity and capability to identify and manage potential events and changing circumstances?
Requirements	Are system requirements well understood?
Architecture and Design	Are the architecture and design sufficient to meet system requirements and provide the desired operational capability?
System Capability	Will the system satisfactorily meet its requirements?
System Integration	Will the system sufficiently integrate and interoperate with other systems when deployed?

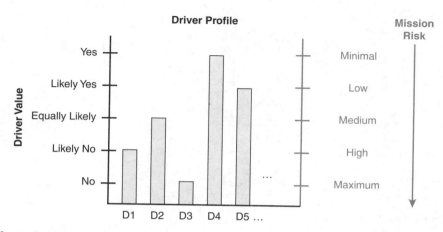

Figure 2.5 *The Relationship Between Driver Value and Mission Risk*

As illustrated in Figure 2.5, a relationship exists between a driver's success state (as depicted in a driver profile) and mission risk. A driver profile shows the probability that drivers are in their success states. Thus, a driver with a high probability of being in its success state (i.e., a high degree of momentum toward the mission) translates to a low degree of mission risk. Likewise, a driver with a low probability of being in its success state (i.e., a high probability of being in its failure state) translates to a high degree of mission risk.

The driver profile thus helps decision makers understand how a system is performing against potential mission risks.

2.4 Security Risk

Security risk is a measure of (1) the likelihood that a threat will exploit a vulnerability to produce an adverse consequence or loss and (2) the magnitude of the loss. Figure 2.6 illustrates the three core components of security risk:

- **Threat**—A cyber act, occurrence, or event that exploits one or more vulnerabilities and leads to an adverse consequence or loss
- **Vulnerability**—A weakness in an information system, system security procedures, internal controls, or implementation that a threat could exploit to produce an adverse consequence or loss; a current condition that leads to or enables security risk

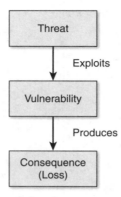

Figure 2.6 *Components of Security Risk*

- **Consequence**—The loss that results when a threat exploits one or more vulnerabilities; the loss is measured in relationship to the status quo (i.e., current state)

From the security perspective, a *vulnerability* is the passive element of risk. It exposes cyber technologies (e.g., software application, software-reliant system) to threats and the losses that those threats can produce. However, by itself, a vulnerability does not cause an entity to suffer a loss or experience an adverse consequence; rather, the vulnerability makes the entity susceptible to the effects of a threat.[8]

The strategy for controlling a risk is based on the measures of the risk (i.e., probability, impact, and risk exposure), which are established during the risk assessment. Decision-making criteria (e.g., for prioritizing risks or deciding when to escalate risks within an organization) can help determine the appropriate strategy for controlling a risk. Common control approaches include the following:

- **Accept**—If a risk occurs, its consequences will be tolerated; no proactive action to address the risk will be taken. When a risk is accepted, the rationale for doing so is documented.
- **Transfer**—Risk mitigation is shifted to another party (e.g., through insurance or outsourcing). The system owner always retains responsibility for managing the risk, even if it is transferred.
- **Avoid**—Activities are restructured to eliminate the possibility of a risk occurring.
- **Mitigate**—Actions are implemented in an attempt to reduce or contain a risk.

---

8. Adapted from the book *Managing Information Security Risks: The OCTAVE Approach* [Alberts 2002].

For any security risk that is not accepted, a security analyst should develop and document a control plan for that risk. A control plan defines a set of actions for implementing the selected control approach. For risks that are being mitigated, plans can include actions from the following categories:

- **Recognize and respond**—Monitor the threat and take action when it is detected.

- **Resist**—Implement protection measures to reduce vulnerability to the threat and minimize any consequences that might occur.

- **Recover**—Recover from the risk if the consequences or losses are realized.

In order to fully address a security risk, it is important to understand the environment in which it resides. The focal point of the environment is the threat actor. A common goal of many threat actors is to inflict harm or loss on a mission's stakeholders. To accomplish that goal, a threat actor first targets data used to support a workflow or mission thread.[9] To access targeted mission data, a threat actor must navigate through the complex network of people, processes, and technologies, looking for weaknesses to exploit in organizational security practices and vulnerabilities in software-reliant systems. Getting to the mission data can be difficult. A threat actor may need to jump from one targeted computer to another when attempting to achieve the goal of the attack. In many cases, an actor may target computers that are owned and maintained by trusted partners and third-party collaborators when conducting a cyberattack.

The threat actor is ultimately looking to violate the security attributes of mission data, with the hope of causing a range of indirect, negative consequences for mission stakeholders. Data have three basic security attributes: confidentiality, integrity, and availability.[10] For a given risk, a threat actor generally tries to produce one or more of the following outcomes:

- Disclosure of data (violation of the confidentiality attribute)

- Modification of data (violation of the integrity attribute)

---

9. A workflow is a collection of interrelated work tasks that achieves a specific result [Leveson 2004]. A workflow includes all tasks, procedures, organizations, people, technologies, tools, data, inputs, and outputs required to achieve the desired objectives. The business literature uses several terms synonymously with *workflow*, including *work process*, *business process*, and *process*. *Mission thread* is essentially the term the military uses in place of *workflow*. A mission thread is a sequence of end-to-end activities and events that takes place to accomplish the execution of a military operation.

10. *Confidentiality* is defined as keeping proprietary, sensitive, or personal information private and inaccessible to anyone who is not authorized to see it. *Integrity* is defined as the authenticity, accuracy, and completeness of data. *Availability* is defined as the extent to which, or frequency with which, data must be present or ready for use. These definitions are adapted from the book *Managing Information Security Risks: The OCTAVE Approach* [Alberts 2002].

- Insertion of false data (violation of the integrity attribute)
- Destruction of data (violation of the availability attribute)
- Interruption of access to data (violation of the availability attribute)
- System destruction, destabilization, or degradation (violation of the availability attribute)

Each outcome maps to a security attribute of the data. As indicated in Figure 2.7, the violation of a security attribute has an impact on the workflow/mission thread and the organization's ability to achieve its mission successfully.

The final basic element of the security risk environment is the impact on mission stakeholders.[11] When a threat actor produces mission degradation or mission failure, the consequence can have a negative impact on various stakeholder groups.

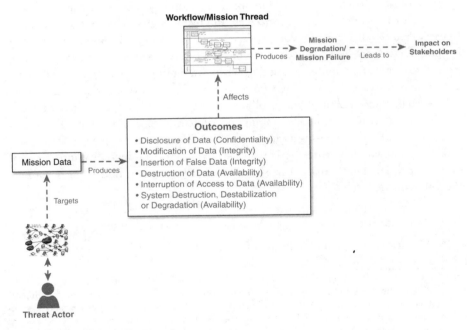

Figure 2.7 *Security Risk Environment*

---

11. A *stakeholder* is defined as a person or group with an interest in a workflow/mission thread and the products it produces or the services it provides.

2.5 Security Risk Analysis[12]

System and software security risk can be evaluated using the Security Engineering
Risk Analysis (SERA) framework [Alberts 2014]. SERA differs from many other
risk-identification methods that are based on brainstorming techniques. When brainstorming is used, participants describe risks based on their tacit understanding of
the operational environment. For security risk-identification methods, people tend to
identify threats with which they have some familiarity. They also tend to describe
consequences based on their personal knowledge of organizational workflows and
associated stakeholders. In lieu of brainstorming, SERA implements a detailed analysis that employs a multi-model approach for establishing operational content. The
SERA evaluation is not limited to the knowledge of the active participants.

The SERA framework defines an approach for analyzing security risk in software-
reliant systems and systems of systems across the software lifecycle. Traditional
security-risk analysis methods are based on a simplified view of security risk, where
a single threat actor exploits a single vulnerability in a single system to cause an
adverse consequence. However, in reality, multiple actors exploit multiple vulnerabilities in multiple systems as part of a complex chain of events.

For SERA, a shared understanding of the system in its operational or production
environment is assembled using multiple models that represent various aspects of
the system that are important to security. If the system is still in development, the
development environment is the targeted environment.

Models representing the views listed in Table 2.3 can be analyzed to establish the
following key aspects of a threat:

- **Critical data**—(subset of the Data view) Important information highlighted
  in workflow/mission thread, use case, and network diagrams. By examining
  these models, analysts can identify which data elements are most critical to the
  workflow/mission thread and its associated mission.

- **Access path**—(connecting Workflow and Network views) How a threat actor
  can gain access to data and violate its security attributes (i.e., create breaches
  of data confidentiality, integrity, and availability). The network and physical models provide insights into potential cyber and physical access paths for
  an attack.

- **Threat outcome**—(identification of Workflow view failures that impact Critical data) The direct consequence caused by the threat. A direct consequence

---

12. The material in this section comes from Microsoft [Microsoft 2013].

Table 2.3 *Views Used to Assemble an Operational System Model*

Task	Description
Workflow/mission thread	The sequence of end-to-end activities and events that take place to achieve a specific result
Stakeholder	The set of people with an interest or concern in the workflow/mission thread and the outcomes (e.g., products, services) produced by it
Data	The data items that are required when executing the workflow/mission and their associated security attributes (confidentiality, integrity, availability)
Network	The projected network topology for the system of interest
Physical	The projected physical layout of the facilities in which components of the system of interest are located
Use case	A description of a set of steps that define the interactions between a role/actor (which can be a human or an external system) and a system to achieve a goal

describes which security attributes of critical data have been breached. Examples of outcomes include data disclosure, data modification, insertion of false data, destruction of data, and interruption of access to data. The data model is used to identify the immediate consequence of a threat.

A threat ends with a description of its direct consequence or outcome. However, a security risk analysis must also account for indirect consequences triggered by the occurrence of a threat. The indirect consequences are used to (1) measure the impact of a security risk and (2) establish a risk's priority for decision makers. Analysts determine indirect consequences using models that represent the workflow/ mission thread and stakeholder views. Mission thread analysis, unlike other techniques, allows consideration of the people and their interactions with technology in addition to the functioning of a system itself.

Using the shared operational model, plausible threat scenarios can be developed and analyzed. The SERA framework requires the following data to be recorded for each security risk:

- Security risk scenario
- Risk statement
- Threat components
- Threat sequence
- Workflow consequences
- Stakeholder consequences
- Enablers

The SERA framework comprises the following four tasks:

1. Establish the operational context
2. Identify risk
3. Analyze risk
4. Develop a control plan

The SERA framework can be self-applied by the person or group that is responsible for acquiring and developing a software-reliant system or facilitated by external parties on behalf of the responsible person or group.[13] In either case, a small analysis team of approximately three to five people is needed to implement the framework and report findings to stakeholders.

The analysis team should be an interdisciplinary team with members providing diverse skill sets. Examples of skills and experience that should be considered when forming a team include security engineering, risk analysis, systems engineering, software engineering, operational cyber security, and physical/facility security. The exact composition of an analysis team depends on the point in the lifecycle at which the SERA framework is being applied and the nature of the engineering activity being pursued. The analysis team begins its work by focusing on the environment in which a software-reliant system will be deployed. Table 2.4 lists the steps involved in task 1.

In task 2 the analysis team transforms a security concern into a distinct, tangible risk scenario that can be described and measured. Table 2.5 lists the steps involved in task 2.

---

13. A facilitated assessment still requires participation from groups that are responsible for acquiring and developing the system of interest. The person facilitating the assessment has expertise in conducting security risk analysis. The facilitator includes others on the team with skills and experience in other areas, such as systems engineering, software engineering, operational cyber security, and physical/facility security.

Table 2.4 *Task 1 (Establish the Operational Context) Steps*

Step	Description	Output
1.1 Determine the system of interest.	The analysis team identifies the system of interest for the analysis. The *system of interest* is the software application or system that is the focus of the analysis. Selecting the system of interest defines the scope of the subsequent analysis.	System of interest
1.2 Select the workflow/ mission thread.	After selecting the system of interest, the analysis team determines which workflows or mission threads to include in the analysis. The system of interest might support multiple workflows or mission threads during operations. Selecting relevant workflows or mission threads helps to refine the scope of the analysis further.	Selected workflows/ mission threads
1.3 Establish operational views.	In the final step of task 1, the analysis team establishes a common view of the operational environment in which the system of interest must function. The team uses one or more models to characterize the following operational views: • Workflow/mission thread • Stakeholder • Data • Network • Physical • Use case These views provide team members with the information they need to begin identifying risk scenarios in task 2.	Operational models

Table 2.5 *Task 2 (Identify Risk) Steps*

Step	Description	Output
2.1 Identify threat.	The analysis team first analyzes the operational models from task 1 to identify critical data that are transmitted, stored, and processed by the system of interest (i.e., critical assets). The team then examines how threat actors might violate the security attributes (i.e., confidentiality, integrity, and availability) of the critical data. For threats the team will analyze further, it documents the components of the threat and the sequence of steps required to execute the threat (i.e., threat sequence).	Threat components Threat sequence
2.2 Establish consequence.	The next step in the analysis is to establish the consequences of each threat identified during the previous step. In this step, the analysis team analyzes the workflow/mission thread and stakeholder models from task 1 to determine how the workflow/mission thread and stakeholders could be affected by that threat.	Workflow consequences Stakeholder consequences
2.3 Identify enablers.	Enablers include vulnerabilities that a threat actor could exploit as well as the conditions and circumstances that are needed for the risk to occur. In this step, the analysis team identifies and documents the enablers of the risk.	Enablers
2.4 Develop a risk scenario.	The team documents a narrative description of the security risk based on the information generated in steps 2.1 through 2.3. Finally, the team documents a risk statement that provides a succinct and unique description of the security risk scenario that is used for tracking purposes.	Risk scenario Risk statement

Table 2.6 *Task 3 (Analyze Risk) Steps*

Step	Description	Output
3.1 Establish probability.	A risk's probability provides a measure of the likelihood that the risk will occur. In step 3.1, the analysis team determines and documents the probability the security risk scenario occurring.	Probability
3.2 Establish impact.	A risk's impact is a measure of the severity of a risk's consequence if the risk were to occur. The analysis team analyzes and documents the impact of the security risk scenario.	Impact
3.3 Determine risk exposure.	Risk exposure is a measure of the magnitude of a risk based on current values of probability and impact. The team determines the risk exposure for the scenario based on the individual values of probability and impact documented in steps 3.2 and 3.1.	Risk exposure

For task 3, the analysis team evaluates each risk in relationship to predefined criteria to determine the risk's probability, impact, and exposure. Table 2.6 lists the steps involved in task 3.

In Task 4, the team establishes a plan for controlling a selected set of risks. First, the analysis team prioritizes the security risk scenarios based on their risk measures (probability and impact). Once priorities have been established, the team determines the basic approach for controlling each risk (i.e., accept or plan[14]), based on

---

14. The SERA framework examines control approaches in steps 4.2 and 4.3. During step 4.2, the analysis team determines which risks will be accepted and no longer considered and which will have control plans. At this point in applying the framework, the analysis team does not identify specific strategies for transferring, avoiding, and mitigating risks. Those strategies are addressed in step 4.3. Security risk scenarios comprise multiple threat steps (as defined in the threat sequence), many enablers, and a range of indirect consequences. An analysis team might employ multiple strategies for addressing a given security risk scenario. For example, some steps in the threat sequence might be avoided through restructuring the workflow/mission thread or changing the network architecture. Certain financial consequences might be transferred to third parties by purchasing insurance. The probability of occurrence for some steps in the threat sequence or some types of consequences might be reduced by implementing mitigation controls. Specific control strategies (e.g., transfer, avoid, mitigate) are considered when the control plan is being developed.

predefined criteria and current constraints (e.g., resources and funding available for control activities). For each risk that is not accepted, the analysis team develops a control plan that indicates the following:

- How the threat can be monitored and the actions taken when it occurs (recognize and respond)

- Which protection measures can be implemented to reduce vulnerability to the threat and minimize any consequences that might occur (resist)

- How to recover from the risk if the consequences or losses are realized (recover)

Table 2.7 lists the steps involved in task 4.

Table 2.7 *Task 4 (Develop a Control Plan) Steps*

	Description	Output
4.1 Prioritize risks.	The analysis team prioritizes all security risk scenarios based on their impact, probability, and risk exposure measures.	Prioritized risk scenarios
4.2 Select the control approach.	During this step, the team determines how it will handle each risk. If a risk is accepted, its consequences will be tolerated; no proactive action to address the risk will be taken. If the team decides to take action to control a risk, it will develop a control plan for that risk in step 4.3.	Control approach
4.3 Establish control actions.	The analysis team defines and documents a plan for all risks that are being controlled. A control plan establishes a range of actions needed to • Recognize and respond to threats • Resist the threat and potential consequences • Recover from consequences when they occur A subset of the control actions will have implications for the software (or system) requirements and design. Any control actions with requirements or design implications are documented for further analysis.	Control plan Candidate design controls

A case study illustrating the use of SERA framework for the Wireless Emergency Alert (WEA) system can be found in Appendix A, "WEA Case Study: Evaluating Security Risks Using Mission Threads."

2.6 Operational Risk Analysis—Comparing Planned to Actual

Assessments should be used to confirm that the implemented system meets the expected levels of risk that were planned in acquisition, design, and development and continues to do so over time. If effective security risk analysis is performed as the system is being developed, this knowledge can be leveraged to focus assessments on confirming that expected mitigations are in place and are appropriately addressing the risks.

Data from actual security incidents can be compared to the risks that were anticipated to identify gaps that may indicate the need to revisit the risk analysis activities to factor in the new information and determine whether changes are needed to meet the realities.

The goal of the risk assessment is to say with certainty that the currently deployed set of controls properly addresses the right threats. The assessment should also demonstrate that those controls continue to be effective, given overall business goals.

In addition to assessments, actual incidents should be collected and compared to anticipated risks to identify gaps for improvements in future system releases.

2.7 Summary

Risk management is a critical element of software assurance. Most organizations are focused only on risk to cost and schedule. The MRD can be used to analyze how organizational risks, which can include lack of capability in risk management, impact the ability of a system to meet its objectives. The SERA framework provides a view from each system of the security risks it may be contributing that can negatively affect a mission. The SERA framework is structured to assemble these risks so they can be prioritized along with other system risks.

Chapter 3

Secure Software Development Management and Organizational Models[1]

with Julia Allen and Dan Shoemaker

In This Chapter

3.1 The Management Dilemma

When managers and stakeholders start a software acquisition or development project, they face a dazzling array of models and frameworks to choose from. Some of those models are general software process models, and others are specific to security or software assurance. Very often the marketing hype that accompanies these models makes it difficult to select a model or set of practices.

In our study of the problem, we realized that there is no single, recognized framework to organize research and practice areas that focuses on building assured systems. Although we did not succeed in defining a single "best" framework, we were

---

1. Many of the models presented in this chapter were initially discussed in Mead [2010b].

able to develop guidance to help managers and stakeholders address challenges such as the following:

- How do I decide which security methods fit into a specific lifecycle activity?

- How do I know if a specific security method is sufficiently mature for me to use on my projects?

- When should I take a chance on a security research approach that has not been widely used?

- What actions can I take when I have no approach or method for prioritizing and selecting new research or when promising research appears to be unrelated to other research in the field?

In this chapter, we present a variety of models and frameworks that managers and stakeholders can use to help address these challenges. We define a framework using the following definitions from Babylon dictionary [Babylon 2009]:

> A framework is a basic conceptual structure used to solve or address complex issues. This very broad definition has allowed the term to be used as a buzzword, especially in a software context.
> A structure to hold together or support something, a basic structure.

3.1.1 Background on Assured Systems

The following topics exhibit varying levels of maturity and use differing terminology, but they all play a role in building assured systems:

- *Engineering resilient systems* encompasses secure software engineering, as well as requirements engineering, architecture, and design of secure systems and large systems of systems, and service, and system continuity of operations.

- *Containment* focuses on the problem of how to monitor and detect a component's behavior to contain and isolate the effect of aberrant behavior while still being able to recover from a false assumption of bad behavior.

- *Architecting secure systems* defines the necessary and appropriate design artifacts, quality attributes, and appropriate trade-off considerations that describe how security properties are positioned, how they relate to the overall system/IT architecture, and how security quality attributes are measured.

- *Secure software engineering* (secure coding, software engineering, and hardware design improvement) improves the way software and hardware are developed by reducing vulnerabilities from software and hardware flaws. This work includes technology lifecycle assurance mechanisms, advanced engineering disciplines, standards and certification regimes, and best practices. Research areas in secure software engineering include refining current assurance mechanisms and developing new ones where necessary, developing certification regimes, and exploring policy and incentive options.

Secure software engineering encompasses a range of activities targeting security. The book *Software Security Engineering* [Allen 2008] presents a valuable discussion of these topics, and further research continues.

Some organizations have begun to pay more attention to building assured systems, including the following:

- Some organizations are participating in the Building Security In Maturity Model [McGraw 2015].

- Some organizations are using Microsoft's Security Development Lifecycle (SDL) [Howard 2006].

- Some organizations are members of the Software Assurance Forum for Excellence in Code (SAFECode) consortium [SAFECode 2010].

- Some organizations are working with Oracle cyber security initiatives and security solutions [Oracle 2016].

- Members of the Open Web Application Security Project (OWASP) are using the Software Assurance Maturity Model (SAMM) [OWASP 2015].

- The Trustworthy Software Initiative in the UK, in conjunction with the British Standards Institution, has produced Publicly Available Specification 754 (PAS 754), "Software Trustworthiness—Governance and Management—Specification" [TSI 2014].

Software assurance efforts tend to be strongest in software product development organizations, which have provided the most significant contribution to the efforts listed above. However, software assurance efforts tend to be weaker in large organizations that develop systems for use in-house and integrate systems across multiple vendors. They also tend to be weaker in small- to medium-sized organizations developing software products for licensed use. It's worth noting that there are many small- and medium-sized organizations that have good cyber security practices, and there are also large organizations that have poor ones. For a while, organizations producing industrial control systems lagged behind large software development firms, but this has changed over the past several years.

Furthermore, there are a variety of lifecycle models in practice. Even in the larger organizations that adopt secure software engineering practices, there is a tendency to select a subset of the total set of recommended or applicable practices. Such uneven adoption of practices for building assured systems makes it difficult to evaluate the results using these practices.

Let's take a look at existing frameworks and lifecycle models for building assured systems. In the literature, we typically see lifecycle models or approaches that serve as structured repositories of practices from which organizations select those that are meaningful for their development projects.

Summary descriptions of several software development and acquisition process models that are in active use appear in Section 3.2, "Process Models for Software Development and Acquisition," and models for software security are summarized in Section 3.3, "Software Security Frameworks, Models, and Roadmaps."

3.2 Process Models for Software Development and Acquisition

A framework for building assured systems needs to build on and reflect known, accepted, common practice for software development and acquisition. One commonly accepted expression of the codification of effective software development and acquisition practices is a process model. Process models define a set of processes that, when implemented, demonstrably improve the quality of the software that is developed or acquired using such processes. The Software Engineering Institute (SEI) at Carnegie Mellon University has been a recognized thought leader for more than 25 years in developing capability and maturity models for defining and improving the process by which software is developed and acquired. This work includes building a community of practitioners and reflecting their experiences and feedback in successive versions of the models. These models reflect commonly known good practices that have been observed, measured, and assessed by hundreds of organizations. Such practices serve as the foundation for building assured systems; it makes no sense to attempt to integrate software security practices into a software development process or lifecycle if this development process is not defined, implemented, and regularly improved. Thus, these development and acquisition models serve as the basis against which models and practices for software security are considered. These development and acquisition models also serve as the basis for considering the use of promising research results. The models described in this section apply to newly developed software, acquired software, and (extending the useful life of) legacy software.

The content in this section is excerpted from publicly available SEI reports and the CMMI Institute website. It summarizes the objectives of Capability Maturity Model Integration (CMMI) models in general, CMMI for Development, and CMMI for Acquisition. We recommend that you familiarize yourself with software development and acquisition process models in general (including CMMI-based models) to better understand how software security practices, necessary for building assured systems, are implemented and deployed.

3.2.1 CMMI Models in General

The following information about CMMI models is from the CMMI Institute [CMMI Institute 2015]:

The Capability Maturity Model Integration (CMMI®) is a world-class performance improvement framework for competitive organizations that want to achieve high-performance operations. Building upon an organization's business performance objectives, CMMI provides a set of practices for improving processes, resulting in a performance improvement system that paves the way for better operations and performance. More than any other approach, CMMI doesn't just help you to improve your organizational processes. CMMI also has built-in practices that help you to improve the way you use any performance improvement approach, setting you up to achieve a positive return on your investment.

CMMI does not provide a single process. Rather, the CMMI framework models what to do to improve your processes, not define your processes. CMMI is designed to compare an organization's existing processes to proven best practices developed by members of industry, government, and academia; reveal possible areas for improvement; and provide ways to measure progress.

The result? CMMI helps you to build and manage performance improvement systems that fit your unique environment.

CMMI is not just for software development. CMMI helps software and services organizations in a variety of industries to align meaningful process improvement with business and engineering goals for cost, schedule, productivity, quality, and customer satisfaction.

CMMI helps companies to improve operational performance by lowering the cost of development, production, and delivery. CMMI provides the framework for you to consistently and predictably deliver the products and services that your customers want, when they want them.

CMMI offers three constellations—CMMI for Acquisition, CMMI for Development, and CMMI for Services—that help to improve specific business needs, plus the People Capability Maturity Model (People CMM), which uses process framework as a foundation to help organizations managing and developing their workforce to become an employer of choice. Across these three constellations and the People CMM, CMMI delivers measurable results for organizations of all sizes in a variety of industries, including aerospace, finance, health services, software, defense, transportation, and telecommunications.

3.2.2 CMMI for Development (CMMI-DEV)

The SEI's CMMI for Development report states the following [CMMI Product Team 2010b]:

> Companies want to deliver products and services better, faster, and cheaper. At the same time, in the high-technology environment of the twenty-first century, nearly all organizations have found themselves building increasingly complex products and services. It is unusual today for a single organization to develop all the components that compose a complex product or service. More commonly, some components are built in-house and some are acquired; then all the components are integrated into the final product or service. Organizations must be able to manage and control this complex development and maintenance process.
>
> The problems these organizations address today involve enterprise-wide solutions that require an integrated approach. Effective management of organizational assets is critical to business success. In essence, these organizations are product and service developers that need a way to manage their development activities as part of achieving their business objectives.
>
> In the current marketplace, maturity models, standards, methodologies, and guidelines exist that can help an organization improve the way it does business. However, most available improvement approaches focus on a specific part of the business and do not take a systemic approach to the problems that most organizations are facing. By focusing on improving one area of a business, these models have unfortunately perpetuated the stovepipes and barriers that exist in organizations.
>
> CMMI® for Development (CMMI-DEV) provides an opportunity to avoid or eliminate these stovepipes and barriers. CMMI for Development consists of best practices that address development activities applied to products and services. It addresses practices that cover the product's lifecycle from conception through delivery and maintenance. The emphasis is on the work necessary to build and maintain the total product.

What Is a Process Area?

A process area is a cluster of related practices in an area that, when implemented collectively, satisfies a set of goals considered important for making improvement in that area.

CMMI-DEV includes the following 22 process areas [CMMI Product Team 2010b]. The 22 process areas appear in alphabetical order by acronym:

- Causal Analysis and Resolution (CAR)
- Configuration Management (CM)
- Decision Analysis and Resolution (DAR)

- Integrated Project Management (IPM)
- Measurement and Analysis (MA)
- Organizational Process Definition (OPD)
- Organizational Process Focus (OPF)
- Organizational Performance Management (OPM)
- Organizational Process Performance (OPP)
- Organizational Training (OT)
- Product Integration (PI)
- Project Monitoring and Control (PMC)
- Project Planning (PP)
- Process and Product Quality Assurance (PPQA)
- Quantitative Project Management (QPM)
- Requirements Development (RD)
- Requirements Management (REQM)
- Risk Management (RSKM)
- Supplier Agreement Management (SAM)
- Technical Solution (TS)
- Validation (VAL)
- Verification (VER)

3.2.3 CMMI for Acquisition (CMMI-ACQ)

The SEI's CMMI for Acquisition (CMMI-ACQ) report states the following [CMMI Product Team 2010a]:

> Organizations are increasingly becoming acquirers of needed capabilities by obtaining products and services from suppliers and developing less and less of these capabilities in-house. This widely adopted business strategy is designed to improve an organization's operational efficiencies by leveraging suppliers' capabilities to deliver quality solutions rapidly, at lower cost, and with the most appropriate technology.
>
> Acquisition of needed capabilities is challenging because acquirers have overall accountability for satisfying the end user while allowing the supplier to perform the tasks necessary to develop and provide the solution.
>
> *(continued)*

Mismanagement, the inability to articulate customer needs, poor requirements definition, inadequate supplier selection and contracting processes, insufficient technology selection procedures, and uncontrolled requirements changes are factors that contribute to project failure. Responsibility is shared by both the supplier and the acquirer. The majority of project failures could be avoided if the acquirer learned how to properly prepare for, engage with, and manage suppliers.

In addition to these challenges, an overall key to a successful acquirer-supplier relationship is communication.

Unfortunately, many organizations have not invested in the capabilities necessary to effectively manage projects in an acquisition environment. Too often acquirers disengage from the project once the supplier is hired. Too late they discover that the project is not on schedule, deadlines will not be met, the technology selected is not viable, and the project has failed.

The acquirer has a focused set of major objectives. These objectives include the requirement to maintain a relationship with end users to fully comprehend their needs. The acquirer owns the project, executes overall project management, and is accountable for delivering the product or service to the end users. Thus, these acquirer responsibilities can extend beyond ensuring the product or service is delivered by chosen suppliers to include activities such as integrating the overall product or service, ensuring it makes the transition into operation, and obtaining insight into its appropriateness and adequacy to continue to meet customer needs.

CMMI® for Acquisition (CMMI-ACQ) enables organizations to avoid or eliminate barriers in the acquisition process through practices and terminology that transcend the interests of individual departments or groups.

CMMI-ACQ has 22 process areas, 6 of which are specific to acquisition practices, and 16 of which are shared with other CMMI models. These are the process areas specific to acquisition practices:

- Acquisition Requirements Development
- Solicitation and Supplier Agreement Development
- Agreement Management
- Acquisition Technical Management
- Acquisition Verification
- Acquisition Validation

In addition, the model includes guidance on the following:

- Acquisition strategy
- Typical supplier deliverables
- Transition to operations and support
- Integrated teams

The 16 shared process areas include practices for project management, organizational process management, and infrastructure and support.

3.2.4 CMMI for Services (CMMI-SVC)

The SEI's CMMI for Services (CMMI-SVC) report states the following [CMMI Product Team 2010c]:

> The service industry is a significant driver for worldwide economic growth. Guidance on developing and improving mature service practices is a key contributor to the service provider performance and customer satisfaction. The CMMI® for Services (CMMI-SVC) model is designed to begin meeting that need.
>
> All CMMI-SVC model practices focus on the activities of the service provider. Seven process areas focus on practices specific to services, addressing capacity and availability management, service continuity, service delivery, incident resolution and prevention, service transition, service system development, and strategic service management processes.

CMMI-SVC contains 24 process areas. Of those process areas, 16 are core process areas, 1 is a shared process area, and 7 are service-specific process areas. Detailed information on the process areas can be found in *CMMI for Services, Version 1.3* [CMMI Product Team 2010c]. The 24 process areas appear in alphabetical order by acronym:

- Capacity and Availability Management (CAM)
- Causal Analysis and Resolution (CAR)
- Configuration Management (CM)
- Decision Analysis and Resolution (DAR)
- Incident Resolution and Prevention (IRP)
- Integrated Work Management (IWM)
- Measurement and Analysis (MA)
- Organizational Process Definition (OPD)
- Organizational Process Focus (OPF)
- Organizational Performance Management (OPM)
- Organizational Process Performance (OPP)
- Organizational Training (OT)
- Process and Product Quality Assurance (PPQA)

- Quantitative Work Management (QWM)
- Requirements Management (REQM)
- Risk Management (RSKM)
- Supplier Agreement Management (SAM)
- Service Continuity (SCON)
- Service Delivery (SD)
- Service System Development (SSD)
- Service System Transition (SST)
- Strategic Service Management (STSM)
- Work Monitoring and Control (WMC)
- Work Planning (WP)

3.2.5 CMMI Process Model Uses

CMMI models are one foundation for well-managed and well-defined software development, acquisition, and services processes. In practice, organizations have been using them for many years to improve their processes, identifying areas for improvement, and implementing systematic improvement programs. Process models have been a valuable tool for executive managers and middle managers. There are many self-improvement programs as well as consultants for this area.

In academia, process models are routinely taught in software engineering degree programs and in some individual software engineering courses, so that graduates of these programs are familiar with them and know how to apply them. In capstone projects, students are frequently asked to select a development process from a range of models.

The next section describes leading models and frameworks that define processes and practices for software security. Such processes and practices are, in large part, in common use by a growing body of organizations that are developing software to be more secure.

3.3 Software Security Frameworks, Models, and Roadmaps

In addition to considering process models for software development and acquisition, a framework for building assured systems needs to build on and reflect known, accepted, common practice for software security. The number of promising frameworks and models for building more secure software is growing. For example,

Microsoft has defined their SDL and made it publicly available. In their recently released version 6, the authors of *Building Security In Maturity Model* [McGraw 2015] have collected and analyzed software security practices in 78 organizations.

The following subsections summarize models, frameworks, and roadmaps and provide excerpts of descriptive information from publicly available websites and reports to provide an overview of the objectives and content of each effort. You should have a broad understanding of these models and their processes and practices to appreciate the current state of the practice in building secure software and to aid in identifying promising research opportunities to fill gaps.

3.3.1 Building Security In Maturity Model (BSIMM)

An introduction on the BSIMM website states the following [McGraw 2015]:

> The purpose of the BSIMM is to quantify the activities carried out by real software security initiatives. Because these initiatives make use of different methodologies and different terminology, the BSIMM requires a framework that allows us to describe all of the initiatives in a uniform way. Our Software Security Framework (SSF) and activity descriptions provide a common vocabulary for explaining the salient elements of a software security initiative, thereby allowing us to compare initiatives that use different terms, operate at different scales, exist in different vertical markets, or create different work products.
>
> We classify our work as a maturity model because improving software security almost always means changing the way an organization works—something that doesn't happen overnight. We understand that not all organizations need to achieve the same security goals, but we believe all organizations can benefit from using the same measuring stick.
>
> BSIMM6 is the sixth major version of the BSIMM model. It includes updated activity descriptions, data from 78 firms in multiple vertical markets, and a longitudinal study.
>
> The BSIMM is meant for use by anyone responsible for creating and executing a software security initiative. We have observed that successful software security initiatives are typically run by a senior executive who reports to the highest levels in an organization. These executives lead an internal group that we call the software security group (SSG), charged with directly executing or facilitating the activities described in the BSIMM. The BSIMM is written with the SSG and SSG leadership in mind.
>
> Our work with the BSIMM model shows that measuring a firm's software security initiative is both possible and extremely useful. BSIMM measurements can be used to plan, structure, and execute the evolution of a software security initiative. Over time, firms participating in the BSIMM show measurable improvement in their software security initiatives.

A maturity model is appropriate for building more secure software—a key component of building assured systems—because improving software security means changing the way an organization develops software over time.

The BSIMM is meant to be used by those who create and execute a software security initiative. Most successful initiatives are run by a senior executive who reports to the highest levels in the organization, such as the board of directors or the chief information officer. These executives lead an internal group that the BSIMM calls the software security group (SSG), charged with directly executing or facilitating the activities described in the BSIMM. The BSIMM is written with the SSG and SSG leadership in mind.

The BSIMM addresses the following roles:

- SSG (software security staff with deep coding, design, and architectural experience)
- Executives and middle management, including line-of-business owners and product managers
- Builders, testers, and operations staff
- Administrators
- Line of business owners
- Vendors

As an organizing structure for the body of observed practices, the BSIMM uses the software security framework (SSF) described in Table 3.1.

3.3.2 CMMI Assurance Process Reference Model

The Department of Homeland Security (DHS) Software Assurance (SwA) Processes and Practices Working Group developed a draft process reference model (PRM) for assurance in July 2008 [DHS 2008]. This PRM recommended additions to CMMI-DEV v1.2 to address software assurance. These also apply to CMMI-DEV v1.3. The "assurance thread" description[2] includes Figure 3.1, which may be useful for addressing the lifecycle phase aspect of building assured systems.

The DHS SwA Processes and Practices Working Group's additions and updates to CMMI-DEV v1.2 and v1.3 are focused at the specific practices (SP) level for the following CMMI-DEV process areas (PAs):

- Process Management
  - Organizational Process Focus
  - Organizational Process Definition
  - Organizational Training

---

2. https://buildsecurityin.us-cert.gov/swa/procwg.html

Table 3.1 *BSIMM Software Security Framework [McGraw 2015]*

Governance **Goal: Transparency, Accountability, Checks, and Balances**	*Intelligence* **Goal: Auditability, Stewardship, Standardization**	*SSDL* Touchpoints* **Goal: Quality Control**	*Deployment* **Goal: Quality Control, Change Management**
Strategy & Metrics Planning; assigning roles and responsibilities; identifying software security goals; determining budgets; identifying metrics and gates	*Attack Models* Capture information to think like an attacker; threat modeling; abuse case development and refinement; data classification; attack patterns	*Architecture Analysis* Capture software architecture; apply risks and threats; adopt an architecture review process; build assessment and remediation plan	*Penetration Testing* Test for vulnerability in final configuration; provide input to defect management and mitigation
Compliance & Policy Identify controls for compliance; develop contractual controls (service level agreements) for externally developed software; set software security policy; audit against policy	*Security Features & Design* Create usable security patterns for major security controls; build middleware frameworks for controls; create and document security guidance	*Code Review* Use code review tools; develop customized rules; develop profiles for tool use by role; perform manual analysis; track/measure results	*Software Environment* Operating system (OS) and platform patching; web application firewalls; installation and configuration documentation; application monitoring; change management; code signing
Training Awareness training; new hire training; SSG office hours; build social network; role-based training; provide specific information on error root causes; annual refresher; on-demand; training for vendors/external parties	*Standards & Requirements* Elicit security requirements; determine commercial, off-the-shelf (COTS); build standards for major security controls; create security standards; creating a standards review board	*Security Testing* Integrate security into standard quality assurance (QA) processes; black box testing; fuzz testing; risk-driven white box testing; apply attack models; code coverage analysis; focus on vulnerabilities in construction	*Configuration Management & Vulnerability Management* Patch and update applications; version control; defect tracking and remediation; incident handling

* Software Security Development Lifecycle

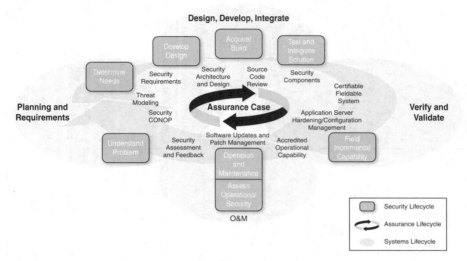

Figure 3.1 *Summary of Assurance for CMMI Efforts*

- Project Management
  - Project Planning
  - Project Monitoring and Control
  - Supplier Agreement Management
  - Integrated Project Management
  - Risk Management

- Engineering
  - Requirements Development
  - Technical Solution
  - Verification
  - Validation

- Support
- Measurement & Analysis

More recently, the CMMI Institute published "Security by Design with CMMI for Development, Version 1.3," a set of additional process areas that integrate with CMMI [CMMI 2013].

3.3.3 Open Web Application Security Project (OWASP) Software Assurance Maturity Model (SAMM)

The OWASP website provides the following information on the Software Assurance Maturity Model (SAMM) [OWASP 2015]:

The Software Assurance Maturity Model (SAMM) is an open framework to help organizations formulate and implement a strategy for software security that is tailored to the specific risks facing the organization. The resources provided by SAMM will aid in:

- Evaluating an organization's existing software security practices
- Building a balanced software security assurance program in well-defined iterations
- Demonstrating concrete improvements to a security assurance program
- Defining and measuring security-related activities throughout an organization

SAMM was defined with flexibility in mind such that it can be utilized by small, medium, and large organizations using any style of development. Additionally, this model can be applied organization-wide, for a single line-of-business, or even for an individual project. Beyond these traits, SAMM was built on the following principles:

- An organization's behavior changes slowly over time—A successful software security program should be specified in small iterations that deliver tangible assurance gains while incrementally working toward long-term goals.
- There is no single recipe that works for all organizations—A software security framework must be flexible and allow organizations to tailor their choices based on their risk tolerance and the way in which they build and use software.
- Guidance related to security activities must be prescriptive—All the steps in building and assessing an assurance program should be simple, well-defined, and measurable. This model also provides roadmap templates for common types of organizations.

The foundation of the model is built upon the core business functions of software development with security practices tied to each [see Table 3.2]. The building blocks of the model are the three maturity levels defined for each of the twelve security practices. These define a wide variety of activities in which an organization could engage to reduce security risks and increase software assurance. Additional details are included to measure successful activity performance, understand the associated assurance benefits, estimate personnel, and other costs.

Practical Measurement Framework for Software Assurance and Information Security provides an approach for measuring the effectiveness of achieving software assurance goals and objectives at an organizational, program, or project level. It addresses how to assess the degree of assurance provided by software, using quantitative and qualitative methodologies and techniques. This framework incorporates existing measurement methodologies and is intended to help organizations and projects integrate SwA measurement into their existing programs.

Table 3.2 *OWASP SAMM Business Functions and Security Practices [OWASP 2015]*

Governance	Construction	Verification	Deployment
Strategy & Metrics	*Threat Assessment*	*Design Review*	*Vulnerability Management*
Overall strategic direction of the software assurance program & instrumentation of processes & activities to collect metrics about an organization's security posture	Identify and characterize potential attacks on software to better understand the risks and facilitate risk management	Inspect artifacts created from the design process to ensure provision of adequate security mechanisms and adherence to expectations for security	Establish consistent process for managing internal and external vulnerability reports to limit exposure and gather data to enhance the security assurance program
Policy & Compliance	*Security Requirements*	*Code Review*	*Environment Hardening*
Set up a security and compliance control and audit framework to achieve increased assurance in software under construction and in operation	Promote the inclusion of security-related requirements during the software development process to specify correct functionality from inception	Assess source code to aid vulnerability discovery and related mitigation activities as well as establish a baseline for secure coding expectations	Implement controls for the operating environment in which software executes to bolster the security posture of applications that have been deployed
Education & Guidance	*Secure Architecture*	*Security Testing*	*Operational Enablement*
Increase security knowledge among personnel in software development through training and guidance on security topics relevant to individual job functions	Bolster the design process with activities to promote secure-by-default designs and control over technologies and frameworks upon which software is built	Test software in its runtime environment in order to discover vulnerabilities and establish a minimum standard for software releases	Identify and capture security-relevant information needed by an operator to properly configure, deploy, and run software

The SAMM presents success metrics for all activities in all 12 practices for all 4 critical business functions. Each practice has 3 objectives, and each objective has 2 activities, for a total of 72 activities.

3.3.4 DHS SwA Measurement Work

Nadya Bartol and Michele Moss, both of whom played important roles in the DHS SwA Measurement Working Group, led the development of several important metrics documents. These documents were published at an earlier time. Note that we discuss more recent work in the measurement area by the SEI in Chapter 6, "Metrics."

According to the DHS SwA Measurement Working Group [DHS 2010]:

> Practical Measurement Framework for Software Assurance and Information Security provides an approach for measuring the effectiveness of achieving software assurance goals and objectives at an organizational, program, or project level. It addresses how to assess the degree of assurance provided by software, using quantitative and qualitative methodologies and techniques. This framework incorporates existing measurement methodologies and is intended to help organizations and projects integrate SwA measurement into their existing programs.

The following discussion is from the *Practical Measurement Framework for Software Assurance and Information Security* [Bartol 2008]:

> Software assurance is interdisciplinary and relies on methods and techniques produced by other disciplines, including project management, process improvement, quality assurance, training, information security/information assurance, system engineering, safety, test and evaluation, software acquisition, reliability, and dependability [as shown in Figure 3.2].
>
> The Practical Measurement Framework focuses principally, though not exclusively, on the information security viewpoint of SwA. Many of the contributing disciplines of SwA enjoy an established process improvement and measurement body of knowledge, such as quality assurance, project management, process improvement, and safety. SwA measurement can leverage measurement methods and techniques that are already established in those disciplines, and adapt them to SwA. The Practical Measurement Framework report focuses on information assurance/information security aspects of SwA to help mature that aspect of SwA measurement.
>
> *(continued)*

Figure 3.2 *Cross-Disciplinary Nature of SwA [Bartol 2008]*

This framework provides an integrated measurement approach, which leverages five existing industry approaches that use similar processes to develop and implement measurement as follows:

- Draft National Institute of Standards and Technology (NIST) Special Publication (SP) 800-55, Revision 1, Performance Measurement Guide for Information Security
- ISO/IEC 27004 Information technology—Security techniques—Information security management measurement
- ISO/IEC 15939, System and Software Engineering—Measurement Process, also known as Practical Software and System Measurement (PSM)
- CMMI Measurement and Analysis Process Area
- CMMI GQ(I)M—Capability Maturity Model Integration Goal Question Indicator Measure

The Practical Measurement Framework authors selected these methodologies because of their widespread use among the software and systems development community and the information security community. The Framework includes a common measure specification table which is a crosswalk of specifications, templates, forms and other means of documenting individual measures provided by the five industry approaches listed above that were leveraged to create the framework.

Measures are intended to help answer the following five questions:

- What are the defects in the design and code that have a potential to be exploited?
- Where are they?
- How did they get there?
- Have they been mitigated?
- How can they be avoided in the future?

A number of representative key measures for different stakeholder groups are included in the framework to help organizations assess the state of their SwA efforts during any stage of a project:

- *Supplier*—an individual or an organization that offers software and system-related products and services to other organizations. This includes software developers, program managers, and other staff working for an organization that develops and supplies software to other organizations.
- *Acquirer*—an individual or an organization that acquires software and system-related products and services from other organizations. This includes acquisition

officials, program managers, system integrators, system owners, information owners, operators, designated approving authorities (DAAs), certifying authorities, independent verification and validation (IV&V), and other individuals who are working for an organization that is acquiring software from other organizations.

Within each supplier and acquirer organization, the following stakeholders are considered:

- *Executive Decision Maker*—a leader who has authority to make decisions and may require quantifiable information to understand the level of risk associated with software to support decision-making processes.
- *Practitioner*—an individual responsible for implementing SwA as a part of their job.

The framework describes candidate goals and information needs for each stakeholder group. The framework then presents examples of supplier measures as a table, with columns for project activity, measures, information needs, and benefits. The framework includes supplier project activities—requirements management (five measures), design (three measures), development (six measures), test (nine measures)—and the entire software development lifecycle (SDLC) (three measures).

Examples of measures for acquirers are also presented and are intended to answer the following questions:

- Have SwA activities been adequately integrated into the organization's acquisition process?
- Have SwA considerations been integrated into the SDLC and resulting product by the supplier?

The acquisition activities are planning (two measures), contracting (three measures), and implementation and acceptance (five measures).

Ten examples of measures for executives are presented. These are intended to answer the question "Is the risk generated by software acceptable to the organization?" The following are some of these examples of measures:

- Number and percentage of patches published on announced date
- Time elapsed for supplier to fix defects
- Number of known defects by type and impact
- Cost to correct vulnerabilities in operations
- Cost of fixing defects before system becomes operational
- Cost of individual data breaches
- Cost of SwA practices throughout the SDLC

Fifteen examples of measures for practitioners are presented. They are intended to answer the question "How well are current SwA processes and techniques mitigating software-related risks?"

3.3.5 Microsoft Security Development Lifecycle (SDL)

The Microsoft Security Development Lifecycle (SDL)[3] is an industry-leading software security process. A Microsoft-wide initiative and a mandatory policy since 2004, the SDL has played a critical role in enabling Microsoft to embed security and privacy in its software and culture. Combining a holistic and practical approach, the SDL introduces security and privacy early and throughout all phases of the development process.

The reliable delivery of more secure software requires a comprehensive process, so Microsoft defined a collection of principles it calls *Secure by Design, Secure by Default, Secure in Deployment, and Communications* (SD3+C) to help determine where security efforts are needed [Microsoft 2010b]:

Secure by Design

Secure architecture, design, and structure. Developers consider security issues part of the basic architectural design of software development. They review detailed designs for possible security issues, and they design and develop mitigations for all threats.

- *Threat modeling and mitigation.* Threat models are created, and threat mitigations are present in all design and functional specifications.
- *Elimination of vulnerabilities.* No known security vulnerabilities that would present a significant risk to the anticipated use of the software remain in the code after review. This review includes the use of analysis and testing tools to eliminate classes of vulnerabilities.
- *Improvements in security.* Less secure legacy protocols and code are deprecated, and, where possible, users are provided with secure alternatives that are consistent with industry standards.

Secure by Default

- *Least privilege.* All components run with the fewest possible permissions.
- *Defense in depth.* Components do not rely on a single threat mitigation solution that leaves users exposed if it fails.
- *Conservative default settings.* The development team is aware of the attack surface for the product and minimizes it in the default configuration.

---

3. More information is available in *The Security Development Lifecycle* [Howard 2006], at the Microsoft Security Development Lifecycle website [Microsoft 2010a], and in the document *Microsoft Security Development Lifecycle Version 5.0* [Microsoft 2010b].

- *Avoidance of risky default changes.* Applications do not make any default changes to the operating system or security settings that reduce security for the host computer. In some cases, such as for security products, it is acceptable for a software program to strengthen (increase) security settings for the host computer. The most common violations of this principle are games that either open firewall ports without informing the user or instruct users to open firewall ports without informing users of possible risks.

- *Less commonly used services off by default.* If fewer than 80 percent of a program's users use a feature, that feature should not be activated by default. Measuring 80 percent usage in a product is often difficult because programs are designed for many different personas. It can be useful to consider whether a feature addresses a core/primary use scenario for all personas. If it does, the feature is sometimes referred to as a P1 feature.

Secure in Deployment

- *Deployment guides.* Prescriptive deployment guides outline how to deploy each feature of a program securely, including providing users with information that enables them to assess the security risk of activating non-default options (and thereby increasing the attack surface).

- *Analysis and management tools.* Security analysis and management tools enable administrators to determine and configure the optimal security level for a software release.

- *Patch deployment tools.* Deployment tools aid in patch deployment.

Communications

- *Security response.* Development teams respond promptly to reports of security vulnerabilities and communicate information about security updates.

- *Community engagement.* Development teams proactively engage with users to answer questions about security vulnerabilities, security updates, or changes in the security landscape.

Figure 3.3 shows what the secure software development process model looks like.

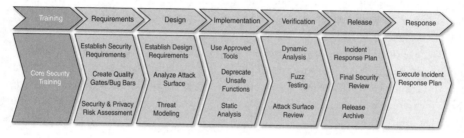

Figure 3.3 *Secure Software Development Process Model at Microsoft [Shunn 2013]*

The Microsoft SDL documentation describes, in great detail, what architects, designers, developers, and testers are required to do during each lifecycle phase. The introduction states, "Secure software development has three elements—best practices, process improvements, and metrics. This document focuses primarily on the first two elements, and metrics are derived from measuring how they are applied" [Microsoft 2010b]. This description indicates that the document contains no concrete measurement-related information; measures would need to be derived from each of the lifecycle-phase practice areas.

3.3.6 SEI Framework for Building Assured Systems

In developing the Building Assured Systems Framework (BASF), we studied the available models, roadmaps, and frameworks. Given our deep knowledge of the MSwA2010 Body of Knowledge (BoK)—the core body of knowledge for a master of software architecture degree from Carnegie Mellon University—we decided to use it as an initial foundation for the BASF.

Maturity Levels

We assigned the following maturity levels to each element of the MSwA2010 BoK:

- **L1**—The approach provides guidance for how to think about a topic for which there is no proven or widely accepted approach. The intent of the area is to raise awareness and aid in thinking about the problem and candidate solutions. The area may also describe promising research results that may have been demonstrated in a constrained setting.

- **L2**—The approach describes practices that are in early pilot use and are demonstrating some successful results.

- **L3**—The approach describes practices that have been successfully deployed (mature) but are in limited use in industry or government organizations. They may be more broadly deployed in a particular market sector.

- **L4**—The approach describes practices that have been successfully deployed and are in widespread use. You can start using these practices today with confidence. Experience reports and case studies are typically available.

We developed these maturity levels to support our work in software security engineering [Allen 2008]. We associated the BoK elements and maturity levels by evaluating the extent to which relevant sources, practices, curricula, and courseware exist for a particular BoK element and the extent to which we have observed the element in practice in organizations.

MSwA2010 BoK with Outcomes and Maturity Levels

We found that the current maturity of the material being proposed for delivery in the MSwA2010 BoK varied. For example, a student would be expected to learn material at all maturity levels. If a practice was not very mature, we would still expect the student to be able to master it and use it in an appropriate manner after completing an MSwA program. We reasoned that the MSwA curriculum body of knowledge could be used as a basis for assessing maturity of software assurance practices, but to our knowledge, it has not been used for this purpose on an actual project, so it remains a hypothetical model. The portion of the table addressing risk management is shown below. The full table is contained in Appendix B, "The MSwA Body of Knowledge with Maturity Levels Added."

---

2. Risk Management

Outcome: Graduates will have the ability to perform risk analysis and tradeoff assessment and to prioritize security measures.

2.1. Risk Management Concepts

    2.1.1. Types and classification [L4]
    Different classes of risks (for example, business, project, technical)

    2.1.2. Probability, impact, severity [L4]
    Basic elements of risk analysis

    2.1.3. Models, processes, metrics [L4] [L3—metrics]
    Models, process, and metrics used in risk management

2.2. Risk Management Process

    2.2.1. Identification [L4]
    Identification and classification of risks associated with a project

    2.2.2. Analysis [L4]
    Analysis of the likelihood, impact, and severity of each identified risk

    2.2.3. Planning [L4]
    Risk management plan covering risk avoidance and mitigation

    2.2.4. Monitoring and management [L4]
    Assessment and monitoring of risk occurrence and management of risk mitigation

2.3. Software Assurance Risk Management

    2.3.1. Vulnerability and threat identification [L3]
    Application of risk analysis techniques to vulnerability and threat risks

    2.3.2. Analysis of software assurance risks [L3]
    Analysis of risks for both new and existing systems

(continued)

2.3.3. Software assurance risk mitigation [L3]
Plan for and mitigation of software assurance risks

2.3.4. Assessment of Software Assurance Processes and Practices [L2/3]
As part of risk avoidance and mitigation, assessment of the identification and use of appropriate software assurance processes and practices

3.3.7 SEI Research in Relation to the Microsoft SDL

More recently, the SEI's CERT Division examined the linkages between CERT research and the Microsoft SDL [Shunn 2013]. An excerpt from this report follows:

Our research has confirmed that **decisions made in the acquisition and development of new software and software-based systems have a major impact on operational security**. The challenge begins with properly stating software requirements and ensuring they clearly and practically define security. This is fundamental to the development and fielding of effectively secure systems. When these systems must interoperate with other systems built at a different time and with varying degrees of security, effective operational security becomes much more complex. Software and systems acquired, designed, and developed with operational security in mind are more resistant to both intentional attack and unintentional failures. The goal is to build and acquire better, minimally defective software and systems that can

- possess, through testing and analysis, some measurable level of assurance of minimal vulnerabilities

- operate correctly in the presence of most attacks by either resisting the exploitation of weaknesses in the software or tolerating the failures that result from such exploits

- recognize an attack and respond with expected behaviors that support resistance and recovery

- limit the damage from failures caused by attack or unanticipated faults and events and recover as quickly as possible

Managing complexity and ensuring survivability requires engineering methods based on solid foundations and the realities of current and emerging systems. A great deal of security response is reactive—addressing security issues in response to an attack. A more effective approach is to reduce the potential of such attacks by removing the vulnerabilities that allow a compromise in the first place. Our efforts to address issues before they become a security problem focus on the following key areas:

Secure Coding addresses tools, techniques, and standards that software developers and software development organizations require to eliminate vulnerabilities resulting from coding errors before software is deployed.

Vulnerability Analysis reduces the security risks posed by software vulnerabilities by addressing both the number of vulnerabilities in software that is being developed and the number of vulnerabilities in software that is already deployed. Our vulnerability analysis work is divided into two areas. Identifying and reducing the number of new vulnerabilities before the software is deployed is the focus of our vulnerability discovery effort, while our vulnerability remediation work deals with existing vulnerabilities in deployed software. We regularly comment on issues of importance to the vulnerability analysis and security community through the CERT/CC Blog.

Cyber Security Engineering addresses research needed to prepare acquirers, managers, developers, and operators of largescale, complex, networked systems to address security, survivability, and software assurance throughout the design and acquisition lifecycles. This research encompasses four areas: Software Assurance, Security Requirements, Software Supply Chain Risk Management (SCRM), and Software Risk Management. Because much of the DoD software is vendor developed, the research addresses both internal development and acquired software sources.

The report thus highlights a sample of CERT results with readily apparent connections to the SDL. Table 3.3 maps the CERT results to Microsoft SDL activities.

3.3.8 CERT Resilience Management Model Resilient Technical Solution Engineering Process Area

As is the case for software security and software assurance, resilience is a property of software and systems. Developing and acquiring resilient[4] software and systems requires a dedicated process focused on this property that encompasses the software and system lifecycle. Version 1.1 of the CERT Resilience Management Model's

---

4. There is substantial overlap in the definitions of assured software (or software assurance) and resilient software (or software resilience). Resilient software is software that continues to operate as intended (including recovering to a known operational state) in the face of a disruptive event (satisfying business continuity requirements) so as to satisfy its confidentiality, availability, and integrity requirements (reflecting operational and security requirements) [Caralli 2011].

Table 3.3 *Summary Mapping and Recommended Use*

CERT Solution	Microsoft SDL																
	Training	Requirements			Design			Implementation			Verification			Release			Response
	Core Security Training	Establish Security Requirements	Create Quality Gates/Bug Bars	Security & Privacy Risk Assessment	Establish Design Requirements	Analyze Attack Surface	Threat Modeling	Use Approved Tools	Deprecate Unsafe Functions	Static Analysis	Dynamic Analysis	Fuzz Testing	Attack Surface Review	Incident Response Plan	Final Security Review	Release Archive	Execute Incident Response Plan
CSIRT Management	X	X												X			X
Secure Coding in Java, C, and C++	X	X	X					X	X								
Source Code Analysis Laboratory (SCALe)		X	X						X	X	X	X			X		
Vulnerability Discovery and Fuzz Testing											X	X	X				
SQUARE Method for Security Requirements and tool	X	X	X	X	X	X	X										
Security Risk Analysis Toolkit		X		X	X								X		X		
Supply Chain Assurance Guidelines and Self-Assessment		X		X	X		X							X	X		

(CERT-RMM's)[5] Resilient Technical Solution Engineering (RTSE) process area defines what is required to develop resilient software and systems [Caralli 2011] (Version 1.2 is available as a free download. The associated release notes describe its updated features.[6]):

- Establish a plan for addressing resiliency as part of the organization's (or supplier's) regular development lifecycle and integrate the plan into the organization's corresponding development process. Plan development and execution includes identifying and mitigating risks to the success of the project.

- Identify practice-based guidelines that apply to all phases such as threat analysis and modeling as well as those that apply to a specific lifecycle phase.

- Elicit, identify, develop, and validate assurance and resiliency requirements (using methods for representing attacker and defender perspectives, for example). Such processes, methods, and tools are performed alongside similar processes for functional requirements.

- Use architectures as the basis for design that reflect a resiliency and assurance focus, including security, sustainability, and operations controls.

- Develop assured and resilient software and systems through processes that include secure coding of software, software defect detection and removal, and the development of resiliency and assurance controls based on design specifications.

- Test assurance and resiliency controls for software and systems and refer issues back to the design and development cycle for resolution.

- Conduct reviews throughout the development life cycle to ensure that resiliency (as one aspect of assurance) is kept in the forefront and given adequate attention and consideration.

- Perform system-specific continuity planning and integrate related service continuity plans to ensure that software, systems, hardware, networks, telecommunications, and other technical assets that depend on one another are sustainable.

- Perform a post-implementation review of deployed systems to ensure that resiliency (as well as assurance) requirements are being satisfied as intended.

- In operations, monitor software and systems to determine if there is variability that could indicate the effects of threats or vulnerabilities and to ensure that controls are functioning properly.

- Implement configuration management and change control processes to ensure software and systems are kept up to date to address newly discovered vulnerabilities and weaknesses (particularly in vendor-acquired products and components) and to prevent the intentional or inadvertent introduction of malicious code or other exploitable vulnerabilities.

---

5. www.cert.org/resilience/

6. Version 1.2 of the Resilience Management Model document [Caralli 2016] can be downloaded from the CERT website (www.cert.org/resilience/products-services/cert-rmm/index.cfm).

Table 3.4 lists RTSE practices.

Organizations should consider the following goals—in addition to RTSE—when developing and acquiring software and systems that need to meet assurance and resiliency requirements [Caralli 2011]:

> Resiliency requirements for software and system technology assets in operation, including those that may influence quality attribute requirements in the development process, are developed and managed in the Resiliency Requirements Development (RRD) and Resiliency Requirements Management (RRM) process areas respectively.
>
> Identifying and adding newly developed and acquired software and system assets to the organization's asset inventory is addressed in the Asset Definition and Management (ADM) process area.
>
> The management of resiliency for technology assets as a whole, particularly for deployed, operational assets, is addressed in the Technology Management (TM) process area. This includes, for example, asset fail-over, backup, recovery, and restoration.
>
> Acquiring software and systems from external entities and ensuring that such assets meet their resiliency requirements throughout the asset life cycle is addressed in the External Dependencies Management process area. That said, RTSE specific goals and practices should be used to aid in evaluating and selecting external entities that are developing software and systems (EXD:SG3.SP3), formalizing relationships with such external entities (EXD:SG3.SP4), and managing an external entity's performance when developing software and systems (EXD:SG4).
>
> Monitoring for events, incidents, and vulnerabilities that may affect software and systems in operation is addressed in the Monitoring (MON) process area.
>
> Service continuity plans are identified and created in the Service Continuity (SC) process area. These plans may be inclusive of software and systems that support the services for which planning is performed.

Table 3.4 *RTSE Practices*

Goal	Practices
RTSE:SG1 Establish Guidelines for Resilient Technical Solution Development	RTSE:SG1.SP1 Identify General Guidelines
	RTSE:SG1.SP2 Identify Requirements Guidelines
	RTSE:SG1.SP3 Identify Architecture and Design Guidelines
	RTSE:SG1.SP4 Identify Implementation Guidelines
	RTSE:SG1.SP5 Identify Assembly and Integration Guidelines

RTSE:SG2 Develop Resilient Technical Solution Development Plans	RTSE:SG2.SP1 Select and Tailor Resiliency Guidelines
	RTSE:SG2.SP2 Integrate Selected Guidelines with a Defined Software and System Development Process
RTSE:SG3 Execute the Plan	RTSE:SG3.SP1 Monitor Execution of the Development Plan
	RTSE:SG3.SP2 Release Resilient Technical Solutions into Production

RTSE assumes that the organization has one or more existing, defined process for software and system development into which resiliency controls and activities can be integrated. If this is not the case, the organization should not attempt to implement the goals and practices identified in RTSE or in other CERT-RMM process areas as described above.

3.3.9 International Process Research Consortium (IPRC) Roadmap

From August 2004 to December 2006, the SEI's process program sponsored a research consortium of 28 international thought leaders to explore process needs for today, the foreseeable future, and the unforeseeable future. One of the emerging research themes was the relationships between processes and product qualities, defined as "understanding if and how particular process characteristics can affect desired product (and service) qualities such as security, usability, and maintainability" [IPRC 2006]. As an example, or instantiation, of this research theme, two of the participating members, Julia Allen and Barbara Kitchenham, developed research nodes and research questions for security as a product quality. This content helps identify research topics and gaps that could be explored within the context of the BASF.

The descriptive material presented in Table 3.5 is excerpted from *A Process Research Framework* [IPRC 2006].

3.3.10 NIST Cyber Security Framework

The NIST Framework for Improving Critical Infrastructure Cybersecurity is the result of a February 2013 executive order from U.S. President Barack Obama titled

Table 3.5 *IPRC Research Nodes and Questions for Security as a Product Quality*

Research Node	Research Questions
Establishing security in the systems or software development lifecycle: Determine the extent to which processes can be used to accurately reflect and cause the instantiation of required security product quality attributes for each SDLC phase.	• How is security expressed in each phase of the SDLC? What are appropriate expressions, from a security perspective, of how the system is to be used?
	• What processes best ensure the instantiation of established security principles?
	• What effective processes and methods ensure that known causes of security vulnerabilities are not present in each phase of the SDLC?
	• What processes and methods can be used to accelerate adoption of known methods for developing low-defect-rate (and thus more secure) software (state of art/state of practice gap)?
	• What are the compelling cost/benefit arguments for using these processes and methods to improve security?
	• Is it possible to build and verify secure software and systems using agile methods?
	• What processes can be used to ensure that security requirements are met for systems composed from existing components? For extensible systems?
Establishing the relationship between process and security as a product quality: Establish whether there is a direct relationship between security as a product quality, and the processes used to develop the product.	• What is the role of process in ensuring that software and systems are engineered such that they continue to function correctly under malicious attacks, failures, and accidents?

Measuring and monitoring security performance: Establish processes to accurately capture meaningful measures that aid in determining whether a system is meeting its security requirements (and how well) during all SDLC phases.	• What are the definitions of meaningful, informative security measures? What processes are needed to reliably collect them? • What measures indicate that a system has met its security requirements for each SDLC phase? What are the processes for collecting, analyzing, and reporting these measures? • What measures and evaluation processes can be used to determine the effectiveness of different secure software development processes?
Verifying and validating of security: Enable managers to select appropriate assessment, evaluation, verification, and validation processes to confirm the achievement of security requirements. Process selection is guided by the nature and complexity of the system being constructed and operated. Methods include the use of scenario-based misuse/abuse cases.	• How is an adequate or acceptable level of security determined, tested, verified, and certified? • What processes are most effective for assessing, evaluating, verifying, and certifying the security of software and systems (including those provided by third parties)? • What processes and methods are most likely to reveal security issues, flaws, and vulnerabilities during each SDLC phase? And with third party, open source, and COTS, or other component software? • In the case where such processes already exist and have empirical evidence to justify their use, what can be done to accelerate their adoption (state of art/state of practice gap)? • What processes and methods allow for building misuse/abuse cases that predictably provide evidence that security product qualities are present?

(continued)

Table 3.5 *Continued*

Research Node	Research Questions
Sustaining adequate security: Enable managers to select processes that result in establishing, sustaining, and evolving an adequate level of security throughout the full product lifecycle.	• How do we define and sustain adequate security in the face of increasingly sophisticated attacks (attack evolution), technology evolution, enterprise evolution, supply chain evolution, and the like (all sources of change that require a system to evolve)?
Enabling usable security: Enable users to effectively apply and use required security mechanisms, to the extent that they are visible to the user.	• What user interface processes and methods result in users applying protection and security mechanisms routinely, automatically, and correctly?
	• What processes result in minimal to no user involvement in security?

Improving Critical Infrastructure Cybersecurity [White House 2013]. The order emphasized that "it is the Policy of the United States to enhance the security and resilience of the Nation's critical infrastructure and to maintain a cyber-environment that encourages efficiency, innovation, and economic prosperity while promoting safety, security, business confidentiality, privacy, and civil liberties" [White House 2013].

The NIST framework provides an assessment mechanism that enables organizations to determine their current cyber security capabilities, set individual goals for a target state, and establish a plan for improving and maintaining cyber security programs [NIST 2014]. There are three components—Core, Profile, and Implementation tiers—as discussed in the following excerpt [NIST 2014]:

> The Core presents the recommendations of industry standards, guidelines, and practices in a manner that allows for communication of cybersecurity activities and outcomes across the organization from the executive level to the implementation/ operations level.

The Core is hierarchical and consists of five cyber security risk functions. Each function is further broken down into categories and subcategories.

The categories include processes, procedures, and technologies such as the following:

- Asset management
- Alignment with business strategy
- Risk assessment
- Access control
- Employee training
- Data security
- Event logging and analysis
- Incident response plans

Each subcategory provides a set of cyber security risk management best practices that can help organizations align and improve their cyber security capability based on individual business needs, tolerance to risk, and resource availability [NIST 2014].

The Core criteria are used to determine the outcomes necessary to improve the overall security effort of an organization. The unique requirements of industry, customers, and partners are then factored into the target profile. Comparing the current and target profiles identifies the gaps that should be closed to enhance cyber security. Organizations must prioritize the gaps to establish the basis for a prioritized roadmap to help make improvements.

Implementation tiers create a context that enables an organization to understand how its current cyber security risk management capabilities rate against the ideal characteristics described by the NIST Framework. Tiers range from Partial (Tier 1) to Adaptive (Tier 4). NIST recommends that organizations seeking to achieve an effective, defensible cyber security program progress to Tier 3 or 4.

3.3.11 Uses of Software Security Frameworks, Models, and Roadmaps

Because software security is a relatively new field, the frameworks, models, and road-maps have not been in use, on average, for as long a time as the CMMI models, and their use is not as widespread. Nevertheless, there are important uses to consider.

Secure development process models are in use by organizations for which security is a priority:

- The Microsoft SDL and variants on it are in relatively wide use.
- BSIMM has strong participation, with 78 organizations represented in BSIMM6. Since its inception in 2008, the BSIMM has studied 104 organizations.
- Elements of CERT-RMM are also widely used.

There is less usage data on secure software process models than on the more general software process models, so the true extent of usage is hard to assess. As organizations and governments become more aware of the need for software security, we expect usage of these models to increase, and we expect to see additional research in this area, perhaps with the appearance of new models.

In academia, in addition to traditional software process models, software security courses often present one or more of the secure development models and processes. Such courses occur at all levels of education, but especially at the master's level. Individual and team student projects frequently use the models or their individual components and provide a rich learning environment for students learning about secure software development.

3.4 Summary

This chapter presents a number of frameworks and models that can be used to help support cyber security decision making. These frameworks and models include process models, security frameworks and models in the literature, and the SEI efforts in this area. We do a deeper dive for some of these topics in Chapter 7, "Special Topics in Cyber Security Engineering," which provides further discussion of governance considerations for cyber security engineering, security requirements engineering for acquisition, and standards.

As noted earlier in this chapter, we developed maturity levels to support our work in software security engineering [Allen 2008]. Since 2008, some of the practice areas have increased in maturity. Nevertheless, we believe you can still apply the maturity levels to assess whether a specific approach is sufficiently mature to help achieve your cyber security goals. Our earlier work [Allen 2008] also included a recommended strategy and suggested order of practice implementation. This work remains valid today, and we reiterate the maturity levels here. They also appear in Chapter 8, "Summary and Plan for Improvements in Cyber Security Engineering Performance," where we rate the maturity levels of the methods presented throughout the book.

Maturity Levels, Revisited

- **L1**—The approach provides guidance for how to think about a topic for which there is no proven or widely accepted approach. The intent of the area is to raise awareness and aid in thinking about the problem and candidate solutions. The area may also describe promising research results that may have been demonstrated in a constrained setting.

- **L2**—The approach describes practices that are in early pilot use and are demonstrating some successful results.

- **L3**—The approach describes practices that have been successfully deployed (mature) but are in limited use in industry or government organizations. They may be more broadly deployed in a particular market sector.

- **L4**—The approach describes practices that have been successfully deployed and are in widespread use. You can start using these practices today with confidence. Experience reports and case studies are typically available.

We encourage you to try using the maturity levels to assess the models presented in this chapter to see which ones work best to support your cyber security goals. Organizations may be able to use one or more of the models directly, or they may need to tailor them to address their own unique organizational cyber security problems and goals for improvement.

Chapter 4

Engineering Competencies

with Tom Hilburn and Dan Shoemaker

In This Chapter

- 4.1 Security Competency and the Software Engineering Profession
- 4.2 Software Assurance Competency Models
- 4.3 The DHS Competency Model
- 4.4 The SEI Software Assurance Competency Model
- 4.5 Summary

4.1 Security Competency and the Software Engineering Profession[1]

Modern society increasingly relies on software systems that put a premium on quality and dependability. The extensive use of the Internet and distributed computing has made software security an ever more prominent and serious problem. So, the interest in and demand for software security specialists have grown dramatically in recent years. The Department of Homeland Security (DHS), the Department of Defense (DoD), the Software Engineering Institute (SEI), and other government, commercial, and educational organizations have expressed a critical need for the education and development of software security specialists.

However, to support this need, we must address some key questions. What background and capability does a software security specialist need? How do individuals assess their capability and preparation for software security work? What's the career path to increased capability and advancement in this area of software development?

---

1. This section is drawn from *The Software Assurance Competency Model: A Roadmap to Enhance Individual Professional Capability* [Mead 2013a].

In this section, we hope to answer these questions and provide guidance to career seekers in software security engineering. These answers might also help employers determine their software security needs and assess and improve their employees' software security capability.

Software was with us long before the creation of FORTRAN [Backus 1957]. The roots of software engineering as a profession go back to the late 1960s and early 1970s, with the emergence of structured programming, structured design, and process models such as the Waterfall model [Royce 1970]. This means that, at a minimum, software engineering has been a regular profession for at least 42 years.

In the past four decades, there have been numerous general attempts to define what a competent software professional should look like. Examples of this range from Humphrey's first published work on capability [Humphrey 1989], through the effort to define software engineering as a profession, accompanied by a Software Engineering Body of Knowledge [Abran 2004] and the People Capability Maturity Model [Curtis 2002].

The success of these efforts is still debatable, but one thing is certain: Up to this point, there have been only a few narrowly focused attempts to define the professional qualities needed to develop a secure software product. The Software Assurance (SwA) Competency Model was developed to address this missing element of the profession.

The obvious question, given all of this prior work, is "Why do we need one more professional competency model?" The answer lies in the significant difference between the competencies required to produce working code and those that are needed to produce software free from exploitable weaknesses. That difference is underscored by the presence of the adversary.

In the 1990s, it was generally acceptable for software to have flaws, as long as those flaws did not impact program efficiency or the ability to satisfy user requirements. So development and assurance techniques focused on proper execution with no requirements errors. Now, bad actors can exploit an unintentional defect in a program to cause all kinds of trouble. So although they are related in some ways, the professional competencies that are associated with the assurance of secure software merit their own specific framework.

A specific model for software assurance competency provides two advantages for the profession as a whole. First and most importantly, a standard model allows prospective employers to define the fundamental capabilities needed by their workforce. At the same time, it allows organizations to establish a general, minimum set of competency requirements for their employees; and more importantly, it allows companies to tailor an exact set of competency requirements for any given project.

From the standpoint of the individual worker, a competency model provides software assurance professionals with a standard roadmap that they can use to improve performance by adding specific skills needed to obtain a position and climb the competency ladder for their profession. For example, a new graduate starting in an entry-level position can map out a path for enhancing his/her skills and planning his/her career advances as a software assurance professional. In many respects, this roadmap feature makes a professional competency model a significant player in the development of the workforce of the future, which, of course, is of interest to software engineering educators and trainers.

4.2 Software Assurance Competency Models[2]

In this section, we discuss the SEI's Software Assurance Competency Model in detail. Before we begin, we provide a list of influential and useful sources—some of the competency models and supporting materials that were studied and analyzed in the development of the SEI's SwA Competency Model:

- **Software Assurance Professional Competency Model (DHS)**—Focuses on 10 SwA specialty areas (e.g., Software Assurance and Security Engineering and Information Assurance Compliance) and describes four levels of behavior indicators for each specialty area [DHS 2012].

- **Information Technology Competency Model (Department of Labor)**— Uses a pyramid model to focus on a tiered set of generic non-technical and technical competency areas (e.g., Personal Effectiveness Competencies for Tier 1 and Industry-Wide Technical Competencies for Tier 4). Specific jobs or roles are not designated [DoLETA 2012].

- *A Framework for PAB Competency Models* **(Professional Advisory Board [PAB], IEEE Computer Society)**—Provides an introduction to competency models and presents guidelines for achieving consistency among competency models developed by the Professional Advisory Board (PAB) of the IEEE Computer Society. Provides a generic framework for a professional that can be instantiated with specific knowledge, skills, and effectiveness levels for a particular computing profession (e.g., Software Engineering practitioner) [IEEE-CS 2014].

- **"Balancing Software Engineering Education and Industrial Needs"**— Describes a study conducted to help both academia and the software industry form a picture of the relationship between the competencies of recent graduates of undergraduate and graduate software engineering programs and the competencies needed to perform as a software engineering professional [Moreno 2012].

---

2. This section is drawn from *Software Assurance Competency Model* [Hilburn 2013a].

- *Competency Lifecycle Roadmap: Toward Performance Readiness* (**Software Engineering Institute**)—Provides an early look at the roadmap for understanding and building workforce readiness. This roadmap includes activities to reach a state of readiness: Assess Plan, Acquire, Validate, and Test Readiness [Behrens 2012].

Other work on competency models includes works from academia and government [Khajenoori 1998; NASA 2016]. Other related work, although it was not reviewed prior to development of the SEI's Software Assurance Competency Model, includes the Skills Framework for the Information Age (SFIA), an international effort related to competencies in information technology.[3]

IEEE Software Engineering Competency Model

Since the SEI's Software Assurance Competency Model was published, IEEE has published the Software Engineering Competency Model (SWECOM) [IEEE-CS 2014]. We highly recommend the SWECOM as a relevant model for the broader topic of software engineering competency.

4.3 The DHS Competency Model[4]

The DHS competency model was developed independently from the SEI's competency model. The structure of the DHS model provides insight into how competency models can differ from one another, depending on the model developers, the intended audience, and so on. There is no single "correct" software assurance competency model; however, use of a competency model benefits organizations, projects, and individuals.

4.3.1 Purpose

The DHS model [DHS 2012] is designed to serve the following needs:

- Interagency and public–private collaboration promotes and enables security and resilience of software throughout the lifecycle.

---

3. www.sfia-online.org/en

4. This section is drawn from *Software Assurance Competency Model* [Hilburn 2013a].

- It provides a means to reduce exploitable software weaknesses and improve capabilities that routinely develop, acquire, and deploy resilient software products.

- Development and publishing of software security content and SwA curriculum courseware are focused on integrating software security content into relevant education and training programs.

- It enables software security automation and measurement capabilities.

4.3.2 Organization of Competency Areas

The DHS organizes its model around a set of "specialty areas" aligned with the National Initiative for Cybersecurity Education (NICE), corresponding to the range of areas in which the DHS has interest and responsibility:

- Software Assurance and Security Engineering
- Information Assurance Compliance
- Enterprise Architecture
- Technology Demonstration
- Education and Training
- Strategic Planning and Policy Development
- Knowledge Management
- Cyber Threat Analysis
- Vulnerability Assessment and Management
- Systems Requirements Planning

4.3.3 SwA Competency Levels

The DHS model designates four "proficiency" levels for which competencies are specified for each specialty area:

- **Level 1—Basic**—Understands the subject matter and is seen as someone who can perform basic or developmental-level work in activities requiring this specialty.

- **Level 2—Intermediate**—Can apply the subject matter and is considered someone who has the capability to fully perform work that requires application of this specialty.

- **Level 3—Advanced**—Can analyze the subject matter and is seen as someone who can immediately contribute to the success of work requiring this specialty.

- **Level 4—Expert**—Can synthesize/evaluate the subject matter and is looked to as an expert in this specialty.

Table 4.1 *Proficiency Targets for the Software Assurance and Security Engineering Specialty Area*

Proficiency Targets		
Project Lead (GS 13)	**Senior (GS 14)**	**Director (GS 15)**
3—Advanced	4—Expert	4—Expert

4.3.4 Behavioral Indicators

For each specialty area, the DHS describes, for each level, how the competency manifests itself in observable on-the-job behavior; these descriptions are called *behavioral indicators*.

The description of each specialty area also designates proficiency targets (which identify the proficiency at which a person in a specific career level should be performing) and aligns with the behavioral indicator descriptions for the specialty area. For example, the Software Assurance and Security Engineering specialty area designates the targets depicted in Table 4.1.

4.3.5 National Initiative for Cybersecurity Education (NICE)

As noted above, the DHS organizes its model around a set of "specialty areas" aligned with the National Initiative for Cybersecurity Education (NICE). A major government initiative in cyber security work descriptions and training, the National Initiative for Cybersecurity Careers and Studies (NICCS) supporting NICE provides the following insight:[5]

> The National Initiative for Cybersecurity Careers and Studies (NICCS) is a key resource of cyber security information. NICCS directly supports the three components of The National Initiative for Cybersecurity Education (NICE) that focus on enhancing awareness, expanding the pipeline and evolving the field. NICCS is a national resource available to anyone from government, industry, academia, and the general public who seeks to learn more about cyber security and opportunities in the field.

An important element of the initiative is the National Cybersecurity Workforce Framework:[6]

---

5. https://niccs.us-cert.gov/home/about-niccs

6. https://niccs.us-cert.gov/training/tc/framework

> The National Cybersecurity Workforce Framework provides a blueprint to categorize, organize, and describe cyber security work into Specialty Areas, tasks, and knowledge, skills and abilities (KSAs). The Workforce Framework provides a common language to speak about cyber roles and jobs and helps define professional requirements in cyber security.

The Workforce Framework organizes cyber security into seven high-level categories, each comprised of several specialty areas. The seven categories are Securely Provision, Operate and Maintain, Protect and Defend, Investigate, Collect and Operate, Analyze, and Oversight and Development.

The SEI's Software Assurance Curriculum Model heavily influenced the Securely Provision section of the NICE framework. Securely Provision includes the following specialty areas: Information Assurance Compliance, Software Assurance and Security Engineering, Systems Development, Systems Requirements Planning, Systems Security Architecture, Technology Research and Development, and Test and Evaluation.

The framework additionally provides a discussion of knowledge, skills, and abilities, competencies, and tasks, in a searchable database. NICE hosts periodic workshops and maintains a training catalog[7]:

> The NICCS Training Catalog provides a robust listing of cyber security and cyber security-related training courses offered in the U.S. The Training Catalog contains over 2,000 courses, with more courses being added every day! The NICCS Training Catalog is meant to serve as a central resource to help people find the information on courses they want or need for a career in cyber. The Training Catalog allows users to search for courses based on: keyword, proficiency level, delivery method, and Workforce Framework Specialty Area.

4.4 The SEI Software Assurance Competency Model[8]

In the SEI Software Assurance Competency Model, the term *competency* represents the set of knowledge, skills, and effectiveness needed to carry out the job activities associated with one or more roles in an employment position [IEEE-CS 2014]:

- Knowledge is what an individual knows and can describe (e.g., can name and define various classes of risks).

- Skills are what an individual can do that involves application of knowledge to carry out a task (e.g., can identify and classify the risks associated with a project).

---

7. https://niccs.us-cert.gov/training/tc/search
8. This section is drawn from *Software Assurance Competency Model* [Hilburn 2013a].

- Effectiveness is concerned with the ability to apply knowledge and skills in a productive manner, characterized by attributes of behavior such as aptitude, initiative, enthusiasm, willingness, communication skills, team participation, and leadership.

As noted above, in the process of developing the SEI's Software Assurance Competency Model, the authors studied and analyzed a number of other competency models and supporting material. A key reference for the SwA Competency Model is the Master of Software Assurance Reference Curriculum [Mead 2010a]. The curriculum underwent both internal and public review and was endorsed by both the ACM and the IEEE Computer Society as being appropriate for a master's degree in software assurance. The curriculum document includes a mapping of the software assurance topic areas to GSwE2009 [Stevens Institute of Technology 2009], thus providing a comparison to software engineering knowledge areas. Since then, elements of the curriculum have been adopted by various universities, including the Air Force Academy [Hadfield 2011, 2012], Carnegie Mellon University, Stevens Institute of Technology, and notably by (ISC)^2, a training and certification organization. As noted below, the MSwA curriculum was the primary source for the knowledge and skills used in the competency model for various levels of professional competency.

The Software Assurance Competency Model provides employers of software assurance personnel with a means to assess the software assurance capabilities of current and potential employees. In addition, along with the MSwA reference curriculum, this model is intended to guide academic or training organizations in the development of education and training courses to support the needs of organizations that are hiring and developing software assurance professionals.

The SwA Competency Model enhances the guidance of software engineering curricula by providing information about industry needs and expectations for competent security professionals [Mead 2010a, 2010c, 2011b]; the model also provides software assurance professionals with direction and a progression for development and career planning. Finally, a standard competency model provides support for professional certification activities.

4.4.1 Model Features

Professional competency models typically feature competency levels, which distinguish between what's expected in an entry-level position and what's required in more senior positions.

In the software assurance competency model, five levels (L1–L5) of competency distinguish different levels of professional capability relative to knowledge, skills, and effectiveness [IEEE-CS 2014]. Individuals can use the competency levels to assess the extent and level of their capability and to guide their preparation for software security work:

- L1—Technician C
  - Possesses technical knowledge and skills, typically gained through a certificate or an associate degree program or equivalent knowledge and experience.
  - May be employed in system operator, implementer, tester, and maintenance positions with specific individual tasks assigned by someone at a higher hierarchy level.
  - Main areas of competency are System Operational Assurance (SOA), System Functional Assurance (SFA), and System Security Assurance (SSA) (see Table 4.2).
  - Major tasks: low-level implementation, testing, and maintenance.

- L2—Professional Entry Level
  - Possesses "application-based" knowledge and skills and entry-level professional effectiveness, typically gained through a bachelor's degree in computing or through equivalent professional experience.
  - May perform all tasks of L1 and, additionally, manage a small internal project, supervise and assign subtasks for L1 personnel, supervise and assess system operations, and implement commonly accepted assurance practices.
  - Main areas of competency are SFA, SSA, and Assurance Assessment (AA) (see Table 4.2).
  - Major tasks: requirements fundamentals, module design, and implementation.

- L3—Practitioner
  - Possesses breadth and depth of knowledge, skills, and effectiveness beyond the L2 level and typically has 2 to 5 years of professional experience.
  - May perform all tasks of L2 personnel and, additionally, set plans, tasks, and schedules for in-house projects; define and manage such projects; and supervise teams on the enterprise level, report to management, assess the assurance quality of a system, and implement and promote commonly accepted software assurance practices.

- Main areas of competency are Risk Management (RM), AA, and Assurance Management (AM) (see Table 4.2).

- Major tasks: requirements analysis, architectural design, tradeoff analysis, and risk assessment.

- L4—Senior Practitioner

- Possesses breadth and depth of knowledge, skills, and effectiveness and a variety of work experiences beyond L3, with 5 to 10 years of professional experience and advanced professional development at the master's level or with equivalent education/training.

- May perform all tasks of L3 personnel and identify and explore effective software assurance practices for implementation, manage large projects, interact with external agencies, etc.

- Main areas of competency are RM, AA, AM, and Assurance Across Lifecycles (AALC) (see Table 4.2).

- Major tasks: assurance assessment, assurance management, and risk management across the lifecycle.

- L5—Expert

- Possesses competency beyond L4; advances the field by developing, modifying, and creating methods, practices, and principles at the organizational level or higher; has peer/industry recognition.

- Typically includes a low percentage of an organization's workforce within the SwA profession (e.g., 2% or less).

4.4.2 SwA Knowledge, Skills, and Effectiveness

The primary source for SwA Competency Model knowledge and skills is the Core Body of Knowledge (CorBoK), contained in *Software Assurance Curriculum Project, Volume I: Master of Software Assurance Reference Curriculum* [Mead 2010a]. The CorBoK consists of the knowledge areas listed in Table 4.2. Each knowledge area is further divided into second-level units, as shown later in this chapter, in Table 4.5. For each unit, competency activities are described for each of the levels L1–L5.

Table 4.2 *CorBoK Knowledge Areas and Competencies*

Knowledge Area (KA)	KA Competency
AALC: Assurance Across Lifecycles L3, L4, L5	The ability to incorporate assurance technologies and methods into lifecycle processes and development models for new or evolutionary system development and for system or service acquisitions.
RM: Risk Management L2, L3, L4, L5	The ability to perform risk analysis and trade-off assessment, and to prioritize security measures.
AA: Assurance Assessment L1, L2, L3, L4	The ability to analyze and validate the effectiveness of assurance operations and create auditable evidence of security measures.
AM: Assurance Management L3, L4, L5	The ability to make a business case for software assurance, lead assurance efforts, understand standards, comply with regulations, plan for business continuity, and keep current in security technologies.
SSA: System Security Assurance L1, L2, L3, L4	The ability to incorporate effective security technologies and methods into new and existing systems.
SFA: System Functionality Assurance L1, L2, L3	The ability to verify new and existing software system functionality for conformance to requirements and to help reveal malicious content.
SOA: System Operational Assurance L1, L2, L3	The ability to monitor and assess system operational security and respond to new threats.

The CorBoK specifies the KAs in greater detail, as illustrated by the specification of the System Security Assurance KA in Table 4.3.

Other than the unit "Ethics and Integrity" in the System Security Assurance Knowledge Area shown in Table 4.3, the CorBoK does not contain topics on competency associated with effectiveness; the effectiveness attributes are listed in Table 4.4 (adapted from [IEEE-CS 2014]). In Table 4.4, for a given attribute, there is no differentiation in effectiveness for the different competency levels; however,

Table 4.3 *The Specification for the System Security Assurance KA*[*]

Unit	Topics	Description
For Newly Developed and Acquired Software for Diverse Systems	Security and safety aspects of computer-intensive critical infrastructure	Knowledge of safety and security risks associated with critical infrastructure systems such as found, for example, in banking and finance, energy production and distribution, telecommunications, and transportation systems
	Potential attack methods	Knowledge of the variety of methods by which attackers can damage software or data associated with that software by exploiting weaknesses in the system design or implementation
	Analysis of threats to software	Analysis of the threats to which software is most likely to be vulnerable in specific operating environments and domains
	Methods of defense	Familiarity with appropriate countermeasures such as layers, access controls, privileges, intrusion detection, encryption, and code review checklists
For Diverse Operational (Existing) Systems	Historic and potential operational attack methods	Knowledge of and ability to duplicate the attacks that have been used to interfere with an application's or system's operations
	Analysis of threats to operational environments	Analysis of the threats to which software is most likely to be vulnerable in specific operating environments and domains

	Design of and plan for access control, privileges, and authentication	Design and plan for effective countermeasures such as layers, access controls, privileges, intrusion detection, encryption, and coding checklists
	Security methods for physical and personnel environments	Knowledge of how physical access restrictions, guards, background checks, and personnel monitoring can address risks
Ethics and Integrity in Creation, Acquisition, and Operation of Software Systems	Overview of ethics, code of ethics, and legal constraints	Knowledge of how people who are knowledgeable about attack and prevention methods are obligated to use their abilities, both legally and ethically, referencing the Software Engineering Code of Ethical and Professional Conduct
	Computer attack case studies	Knowledge of the legal and ethical considerations involved in analyzing a variety of historical events and investigations

*This table is from "Building Security In: A Road to Competency" [Hilburn 2013b].

Table 4.4 *Competency Attributes of Effectiveness*

Competency Attribute	Description	Competency Level
Aptitude	Exhibited by the ability to do a certain software assurance activity at a certain level of competence. Aptitude is not the same as knowledge or skill but rather indicates the ability to apply knowledge in a skillful way.	L2–L5
Enthusiasm	Exhibited by being interested in and excited about performing a software assurance work activity.	L1–L5
Willingness	Exhibited by undertaking a work activity, when asked, even if it is an activity the individual is not enthusiastic about performing.	L1–L5
Communication	Exhibited by expressing thoughts and ideas in both oral and written forms in a clear and concise manner while interacting with team members, managers, project stakeholders, and others.	L2–L5
Teamwork	Exhibited by working enthusiastically and willingly with other team members while collaborating on work activities.	L1–L5
Leadership	Exhibited by effectively communicating a vision, strategy, or technique that is accepted and shared by team members, managers, project stakeholders, and others.	L3–L5

professionals would be expected to show an increase in the breadth and depth of capability in these areas of effectiveness as they proceed through their careers and move to higher competency levels.

4.4.3 Competency Designations

Table 4.5 presents a portion of the CorBoK knowledge areas and second-level units, along with a description of the appropriate knowledge and skills for each competency level and the effectiveness attributes. The complete table can be found in the competency report [Hilburn 2013a]. A designation of L1 applies to levels L1 through L5; a designation of L2 applies to L2 through L5; and so on. The level descriptions indicate the competency activities that are demonstrated at each level.

Table 4.5 *SwA Competency Designations*

KA	Unit	Knowledge/Skill/Effectiveness Competency Activities
Assurance Across Lifecycles	Software Lifecycle Processes	L1: Understand and execute the portions of a defined process applicable to their assigned tasks.
		L2: Manage the application of a defined lifecycle software process for a small internal project.
		L3: Lead and assess process application for small and medium-sized projects, over a variety of lifecycle phases, such as new development, acquisition, operation, and evolution.
		L4: Manage the application of a defined lifecycle software process for a large project, including selecting and adapting existing SwA practices by lifecycle phase.
		L5: Analyze, design, and evolve lifecycle processes that meet the special organizational or domain needs and constraints.
	Software Assurance Processes and Practices	L1: Possess general awareness of methods, procedures, and tools used to assess assurance processes and practices.
		L2: Apply methods, procedures, and tools to assess assurance processes and practices.
		L3: Manage integration of assurance practices into typical lifecycle phases.
		L4: Lead the selection and integration of lifecycle assurance processes and practices in all projects, across an organization.
		L5: Analyze assurance assessment results to determine best practices for various lifecycle phases.

(Continued)

Table 4.5 *Continued*

KA	Unit	Knowledge/Skill/Effectiveness
		Competency Activities
Risk Management	Risk Management Concepts	L1: Understand the basic elements of risk analysis.
		L2: Explain how risk analysis is performed.
		L3: Determine the models, process, and metrics to be used in risk management for small internal projects.
		L4: Develop the models, processes, and metrics to be used in risk management of any sized project.
		L5: Analyze the effectiveness of the use and application of risk management concepts across an organization.
	Risk Management Process	L1: Describe an organizational risk management process.
		L2: Identify and classify the risks associated with a project.
		L3: Analyze the likelihood, impact, and severity of each identified risk for a project. Plan and monitor risk management for small to medium-sized projects.
		L4: Plan and monitor risk management for a large project.
		L5: Develop a program for analyzing and enhancing risk management practices across an organization.
	Software Assurance Risk Management	L1: Describe risk analysis techniques for vulnerability and threat risks.
		L2: Apply risk analysis techniques to vulnerability and threat risks.
		L3: Analyze and plan for mitigation of software assurance risks for small systems.
		L4: Analyze and plan for mitigation of software assurance risks for both new and existing systems.
		L5: Assess software assurance processes and practices across an organization and propose improvements.

4.4.4 A Path to Increased Capability and Advancement[9]

The SwA Competency Model can provide direction on professional growth and career advancement. Each competency level assumes competency at the lower levels. The model also provides a comprehensive mapping between the CorBoK (KAs and units) and the competency levels. The complete mapping can be found in Appendix D, "The Software Assurance Competency Model Designations." Table 4.6 illustrates this mapping for the System Security Assurance KA.

4.4.5 Examples of the Model in Practice[10]

There are a number of ways the Software Assurance Competency Model can be applied in practice. An organization in which software assurance is critical could use the type of information in Table 4.6 to do all of the following:

- Structure its software assurance needs and expectations
- Assess its software assurance personnel's capability
- Provide a roadmap for employee advancement
- Use as a basis for software assurance professional development plans

For example, an organization intending to hire an entry-level software assurance professional could examine the L1–L2 levels and incorporate elements of them into job descriptions. These levels could also be used during the interview process by both the employer and the prospective employee to assess the actual expertise of the candidate.

Another application is by faculty members who are developing courses in software assurance or adding software assurance elements to their software engineering courses. The levels allow faculty to easily see the depth of content that is suitable for courses at the community college, undergraduate, and graduate levels. For example, undergraduate student outcomes might be linked to the L1 and L2 levels, whereas graduate courses aimed at practitioners with more experience might target higher levels. In industry, the model could be used to determine if specific competency areas were being overlooked. These areas could point toward corresponding training needs. With a bit of effort, trainers can tailor their course offerings to the target audience. The model eliminates some of the guesswork involved in deciding what level of material is appropriate for a given course.

---

9. This section is drawn from "Building Security In: A Road to Competency" [Hilburn 2013b].
10. This section is drawn from *The Software Assurance Competency Model: A Roadmap to Enhance Individual Professional Capability* [Mead 2013a].

Table 4.6 *The Competency Specification for the System Security Assurance KA*

Unit	Competency Activities
For Newly Developed and Acquired Software for Diverse Applications	L1: Possess knowledge of security and safety risks associated with critical infrastructure systems (e.g., in banking and finance, energy production and distribution, telecommunications, and transportation systems).
	L2: Describe the variety of methods by which attackers can damage software or data associated with that software by exploiting weaknesses in the system design or implementation.
	L3: Apply software assurance countermeasures such as layers, access controls, privileges, intrusion detection, encryption, and code review checklists.
	L4: Analyze the threats to which software is most likely to be vulnerable in specific operating environments and domains.
	L5: Perform research on security risks and attack methods, and use it to support modification or creation of techniques used to counter such risks and attacks.
For Diverse Operational (Existing) Systems	L1: Possess knowledge of the attacks that have been used to interfere with an application's or system's operations.
	L2: Possess knowledge of how gates, locks, guards, and background checks can address risks.

	L3: Design and plan for access control and authentication.
	L4: Analyze the threats to which software is most likely to be vulnerable in specific operating environments and domains.
	L5: Perform research on security risks and attack methods, and use it to support modification or creation of techniques used to counter such risks and attacks.
Ethics and Integrity in Creation, Acquisition, and Operation of Software Systems	L1: Possess knowledge of how people who are knowledgeable about attack and prevention methods are obligated to use their abilities, both legally and ethically.
	L2: Possess knowledge of the legal and ethical considerations involved in analyzing a variety of historical events and investigations.
	L3: Follow legal and ethical guidelines in the creation and maintenance of software systems.
	L4: Play a leadership role in the practice of ethical behavior for software security.
	L5: Create new case studies for use in education about ethical and legal issues.

It can also be used by faculty who are already teaching such courses to assess whether the course material is a good fit for the target audience. The authors of this chapter are currently teaching software assurance courses and use the model to revisit and tailor their syllabi accordingly.

4.4.6 Highlights of the SEI Software Assurance Competency Model[11]

The Software Assurance Competency Model was developed to create a foundation for assessing and advancing the capability of software assurance professionals. The span of competency levels L1 through L5 and the decomposition into individual competencies based on the knowledge and skills described in the SwA CorBoK [Mead 2010a] provide the detail necessary for an organization or individual to determine SwA competency across the range of knowledge areas and units. The model also provides a framework for an organization to adapt its features to the organization's particular domain, culture, or structure.

The model was reviewed by invited industry reviewers and mapped to actual industry positions. These mappings are included in the SEI's report; the model also underwent public review prior to publication. Dick Fairley, chair of the Software and Systems Engineering Committee of the IEEE Computer Society (IEEE-CS) Professional Activities Board (PAB), endorsed the SEI Software Assurance Competency Model "as appropriate for software assurance roles and consistent with A Framework for PAB Competency Models."[12] In presentations and webinars delivered by the author on software assurance, only about half of the participants had a plan for their own SwA competency development. However, more than 80% said they could use the SwA Competency Model in staffing a project.

The most important outcome of this model is a better trained and educated workforce. As the needs of the software industry for more secure applications continue, the recommendations of this model can be used to ensure better and more trustworthy practice in the process of developing and sustaining an organization's software assets. That guidance going forward is a linchpin in the overall effort to create trusted systems and provides the necessary reference to allow organizations and individuals to help achieve cyber security.

---

11. This section is drawn from *The Software Assurance Competency Model: A Roadmap to Enhance Individual Professional Capability* [Mead 2013a].

12. http://www.cert.org/news/article.cfm?assetid=91675&article=156&year=2014.

Case Study 1: Using the SwA Competency Model to Staff a Project

Sam is a project manager for a new development project. He is in the automotive industry and knows that the "smart" features being added to new cars often involve significant amounts of software, as well as external communications. In this particular case, the new software uses GPS capabilities as well as cameras, and it communicates vehicle position information to a central processor. Sam knows that he should be concerned about sensitive communications being intercepted by hackers who may wish to track certain vehicles, such as those used by high-profile political figures. This data could then be used for a number of purposes, ranging from financial gain to terrorist attacks. Obviously, in the automotive industry, safety is a primary risk area that must be considered in addition to security.

Sam therefore wants to build a team with the appropriate software assurance competencies, so that software assurance, especially cyber security and safety, is considered from the outset and built into the software. Luckily, threats and failure modes have been under analysis on a number of the company's projects for some time, so Sam can build on prior work and does not need to create new analysis methods. This means that he does not need Level 5 (Expert) competency skills for a successful project. Looking at the other end of the scale, he realizes that there is little opportunity to use staff with Level 1 (Technician) skills, so he focuses primarily on Levels 2–4, Professional Entry Level, Practitioner, and Senior Practitioner. He can now compare the needed skills with the skills his team already has.

It turns out that a year or so ago, the company started to develop skills profiles jointly with the individual staff members, so comparing the existing skills to the needed skills is not the arduous task that it might be otherwise. Nevertheless, after performing the gap analysis, Sam finds there are some gaps between the team's existing software assurance skills and the skills needed to perform the project. Sam can address some of these gaps fairly easily through training, but he really needs a staff member with deep experience in threat modeling, so he realizes he must look for someone elsewhere in the company with those skills or hire a new employee or consultant to fill the gap. The company has a department that specializes in software security, so he is hopeful that one of its staff members has the needed experience and can be assigned to his project.

Since Sam is able to identify the gap areas up front, it is more likely that the new project can successfully address software assurance. Otherwise, he might have been partway through the project before he recognized the need, or, worse yet, the software could have been operational and vulnerable to attack.

4.5 Summary

This chapter discussed the SEI's Software Assurance Competency Model in detail. It also discusses the DHS Competency Model and the related NICE, and it provides pointers to a number of other competency models in the literature. Competency models can be useful in many fields. In software assurance, these models are particularly useful for organizations and individuals trying to assess and improve their own software assurance skills. We recommend that you peruse these models and select one or more for your individual and organizational use. Competency models are essential for gap analysis and development of an overall software assurance improvement plan.

Competency models need to evolve as new methods are developed. Some newer technical topics are discussed in more depth in Chapter 7, "Special Topics in Cyber Security Engineering." These topics include DevOps, a convergence of concerns from both the development and operations communities, and MORE, a research project that uses malware analysis—an operational technique—to help identify overlooked security requirements to include in future systems.

Chapter 5

Performing Gap Analysis

with Tom Hilburn

In This Chapter

- 5.1 Introduction
- 5.2 Using the SEI's SwA Competency Model
- 5.3 Using the BSIMM
- 5.4 Summary

5.1 Introduction

The preceding chapters present a number of management (organizational) and engineering capability and competency models. These models can be used effectively at the management and engineering levels to perform gap analysis and lay out an improvement plan.

The first task to be completed is selecting a model or models for this purpose. One strategy might be to pick one model at the management level and a second model at the engineering level. A slightly different approach might be to pick one model at the organizational level and a second model for individuals to use.

In business process modeling, it is a common practice to identify the "as-is," or current process, state and also the "to-be," or desired future, state. This approach can be used for many processes, and there are lots of ways to do it. Organizations must identify the process stakeholders, and documentation and discussion or brainstorming can help to document the as-is state. Depending on the organization, such a document may already exist as part of a larger process activity, or the organization may need to develop it. The next order of business is to document the to-be state, which often involves relevant stakeholders and a brainstorming activity. It's important to note that staff and budget considerations should not initially constrain the to-be state, although those considerations may come into play later. The documentation of the as-is and to-be states can be done as a first activity prior to doing software assurance gap analysis.

One way to perform gap analysis is to assess the current (as-is) state using the selected model, identify a desired (to-be) state using the same model, and thus identify the gaps between the current state and the desired state. Once the organization has identified those gaps, it can develop a strategy and an associated plan to address them.

In this chapter, we provide examples of gap analysis using the SEI's Software Assurance (SwA) Competency Model and Cigital's Building Security In Maturity Model (BSIMM). Organizations can use the SwA Competency Model at the organizational, project, or individual level, and as noted earlier, that model focuses on software assurance competencies needed to support software assurance goals. BSIMM is intended to assess software assurance practices at the organizational level and across a number of projects. Organizations compare results to a benchmark of industry best practices for software assurance. Organizations can then develop a plan to address the gaps in their software assurance practices and participate in a follow-up BSIMM assessment to measure their improvement. BSIMM provides a powerful approach that is independent of an organization's specific software development process and thus is process-agnostic.

5.2 Using the SEI's SwA Competency Model

In Chapter 4, "Engineering Competencies," we introduced the SEI's Software Assurance Competency Model [Hilburn 2013a]. To use the competency model, organizations must first map their cyber security positions to the model.

When we developed the model, we mapped it to the DHS Competency Model levels. We also asked (ISC)² Application Security Advisory Board members to produce a mapping of their organizations' software assurance jobs and roles to the competency model levels. These mappings are extremely useful because they account for a wide range of positions, thus validating the content of the competency model and helping organizations see where they have competency gaps. In addition, individuals with similar job titles can see how their competencies compare with expected competencies elsewhere. We reproduce a segment of the mappings in Table 5.1. In Table 5.1, the organizations mapped the knowledge areas and units from the competency model to job titles in their organization(s). In this mapping, the organizations added four levels of behavioral indicators denoting expertise. The full mapping and a second detailed mapping showing a comprehensive list of job titles can be found in Appendix E, "Proposed SwA Competency Mappings."

The first order of business is for an organization to develop an equivalent table for its own software assurance job positions or to modify Table 5.1 as needed to reflect its positions.

Table 5.1 *Proposed SwA Competency Mappings from the (ISC)² Applications Security Advisory Board (Abridged) [Hilburn 2013a]*

KA	Knowledge/Skill/Effectiveness		
	Unit	Job Titles	Behavioral Indicators
Assurance Across Lifecycles	Software Lifecycle Processes	L1: Application Security Analyst	2—Intermediate 3—Advanced
		L2: Application Security Engineer	2—Intermediate 3—Advanced
		L3: Software Architect	3—Advanced
		L4: Application Security Architect, Senior Software Architect, Information Assurance Architect	3—Advanced 4—Expert
		L5: Software Team Lead, Principal Security Architect	4—Expert
	Software Assurance Processes and Practices	L1: QA Analyst	2—Intermediate 3—Advanced
		L2: QA Engineer	2—Intermediate 3—Advanced
		L3: Senior QA Engineer	3—Advanced 4—Expert
		L4: Lead QA Engineer	3—Advanced 4—Expert
		L5: Principal QA Engineer, QA Engineer Manager	4—Expert

One way to use this information on a specific project is to supplement the current table with the following:

- An as-is state, represented by the job titles and associated behavioral indicators of the current staff. Undoubtedly position descriptions exist for the job titles.

- A to-be state, showing the needed job titles for the project, thus identifying the gaps in staffing. The to-be job titles should also have position descriptions.

It should be relatively easy to document the as-is state, as it corresponds to the existing staff and their current skills. Arriving at the to-be state of job titles needed for the project is more challenging. Useful inputs in making this determination could include the schedule, size, and complexity of the project, which are considered as part of the project cost estimation activity. Project risk assessment, as discussed in Chapter 2, "Risk Analysis—Identifying and Prioritizing Needs," is an important input to determining the needed project job titles when we are talking about software assurance positions. Many projects have failed because management underestimated the skills that would be needed to complete the project or because they were unable to acquire staff with the needed skills, either within their organization or from the outside.

In this case, we would expect the project manager and lead personnel to determine which positions are needed on the project, their associated skills, and therefore what level of staff member is needed. Depending on the size and criticality of the project, executive management might also be involved in the process. The result of this exercise leads us to a revision of Table 5.1. Table 5.2 shows a revision of a fragment of Table 5.1, using a simple design to illustrate an example of how to use such a table. Note that in this example, the organization has determined that some positions are not needed for the project; those positions are shown as N/A in the two right columns. When N/A appears in the "Current Staff on Hand" column and a position title appears in the "Needed Staff for the Project" column, this means a staff member with the position title shown must be added to the project. On the other hand, if a position title appears in the "Current Staff on Hand" column, and N/A appears in the "Needed Staff for the Project" column, this means the position is staffed appropriately, and no hiring is needed for that role.

The example in Table 5.2 shows a software architect on hand, but the project calls for the skills of a senior software architect. The organization should determine whether there is enough lead time for the existing software architect to acquire the needed skills or whether a senior software architect needs to be transferred into the project or hired from the outside.

Developing such a table is an important part of project planning, but one that organizations often overlook in favor of staffing projects with personnel who are

Table 5.2 *Proposed SwA Competency Mappings from the (ISC)^2 Application Security Advisory Board, Augmented by Project Needs (Abridged) [Hilburn 2013a]*

KA	Knowledge/Skill/Effectiveness		Behavioral Indicators	Current Staff on Hand	Needed Staff for the Project
	Unit	**Job Titles**			
Assurance Across Lifecycles	Software Lifecycle Processes	L1: Application Security Analyst	2—Intermediate 3—Advanced	N/A	N/A
		L2: Application Security Engineer	2—Intermediate 3—Advanced	Application Security Engineer	Application Security Engineer
		L3: Software Architect	3—Advanced	Software Architect	N/A
		L4: Application Security Architect, Senior Software Architect, Information Assurance Architect	3—Advanced 4—Expert	N/A	Senior Software Architect
		L5: Software Team Lead, Principal Security Architect	4—Expert	Software Team Lead	Software Team Lead
	Software Assurance Processes and Practices	L1: QA Analyst	2—Intermediate 3—Advanced	N/A	N/A
		L2: QA Engineer	2—Intermediate 3—Advanced	QA Engineer	QA Engineer
		L3: Senior QA Engineer	3—Advanced 4—Expert	Senior QA Engineer	Senior QA Engineer
		L4: Lead QA Engineer	3—Advanced 4—Expert	Lead QA Engineer	Lead QA Engineer
		L5: Principal QA Engineer, QA Engineer Manager	4—Expert	N/A	N/A

available at the time—even though they may not have the needed skills, and there may not be enough lead time on the project for the skills to be acquired.

Another way to use Table 5.1 is to develop an as-is state for competencies, assuming that employees with those job titles possess the designated competencies. You can take several approaches to move up to the desired, or to-be, state.

The organization must first identify positions where more staff are needed. For example, perhaps there are a lot of staff at the middle levels of the competency, but more are needed at the higher levels. In that case, the organization can decide to hire more staff at the higher levels, grow the staff at the intermediate levels so that they achieve the higher levels, or do some combination of the two. The organization might choose the approach based on whether the staffing needs are immediate or part of a longer-term strategy.

Example Case Study: Using SwA Competency and Curriculum Models to Meet Organizational Needs

GoFast Automotive needs new software each year to support its latest automotive models. Although much of the software it uses is from vendors, GoFast staff members perform some software customization. The company wants to make sure that the software for its automotive systems is secure: GoFast doesn't want a failure in an anti-lock brake system or other safety-critical on-board system as a result of malicious tampering.

Although GoFast has very good staff, its management team feels that their security risk analysis may not be as strong as it could be; they would like to improve the organization's expertise in that area. They puzzle over whether to grow the expertise of an existing staff member or hire a new staff member.

On the one hand, they are not in crisis mode, as only a subset of the software changes each year. GoFast can afford to take time to develop the expertise in house. On the other hand, if a new requirement comes up, they don't expect that someone who has just acquired advanced skills will be able to go it alone.

Larry is a GoFast security expert with some background in risk analysis. He has been exposed to it in his software engineering courses, as part of his degree program, and he has also completed some security certifications.

After some exploration and discussions with Larry, the team identifies a course in advanced risk analysis that could be helpful to him; professional resources—books and blogs—are also available. Larry is enthusiastic about this career growth opportunity, and a plan is put in place for him to acquire the additional expertise and to start to apply it on selected future projects.

To assist in addressing any immediate needs, the team identifies a consultant who is put on contract to help projects needing advanced risk analysis over the next few months.

At an individual level, staff members could use the competency model directly along with Table 5.1 to identify their own gap areas and initiate discussion of a career growth strategy with their management.

An individual could also use Table 5.3 to assess his or her current skill level and areas needed to support career growth. Table 5.3 is an extract from core body of knowledge (BoK) for the Master of Software Assurance Reference Curriculum, showing the knowledge unit, associated topics, and description, including Bloom's level. An individual could assess whether he or she has the needed knowledge associated with specific topics and units and identify gap areas from it.

Table 5.3 *The Specification for the System Security Assurance Knowledge Area [Hilburn 2013b]*

Unit	Topics	Description
For Newly Developed and Acquired Software for Diverse Systems	Security and safety aspects of computer-intensive critical infrastructure	Knowledge of safety and security risks associated with critical infrastructure systems such as found, for example, in banking and finance, energy production and distribution, telecommunications, and transportation systems
	Potential attack methods	Knowledge of the variety of methods by which attackers can damage software or data associated with that software by exploiting weaknesses in the system design or implementation
	Analysis of threats to software	Analysis of the threats to which software is most likely to be vulnerable in specific operating environments and domains
	Methods of defense	Familiarity with appropriate countermeasures such as layers, access controls, privileges, intrusion detection, encryption, and code review checklists

(continued)

Table 5.3 *Continued*

Unit	Topics	Description
For Diverse Operational (Existing) Systems	Historic and potential operational attack methods	Knowledge of and ability to duplicate the attacks that have been used to interfere with an application's or system's operations
	Analysis of threats to operational environments	Analysis of the threats to which software is most likely to be vulnerable in specific operating environments and domains
	Design of and plan for access control, privileges, and authentication	Design and plan for effective countermeasures such as layers, access controls, privileges, intrusion detection, encryption, and coding checklists
	Security methods for physical and personnel environments	Knowledge of how physical access restrictions, guards, background checks, and personnel monitoring can address risks
Ethics and Integrity in Creation, Acquisition, and Operation of Software Systems	Overview of ethics, code of ethics, and legal constraints	Knowledge of how people who are knowledgeable about attack and prevention methods are obligated to use their abilities, both legally and ethically, referencing the Software Engineering Code of Ethical and Professional Conduct
	Computer attack case studies	Knowledge of the legal and ethical considerations involved in analyzing a variety of historical events and investigations

Of course, not every software security job requires knowledge and competency across the entire core body of knowledge. For example, a position might require deep capability in one or more areas but only a lower level of awareness across the other areas. Also, different application domains (for example, financial or transportation systems) and application types (for example, web or embedded systems) typically require software security specialists to have competency beyond the body of knowledge.

The core body of knowledge not only structures and organizes software assurance knowledge (into KAs, units, and topics) but also details how to understand and use that knowledge. For example, Table 5.3 specifies that a SwA professional should be able to perform "analysis of the threats to which software is most likely to be vulnerable in specific operating environments and domains" and have the "ability to duplicate the attacks that have been used to interfere with an application's or system's operations." This level of detail can help individuals determine their state of knowledge and plan for professional development.

Example Case Study: Using SwA Competency and Curriculum Models to Improve Individual Competencies

Joan graduated with a bachelor's degree in computer science a few years ago and is a software engineer for Fly-By-Night Airlines. As part of a team directed by the system architect, she develops and maintains small and mid-sized modules for a software system that provides services for passengers and flight crews.

In her undergraduate education, Joan acquired most of the SwA skills and knowledge described in the Computer Science I and II courses, which are part of Volume II in the SwA Curriculum Reports [Mead 2010a]; examples of these skills and knowledge include foundations of information security, design concepts and principles, design by contract, exception handling, secure programming, coding standards, algorithm and code review, unit test design, penetration testing, program metrics, and quality assessment. In her current position, Joan has practiced these skills and participated in employer-sponsored workshops and training sessions.

However, Joan would like to advance and acquire additional SwA knowledge and skills. She has looked through the SwA Competency Model [Hilburn 2013a] and identified where she needs further professional development. In looking at the topic areas in the model, she would like to be able to perform threat analysis, analyze risk, and plan and monitor risk management for her projects. In addition, she knows that she has only a fuzzy notion of how to do security analysis at the architectural level. So, she reads through Volumes I and III in the SwA Curriculum Reports [Mead 2010a, 2011a] to see what to study.

Joan notices that the *Assured Software Development 1* course covers several topics in which she is weak, and she would like to learn more about software processes, requirements engineering, software architecture, and software security topics such as assurance risk assessment, attack trees, and misuse or abuse cases.

(continued)

> Based on her analysis of Volumes I and III, Joan examines a local university's courses, looking for ones that can help her in the areas she would like to study. She finds courses that cover software process, requirements engineering, and software architecture. However, she can't find anything that includes the other topics on her wish list.
>
> Joan looks back at *Assured Software Development 1* and reviews the description of the primary sources recommended for it. She purchases both books listed and uses them as part of her study plan. She consults with her supervisor about taking courses at the local university and pursuing self-study using those books. Her supervisor makes a few minor suggestions and strongly encourages her to proceed with her plan.
>
> As Joan proceeds through her self-study, she improves her software security knowledge and capability and can apply it in her work. Her supervisor notices and comments on Joan's improved SwA competency.

As we've discussed, competency models can be used in many different ways. Organizations and projects can use them to determine the roles and corresponding skill sets needed across the organization. Individual staff members can use them to develop a plan for growth and development. One approach is to make an informal assessment part of annual planning, both at the management level and for individual staff members. The plan can then be revisited periodically over the course of the year. In addition, the start of a new project can trigger an assessment of the skills and roles needed on the project. This can be done for any cross-section of skills, but our primary interest is in software assurance skills.

5.3 Using the BSIMM

5.3.1 BSIMM Background

In Chapter 3, "Secure Software Development Management and Organizational Models," we introduced the BSIMM as a model that can be used to assess organizational software security initiatives. The work began in 2008 with an assessment of 9 firms to create BSIMM Version 1. There are now some 78 participants in BSIMM Version 6 [McGraw 2015]. As a consequence, the BSIMM has a substantial practice database organizations can leverage when performing assessments. The BSIMM provides organizations with an external assessment of their security practices relative to other participating organizations. The BSIMM comprises 12 practices, each containing a number of activities, for a total of 112 activities.

The 78 organizations that participated in BSIMM6 include (with some overlap) organizations from the following sectors: financial services (33), independent software vendors (27), consumer electronics (13), and healthcare (10) [McGraw 2015].

On average, the 78 participating firms had practiced software security for 3.98 years at the time of assessment (ranging from less than a year to 15 years as of October 2015). All 78 firms agree that the success of their initiative hinges on having an internal group, the SSG (Software Security Group), devoted to software security. SSG size on average is 13.9 people (smallest 1, largest 130, median 6) with a "satellite" of others (developers, architects, and people in the organization directly engaged in and promoting software security) of 27.1 people (smallest 0, largest 400, median 3).

The average number of developers among our targets was 3,680 people (smallest 23, largest 35,000, median 1,200), yielding an average percentage of SSG to development of 1.51% (median 0.7%).

All told, the BSIMM describes the work of 1,084 SSG members working with a satellite of 2,111 people to secure the software developed by 287,006 developers.

It is interesting to note that "according to our observations, the first step of a Software Security Initiative is forming an SSG" [McGraw 2015].

Example Case Study: Using the BSIMM for Software Security Improvement

Sarah has been hired by GoFast Automotive to head up the Software Security Group. Although she has a software security background and is pleased that GoFast has an SSG, she is having difficulty getting a handle on all of the SSG's activities. Also, she is unsure as to whether the current set of SSG activities and strategies are optimal in terms of cost–benefit to the company. The automotive sector is new to her, and given the importance and visibility of the SSG within the company, she wants to make sure that she has a good understanding of the current software security practices *and* areas where they could improve, especially compared to other automotive companies. She also has observed that some of the staff are reluctant to tell her anything that could be construed as bad news, so she would like to get an independent assessment of their software security practices. She does some research and decides that a BSIMM assessment would provide her with the information she needs. At the same time, any suggestions for improvement (change) would come from an objective and experienced external organization, so that she would not be seen as the "bad guy" for pointing out areas where change is needed. She discusses the idea of a BSIMM assessment with her direct reports. They look at the BSIMM and feel that a BSIMM assessment could be very beneficial. They put a schedule in place for the assessment and follow-on planning. It becomes a team-building process that everyone buys into, and Sarah's collaborative leadership style is viewed favorably by the staff.

During BSIMM data gathering at an organization, interviews are conducted, and documentation may be reviewed. Typically, the SSG owner and some of their direct reports are interviewed along with others involved in Software Security Initiative (SSI) activities. Cigital experts conduct the interviews and perform the document review. The outputs from the activities result in the inputs to the BSIMM tool. The BSIMM tool in turn provides insight into how the organization's current software security initiatives compare to the BSIMM benchmark data. Benchmarking is a well-known good management process—"the process of comparing one's business processes and performance metrics to industry bests or best practices from other companies."[1] In this case, the benchmarking data for industry bests and best practices in software assurance resides in the BSIMM database.

The resulting BSIMM report includes an executive summary, a data gathering discussion, a high-water mark, BSIMM practices, a BSIMM scorecard, a comparison within verticals, and a conclusion. The data gathering section includes the names and roles of the people who were interviewed. The *high-water mark* refers to the highest-level activity observed in each of the 12 BSIMM practices. The high-water mark section in the report shows how the high-water mark for the company under study compares to the average high-water mark for all participants in that edition of BSIMM, for each practice area. Next, a more detailed view of the BSIMM practices observed is provided. The BSIMM scorecard section provides detailed information about each activity in the company's Software Security Initiative (SSI). The comparison within verticals section provides a comparison between the company being studied and other companies in the same business sector. The BSIMM data for the companies in the same business sector (e.g., financial) provide a vertical slice of the complete set of BSIMM data. The conclusion provides a summary and suggestions for where the company might focus its software security improvement activities. The Appendixes provide background on the BSIMM and a discussion of BSIMM activities.

5.3.2 BSIMM Sample Report

A complete example of a BSIMM Assessment Final Report, based on BSIMM6 data, appears in Appendix F, "Sample BSIMM Assessment Report." In that example, a fictitious firm and dummy interview data are used; however, the sections in the report and the benchmark data used for comparison are real.

Figure 5.1 shows the BSIMM scorecard that appears in the report, along with an explanation. (**Note:** The actual BSIMM reports use color; as the print book is grayscale, not color, we have modified slightly.) This scorecard is for FakeFirm; 37 software security activities were observed for this fake organization during the example assessment.

---

1. https://en.wikipedia.org/wiki/Benchmarking

Figure 5.1 provides detailed information about FakeFirm's SSI. Primarily, it lists in the four "FakeFirm" columns the 37 activities the assessment team observed during this assessment. In the "BSIMM6 FIRMS" columns, the scorecard provides the count of firms (out of 67) in which the assessment team observed each activity. See Figure F.8 in Appendix F for more explanation. In addition, see the section "BSIMM Activities" in Appendix F for the short name associated with each BSIMM activity (e.g., SM1.3 is "Educate executives").

The scorecard shown in Figure 5.1 includes the following columns:

- **Activity columns**—List each of the 112 activities included in BSIMM6. For names of each activity, see Appendix F or see http://bsimm.com for an interactive chart of long descriptions.
- **BSIMM6 Firms columns**—Give the count of BSIMM6 participants in which the activity was observed, providing an indication of the prevalence of an activity in the current data pool.
- **FakeFirm columns**—Indicates with a "1" each activity observed during this assessment.

The scorecard also lists a number of common activities and practices:

- The most common activity in each BSIMM6 practice:
- Common activities also observed in FakeFirm, including the following:
  - SM1.4: Identify gate locations, gather necessary artifacts
  - T1.1: Provide awareness training
  - SR1.1: Create security standards
  - AA1.1: Perform security feature review
  - CR1.4: Use automated tools along with manual review
  - ST1.3: Drive tests with security requirements and security features
  - PT1.1: Use external penetration testers to find problems
  - SE1.2: Ensure host and network security basics are in place

- Common activities not observed in FakeFirm, including the following:
  - CP1.2: Identify PII obligations

BSIMM6 Scorecard for: FakeFirm   **Observations: 37**

GOVERNANCE			INTELLIGENCE			SSDL TOUCHPOINTS			DEPLOYMENT		
ACTIVITY	BSIMM6 FIRMS	FakeFirm	ACTIVITY	BSIMM6 FIRMS	FakeFirm	ACTIVITY	BSIMM6 FIRMS	FakeFirm	ACTIVITY	BSIMM6 FIRMS	FakeFirm
Strategy and Metrics			Attack Models			Architecture Analysis			Penetration Testing		
[SM1.1]	41	1	[AM1.1]	17	1	[AA1.1]	67	1	[PT1.1]	69	1
[SM1.2]	40		[AM1.2]	61		[AA1.2]	29	1	[PT1.2]	47	1
[SM1.3]	36	1	[AM1.3]	31		[AA1.3]	22	1	[PT1.3]	47	
[SM1.4]	66	1	[AM1.4]	8	1	[AA1.4]	46		[PT2.2]	20	1
[SM2.1]	36		[AM1.5]	46	1	[AA2.1]	12		[PT2.3]	17	
[SM2.2]	29		[AM1.6]	11		[AA2.2]	9	1	[PT3.1]	10	1
[SM2.3]	30		[AM2.1]	6		[AA2.3]	13		[PT3.2]	8	
[SM2.5]	17		[AM2.2]	8	1	[AA3.1]	6				
[SM2.6]	29		[AM3.1]	4		[AA3.2]	1				
[SM3.1]	15		[AM3.2]	2							
[SM3.2]	7										
Compliance and Policy			Security Features and Design			Code Review			Software Environment		
[CP1.1]	45	1	[SFD1.1]	61		[CR1.1]	18		[SE1.1]	37	
[CP1.2]	61		[SFD1.2]	59	1	[CR1.2]	53	1	[SE1.2]	69	1
[CP1.3]	41	1	[SFD2.1]	24		[CR1.4]	55	1	[SE2.2]	31	1
[CP2.1]	19		[SFD2.2]	39		[CR1.5]	24		[SE2.4]	25	
[CP2.2]	23		[SFD3.1]	8		[CR1.6]	27	1	[SE3.2]	10	
[CP2.3]	25		[SFD3.2]	11		[CR2.2]	7		[SE3.3]	5	
[CP2.4]	29		[SFD3.3]	2		[CR2.5]	20				
[CP2.5]	33	1				[CR2.6]	16				
[CP3.1]	18					[CR3.2]	3	1			
[CP3.2]	11					[CR3.3]	5				
[CP3.3]	6					[CR3.4]	3				
Training			Standards and Requirements			Security Testing			Config. Mgmt. and Vuln. Mgmt.		
[T1.1]	59	1	[SR1.1]	57	1	[ST1.1]	61	1	[CMVM1.1]	71	1
[T1.5]	26		[SR1.2]	50		[ST1.3]	66	1	[CMVM1.2]	73	
[T1.6]	17	1	[SR1.3]	52	1	[ST2.1]	24	1	[CMVM2.1]	64	1
[T1.7]	36		[SR2.2]	27	1	[ST2.4]	8		[CMVM2.2]	61	
[T2.5]	10		[SR2.3]	21		[ST2.5]	10		[CMVM2.3]	31	
[T2.6]	15	1	[SR2.4]	19		[ST2.6]	11		[CMVM3.1]	4	
[T2.7]	6		[SR2.5]	20		[ST3.3]	4		[CMVM3.2]	6	
[T3.1]	3		[SR2.6]	23	1	[ST3.4]	4		[CMVM3.3]	6	
[T3.2]	3		[SR3.1]	6		[ST3.5]	5		[CMVM3.4]	3	
[T3.3]	3		[SR3.2]	11							
[T3.4]	8										
[T3.5]	4										

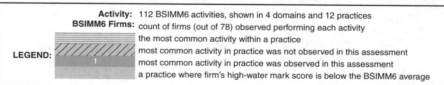

LEGEND:

Activity: 112 BSIMM6 activities, shown in 4 domains and 12 practices
BSIMM6 Firms: count of firms (out of 78) observed performing each activity
the most common activity within a practice
most common activity in practice was not observed in this assessment
most common activity in practice was observed in this assessment
a practice where firm's high-water mark score is below the BSIMM6 average

Figure 5.1 *BSIMM Scorecard with the Entire BSIMM Database ("Earth Data")*[2]

---

2. From a BSIMM sample report.

- SFD1.1: Build and publish security features

- CMVM1.2: Identify software bugs found in operations monitoring and feed them back to development

- Practices where FakeFirm has not reached the same high-water mark as the average of the current participants (i.e., where FakeFirm's high-water mark is "inside" that of the data pool average in Figure 5.1), including the following:

  - Strategy & Metrics

  - Compliance & Policy

  - Security Features & Design

  - Configuration Management & Vulnerability Management

Remember that this scorecard represents Cigital's observations specific to software security activity, as measured by the BSIMM. Observation—or the lack of observation—of a given activity is inherently neither good nor bad. Judging sufficiency and effectiveness for the activities observed requires a deeper analysis of FakeFirm's business objectives, processes, and software. Results of such an analysis can form a cornerstone for strategic broadening and deepening of the current SSI.

Since the BSIMM collects information from companies in a number of domains, the report includes a comparison of FakeFirm's initiatives with the performance of other organizations in the financial sector participating in the BSIMM6. Figure 5.2 presents and explains these results. This figure summarizes the level reached by Fake-Firm in each practice and compares it to the levels reached by BSIMM6 participants in the financial industry (FI) vertical.

In Figure 5.2, the dark line depicts the average high-water marks from 0 to 3 achieved by BSIMM6 participants in a vertical. The gray line depicts the high-water marks from 0 to 3 achieved by FakeFirm. Compared to the average high-water marks of financial industry BSIMM6 participants, FakeFirm's marks appear above average in Training, Attack Models, Code Review, and Penetration Testing. FakeFirm's marks appear near the average in Standards & Requirements, Architecture Analysis, Security Testing, Software Environment, and Configuration Management & Vulnerability Management. FakeFirm's marks appear below the average in Strategy & Metrics, Compliance & Policy, and Security Features & Design.

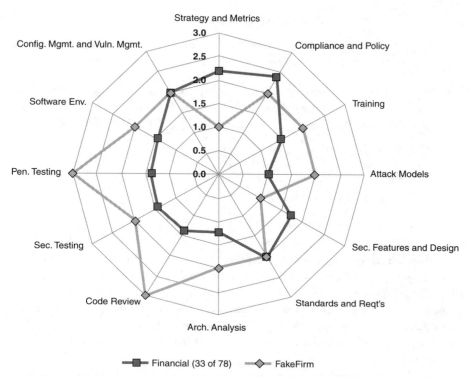

Figure 5.2 *High-Water Mark per Practice Compared to Participants in a Vertical*

Compared to the averages shown in Figure 5.2 for the entire BSIMM data pool, the most significant differences are in the following areas:

- **Standards & Requirements, Compliance & Policy, Training, Strategy & Metrics, and Code Review**—The high-water mark average is higher among financial industry organizations than for the entire data pool (known in BSIMM terminology as BSIMM Earth).

- **Configuration Management & Vulnerability Management**—The average is lower.

The conclusion section in a BSIMM report suggests areas that might be appropriate for strengthening the organization's SSI. We recommend that you go through the full report in Appendix F to get a better picture of BSIMM results. These results are very powerful and use a proven method built on years of experience and benchmark data. Keeping in mind that a single organization is not expected to include all

112 activities among its practices; as noted above, Cigital observed 37 activities at FakeFirm.

The following are some of the improvement recommendations for FakeFirm:

- **Secure Software Development Life Cycle (SDLC)**—FakeFirm has created an SDLC overlay that includes two security gates: one for "Permit to Build" and one for "Permit to Deploy." However, the Software Security Group (SSG) is not involved in all development projects. In addition, the software security gates are voluntary even in large, critical projects. Over the next 12 months, Fake-Firm should institute process improvements to ensure that the SSG is aware of all development and software acquisition projects worldwide. At the same time, FakeFirm should phase in mandatory compliance with various aspects of the SDLC security gates. For example, FakeFirm could immediately require remediation of critical security defects, while phasing in remediation of high- and medium-security defects over a period of months. Similarly, static analysis and penetration testing should quickly become mandatory for all critical applications and should become mandatory for all applications over the next 12–18 months.

- **Inventory**—FakeFirm does not have a robust inventory of applications, personally identifiable information (PII), or open-source software. Ensuring that all software flows appropriately through various SDLC gates becomes complicated when the inventory is unknown. Without a data classification scheme, prioritizing projects and making a PII inventory is effectively impossible. Fake-Firm should immediately begin an inventory initiative that accounts for all applications in the SSG's purview, ensures each application receives a criticality rating, and associates each application with data levels. Over the next 12 months, it should expand the inventory to include the open-source software in use and the current security status for each application. In addition, Fake-Firm should begin including software security waiver information for each application.

- **Training**—FakeFirm has a small amount of software security training that it uses to improve awareness. However, FakeFirm provides only in-person training, and only to developers, and only at onboarding time. Over the next six months, FakeFirm should begin providing on-demand, role-based software security training to all roles involved in the SDLC. Such a plan can increase global awareness and technical skill in the major engineering roles, such as requirements analysis, architecture, development, and testing. FakeFirm should also investigate the opportunity to provide training in the developer environment using Integrated Development Environment (IDE)–based tools.

5.4 Summary

This chapter shows how organizations can use two models introduced in Chapters 3 and 4 to perform gap analysis and thus to identify and implement improvements at organizational, project, and individual levels. The BSIMM is aimed at organizational practices, whereas the SEI SwA Competency Model focuses more on individual competencies and competencies needed to support a specific project.

These kinds of analyses can help to identify an improvement path that is based on actual data, and not solely on brainstorming or other less reliable means of identifying gaps.

Chapters 3 and 4 introduce many models that this chapter does not discuss. By doing some exploration, you could also use those other models to lay out a path for improvement. In addition, new models and frameworks are under development at the SEI and elsewhere that may be suitable for this purpose once they have been validated in the field.

Chapter 6

Metrics

In This Chapter

- 6.1 How to Define and Structure Metrics to Manage Cyber Security Engineering
- 6.2 Ways to Gather Evidence for Cyber Security Evaluation

6.1 How to Define and Structure Metrics to Manage Cyber Security Engineering

A *measure* is defined as "an amount or degree of something"; it is an operation for assigning a value to something.[1] A *metric* is defined as "a standard of measurement"; it is the interpretation of assigned values.[2] Scientist Lord Kelvin said, "When you can measure what you are speaking about, and express it in numbers, you know something about it; but when you cannot measure it, when you cannot express it in numbers, your knowledge is of a meager and unsatisfactory kind; it may be the beginning of knowledge, but you have scarcely in your thoughts advanced to the stage of science."[3]

Software assurance measurement assesses the extent to which a system or software item possesses desirable characteristics [NDIA 1999]. The desires could be

---

1. www.merriam-webster.com/dictionary/measure

2. www.merriam-webster.com/dictionary/metric

3. https://en.wikiquote.org/wiki/William_Thomson

115

expressed as one or all of the following: requirements, standards, compliance mandates, operational qualities, threats to be addressed, and risks to be avoided. The purpose of software assurance measurement is to "establish a basis for gaining justifiable confidence (trust, if you will) that software will consistently demonstrate one or more desirable properties" [Bartol 2009]. This basis includes properties such as quality, reliability, correctness, dependability, usability, interoperability, safety, fault tolerance, and security [Bartol 2009].

6.1.1 What Constitutes a Good Metric?

Jaquith posits that a good metric has three characteristics [Jaquith 2007]:

- Simple to explain and straightforward to determine so the meaning can be widely understood

- Expressible in time, money, or something that can be converted into these readily accepted parameters

- Readily structured for benchmarking so that change can be quickly identified and evaluated

Further, a good metric must be consistently measurable, able to be gathered at a low cost (preferably automated), preferably quantitative (expressed as a number or percentage), and contextually specific to be relevant for decision makers to take action.

Metrics such as the age of an automobile driver, which an insurance company uses to determine an annual cost for automobile insurance, are backed by decades of statistically analyzed data of actual accident rates for drivers of every age. Likewise, a doctor estimates a patient's risk of a heart attack by looking at metrics such as age, deviation of weight from the norm, and whether the patient engages in behaviors such as smoking—health information that has been assembled, along with data on actual heart attacks, for decades across major sectors of the population.

Cyber security does not have this kind of historical data from which to structure standardized metrics, but that does not mean we cannot establish good metrics for decision making. We suggest following a well-established methodology called Goal-Question-Metric (GQM), introduced and described by Basili and Rombach [Basili 1984, 1988]. This process for deriving meaningful metrics is to define the objectives/goals, formulate questions relevant to the goal, collect data and indicators that inform the answers to the questions, define metrics, and report metrics (customized to target audiences).

To be useful, software assurance metric data must be consistently valid, retrievable, relevant, and cost-effective. In order to be practically effective, the data must be retrievable, understandable, and relevant. Data must provide concrete values. Consequently, data collection must be based on consistent units of measure that can be normalized. Moreover, once data have been collected, they must be stored so that they retain their usefulness. These are the generic requirements for metrics-based assurance:

- Agreed-on metrics to define the assurance
- Scientifically derived data for each metric
- Sufficient justification for collecting data to account for the added costs of collection

Organizations must define and adopt a frame of reference before assessors can select the particular metrics to use for data collection. The frame of reference provides the practical justification for the metric selection process. A frame of reference is nothing more than the logic (or justification) for choosing the metrics that are eventually used. For instance, there are no commonly agreed on measures to assess security; however, a wide range of standard metrics, such as defect counts or cyclomatic complexity, could be used to measure that characteristic. The metric that is selected depends on the context of its intended use.

The only rule that guides the selection and adoption process is that the metrics must be objectively measurable, produce meaningful data, and fit the frame of reference that has been adopted [Shoemaker 2013].

6.1.2 Metrics for Cyber Security Engineering

Cyber security is not something for which we can assemble a standard set of metrics, such as height, width, length, and weight. A seemingly endless list of metrics could be collected for cyber security, such as the number of security requirements, lines of validated code, vulnerabilities found by code checkers, process steps that include security considerations, hours needed to fix a security bug, and data validation tests passed and failed. Collecting each of these metrics involves time and effort, so the benefit to organizations, projects, and even individuals must be clear. We may already be collecting related metrics (e.g., for quality, safety, reliability, usability, and a whole host of other system and software qualities) that could tell us something about cyber security.

System and software engineering is composed of many aspects that can be evaluated independently but need to be considered collectively. We need security measures for the product, the processes used to create and maintain that product, the capabilities of the engineers performing the construction or those of the vendor for an acquisition, the trust relationships from the product to other products and the controls on those connections, and the operational environment in which the product executes. In addition, we need to establish that the engineering steps we are performing are moving toward the desired cyber security results.

Why is this so difficult? The responsibilities for these various segments can be scattered across teams, divisions, or even separate organizations, depending on how an engineering effort is structured. The control we have over each segment and access to information about it can vary widely and may impact measurement options. The needs for security and available solutions can also vary widely, depending on the operational mission, languages and frameworks used in development of the product, and operational infrastructure choices. There are currently no established standards for assignment of these responsibilities.

Let's consider software measurement in general. Although it is possible for software to be both incorrect and secure, it is generally the case that incorrect software is also more likely to contain security vulnerabilities. Organizations should establish a broad software measurement program in place and add assurance considerations to it rather than just consider software assurance measures in a vacuum. Software product measurement assesses two related but distinctly different attributes: functional correctness and structural correctness. *Functional correctness* measures how the software performs in its environment. *Structural correctness* assesses the actual product and process implementation.

Software functional correctness describes how closely the behavior of the software complies with or conforms to its functional design requirements or specifications. In effect, functional correctness characterizes how completely the piece of software achieves its contractual purpose. Functional correctness is typically implemented, enforced, and measured through software testing. The testing for correctness is done by evaluating the existing behavior of the software against a logical point of comparison. In essence, the logical point of comparison is the basis that a particular decision maker adopts to form a conclusion [IEEE 2000]. Logical points of comparison include diverse things such as "specifications, contracts, comparable products, past versions of the same product, inferences about intended or expected purpose, user or customer expectations, relevant standards, applicable laws, or other criteria" [Shoemaker 2013].

Measurements of structural correctness assess how well the software satisfies environmental or business requirements, which support the actual delivery of the functional requirements. For instance, structural correctness characterizes qualities such as the robustness or maintainability of the software, or whether the software was produced properly. Structural correctness is evaluated through the analysis of the software's fundamental infrastructure and through the validation of its code against defined acceptability requirements at the unit, integration, and system levels. Structural measurement also assesses how well the architecture adheres to sound principles of software architectural design [OMG 2013].

Consider an example of how metrics were selected and applied.[4] The SEI maintains detailed size, defect, and process data for more than 100 software development projects. The projects include a wide range of application domains and project sizes. Five of these projects focus on specific security- and safety-critical outcomes. Let's take a look at the security results for these projects. Four of these projects reported no post-release safety-critical or security defects in the first year of operation, but the remaining one project had 20 such defects. On one of the projects with no safety-critical or security defects, further study revealed that staff members had been trained to recognize common security issues in development and had been required to build this understanding into their development process. Metrics were collected using review and inspection checklists along with productivity data. These metrics enabled staff to accurately predict the effort and quality required for future components using actual historical data.

The teams performed detailed planning for each upcoming code-release cycle and confirmation planning for the overall schedule. For the project with the largest code base, teams conducted a Monte Carlo simulation to identify a completion date within the 84th percentile (i.e., 84% of the project simulated finished earlier than this completion date). The team included estimates for the following:

- Incoming software change requests (SCRs) per week
- Triage rate of SCRs
- Percentage of SCRs closed
- Development work (SCR assigned) for a cycle
- SCR per developer (SCR/Dev) per week
- Number of developers
- Time to develop test protocols
- Software change requests per security verifier and validator (SCR/SVV) per week
- Number of verification persons

The team then committed to complete the agreed work for the cycle, planned what work was being deferred into future cycles, and projected that all remaining work would still fit the overall delivery schedule. The team tracked all defects throughout

---

4. This example is drawn from *Predicting Software Assurance Using Quality and Reliability Measures* [Woody 2014].

the projects in all phases (injection, discovery, and fix data). Developers used their actual data to plan subsequent work and reach agreement with management on the schedule, content, process used, and resources required so that the plan could proceed without compromising the delivery schedule.

This example uses several measures collected from various aspects of engineering to assemble a basis of confidence constructed from historical information that can be used in making a decision. Each measure by itself is insufficient, but the collection can be useful. The metrics collected were selected based on information needs to support a specific goal (workload planning) and addressed a range of questions related to the goal, such as productivity of the resources performing the work and level of expected churn in the workload. This follows the GQM methodology [Basili 1984, 1988].

Another important element that can be measured is organizational capability to address cyber security. The National Institute of Standards and Technology (NIST) has developed a framework for improving critical infrastructure cyber security [NIST 2014]. The NIST framework focuses on the operational environment that influences the level of cyber security responsibility, enabling organizations to identify features or characteristics of the infrastructure that support cyber security as opposed to what needs to be engineered directly into the system and software. The framework provides an assessment mechanism that enables organizations to determine their current cyber security capabilities, set individual goals for a target state, and establish a plan for improving and maintaining cyber security programs. After using the assessment mechanism to determine goals and plans for cyber security, organizations can use metrics to monitor and evaluate results. Metrics are collected and analyzed to support a decision so that a decision can determine an action [Axelrod 2012].

Measurement frameworks for security are not new, but broad use of available standards in the lifecycle has been limited by the lack of system and software engineering involvement in security beyond authentication and authorization requirements. With the growing recognition of the ways in which engineering decisions impact security, metrics that support the monitoring and managing of these concerns should be incorporated into the lifecycle.

Standards such as NIST's *Performance Measurement Guide for Information Security* [Chew 2008] propose a wide range of possible metrics that can support an information security measurement effort. These metrics are proposed to verify that selected security controls are appropriately implemented and that appropriate federal legislative mandates have been addressed. An international standard, ISO/IEC 27004, "provides guidance on the development and use of measures and measurement in order to assess the effectiveness of an implemented information security management system (ISMS)."[5]

---

5. www.iso.org/iso/catalogue_detail?csnumber=42106

6.1.3 Models for Measurement[6]

An organization might already have a measurement model that structures metrics to address selected goals. There are three major categories of measurement models: descriptive, analytic, and predictive.

Measurement models of any type can be created based on equations, or analysis of sets of variables, that characterize practical concerns about the software. A good measurement model allows users to fully understand the influence of all factors that affect the outcome of a product or process, not just primary factors. A good measurement model also has predictive capabilities; that is, given current known values, it predicts future values of those attributes with an acceptable degree of certainty.

Assurance models measure and predict the level of assurance of a given product or process. In that respect, assurance models characterize the state of assurance for any given piece of software. They provide a reasonable answer to questions such as "How much security is good enough?" and "How do you determine when you are secure enough?" In addition, assurance measurement models can validate the correctness of the software assurance process itself. Individual assurance models are built to evaluate everything from error detection efficiency to internal program failures, software reliability estimates, and degree of availability testing required. Assurance models can also be used to assess the effectiveness and efficiency of the software management, processes, and infrastructure of an organization.

Assurance models rely on maximum likelihood estimates, numerical methods, and confidence intervals to make their assumptions. Therefore, it is essential to validate the correctness of a model. Validation involves applying the model to a set of historical data and comparing the model's predicted outcomes to the actual results. The output from a model should be a metric, and that output should be usable as input to another model.

Assurance modeling provides a quantitative estimate of the level of trust that can be assumed for a system. Models that predict the availability and reliability of a system include estimates such as initial error counts and error models incorporating error generation, uptime, and the time to close software error reports.

Software error detection models characterize the state of debugging the system, which encompasses concerns such as the probable number of software errors that are corrected at a given time in system operation, plus methods for developing programs with low error content and for developing measures of program complexity.

Models of internal program structure include metrics such as the number of paths (modules) traversed, the number of times a path has been traversed, and the probability of failure, as well as advice about any automated testing that might be required to execute every program path.

---

6. This section is drawn from *Software Assurance Measurement—State of the Practice* [Shoemaker 2013].

Testing effectiveness models and techniques provides an estimate of the number of tests necessary to execute all program paths and statistical test models. Software management and organizational structure models contain statistical measures for process performance. These models can mathematically relate error probability to the program testing process and the economics of debugging due to error growth.

Because assurance is normally judged against failure, the use of a measurement model for software assurance requires a generic and comprehensive definition of what constitutes "failure" in a particular measurement setting. That definition is necessary to incorporate considerations of every type of failure at every severity level. Unfortunately, up to this point, a large part of software assurance research has been devoted to defect identification, despite the fact that defects are not the only type of failure. This narrow definition is due partly to the fact that defect data is more readily available than other types of data, but it is mostly due to the lack of popular alternatives for modeling the causes and consequences of failure for a software item. With the advent of exploits against software products that both run correctly and fulfill a given purpose, the definition of *failure* must be expanded. That expansion would include incorporating into the definition of *failure* intentional (backdoors) or unintentional (defects) vulnerabilities that can be exploited by an adversary as well as the mere presence of malicious objects in the code.

Existing security standards can be leveraged to fill this measurement need [ISO/IEC 2007]. *Practical Measurement Framework for Software Assurance and Information Security* [Bartol 2008] identifies similarities and differences among five different models for measurement and would be a useful resource to assist in selecting measurements appropriate to an organization's cyber security engineering needs.

What Decisions About Cyber Security Need to Be Supported by Metrics?

In this chapter we have focused on metrics for development planning with expected cyber security results. Let's now take a look at software that is being reused, as opposed to software that is being newly developed. If we plan to reuse software such as a commercial product, open source, or code developed for another purpose, is there something inherent in product cyber security that would motivate us to choose one software product over another? If we can scan the code, we can use software tools to find out what vulnerabilities the code contains as well as the severity of each vulnerability, according to a metrics standard established in the Common Vulnerability Enumeration (CVE). We could use other tools to evaluate the binaries for malware. Each piece of information becomes evidence that supports or refutes a claim about an option.

At the start of a development cycle, we have a limited basis for determining our confidence in the behavior of the delivered system; that is, we have a large gap between our initial level of confidence and the desired level of confidence. Over the

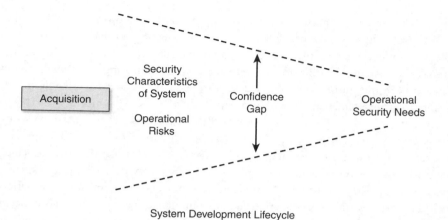

Security
Characteristics
of System

Acquisition

Operational
Risks

Confidence
Gap

Operational
Security Needs

System Development Lifecycle

Figure 6.1 *Confidence Gap*

development lifecycle, we need to reduce that confidence gap, as shown in Figure 6.1, to reach the desired level of confidence for the delivered system [Woody 2014].[7]

In Chapter 1, "Cyber Security Engineering: Lifecycle Assurance of Systems and Software," we discussed confidence in the engineering of software. To review, we must have evidence to support claims that a system is secure. An *assurance case* is a documented body of evidence that provides a convincing and valid argument that a specified set of critical claims about a system's properties are adequately justified for a given application in a given environment. Quality and reliability can be incorporated as evidence into an argument about predicted software security. Details about an assurance case structure and how to build an assurance case can be found in *Predicting Software Assurance Using Quality and Reliability Measures* [Woody 2014].

6.2 Ways to Gather Evidence for Cyber Security Evaluation

6.2.1 Process Evidence

Table 6.1 presents a few examples of lifecycle-phase measures that can aid in demonstrating required levels of software security. Increases in percentages for these measures over time can indicate an expanded focus on security and process improvement for performing security analysis, but they provide no evidence about

---

7. This section is drawn from *Predicting Software Assurance Using Quality and Reliability Measures* [Woody 2014].

the actual product. A more extensive list can be found in Appendix G, "Examples of Lifecycle-Phase Measures." Because of the volume of data that needs to be handled to produce effective measures across an organization, consideration of automation for consistency in collection and effectiveness in monitoring and management is critical. Without automation, labor costs can be expected to be very high and the ability to achieve timely input will be greatly reduced.

Alberts, Allen, and Stoddard [Alberts 2010] suggest a set of questions to use to assess key lifecycle areas of security risk. Security experts identified 17 process-related areas from across the lifecycle as being important for security. The associated security questions provide a means of evaluating security risk. Many of the terms within the questions, such as "sufficient," are not absolute and must be defined based on organization-specific criteria. For example, addressing a frequently occurring security problem may mean once a year for one organization and once a minute for another, depending on what the organization is doing. Table 6.2 shows an extract of a full table provided in Appendix G.

Table 6.1 *Examples of Lifecycle-Phase Measures*

Lifecycle Phase	Examples of Software Security Measures
Requirements Engineering	Percentage of relevant software security principles reflected in requirements-specific actions (assuming that security principles essential for a given development project have been selected)
	Percentage of security requirements that have been subject to analysis (risk, feasibility, cost–benefit, performance trade-offs) prior to being included in the specification
	Percentage of security requirements covered by attack patterns, misuse/abuse cases, and other specified means of threat modeling and analysis
Architecture and Design	Percentage of architectural/design components subject to attack-surface analysis and measurement
	Percentage of architectural/design components subject to architectural risk analysis
	Percentage of high-value security controls covered by a security design pattern

Table 6.2 *Examples of Questions for Software Security [Alberts 2010]*

Security Risk Focus Area	Principle
1 Program Security Objectives	Are the program's security objectives realistic and achievable?
2 Security Plan	Does the plan for developing and deploying the system sufficiently address security?
3 Contracts	Do contract mechanisms with partners, collaborators, subcontractors, and suppliers sufficiently address security?
4 Security Process	Does the process being used to develop and deploy the system sufficiently incorporate security?

Table 6.3 *Mapping Between Security Risk Focus Areas and Principles for Software Security [Mead 2013b]*

Security Risk Focus Area		Supporting Principles
1 Program Security Objectives	6	Well planned and dynamic; also influenced by principles 1 and 4
2 Security Plan	6	Well planned and dynamic; also influenced by principle 1
3 Contracts	2	Interactions; also influenced by principles 1 and 3
4 Security Process	6	Well planned and dynamic; also influenced by principles 1 and 3

Process-related areas can map to the updated security principles described earlier. Table 6.3 is an extract of such a mapping, from the full table presented in Appendix G.

A framework of measures linked to the seven principles of evidence defined in *Common Weakness Enumeration* [MITRE 2014] can provide evidence that organizations are effectively addressing the security risk focus areas [Mead 2013b]. Table 6.4 shows an extract of a full table from Appendix G.

Table 6.4 *Example Measures Based on the Seven Principles of Evidence [MITRE 2014]*

Principle	Description
Risk	Number of active and latent threats, categorized
	Incidents reported by category of threat
	Likelihood of occurrence for each threat category
	Financial and/or human safety estimate of impact for each threat category
Trusted Dependencies	Number of levels of subcontracting in the supply chain (in other words, have the subcontractors, in turn, executed subcontracts, and what is the depth of this activity)
	Number of suppliers by level
	Hierarchical and peer dependencies between suppliers by level
	Number of (vetted) trusted suppliers in the supply chain by level

---

Example Case Study: Using Subcontracting Measures to Evaluate Trusted Dependencies

GoFast automotive is planning a new entertainment system for the Tiger sports car. Traditional entertainment systems cannot be readily adapted to the smaller space of a sport automobile, and GoFast management feels that this newly engineered system will give the company a competitive edge (and thus a financial benefit). After performing risk analysis on the project, executive management decided that this system would receive extra attention to software security.

Traveling Audio Video (TAV), a subcontractor with expertise in automotive entertainment systems, is developing some of the software subsystems. Naturally, GoFast is concerned about industrial espionage and wants to make sure that its competitors cannot get access to company confidential information about its plans and designs or, worse yet, pirate the software and use it themselves.

The security group, as part of its work in support of this project, decides to look at the trusted dependencies principle. Much to their chagrin, they find out that TAV uses other subcontractors in its supply chain, and GoFast must vet all of those subcontractors to ensure that the entire supply chain is trustworthy. It turns out that one of the subcontractors to TAV also contracts with one of GoFast's competitors. Fortunately, GoFast discovers this relationship early on and can assess the risk and determine whether the supply chain needs to be modified in order to reduce the risk or whether the supply chain is, in fact, trustworthy based on prior observations and security measures in place.

If the subcontractor has a unique needed skill set, appropriate nondisclosure agreements may provide the needed level of confidence. On the other hand, if the subcontractor is known to have engaged in questionable practices (an extreme example would be accepting bribes to provide inside information about competitive products to its customers), it might be best to replace that subcontractor with another company, even if the replacement company is less experienced in these types of products. Another option would be to decide to do that part of the development in-house, thus reducing the risk of industrial espionage. Of course, this last option assumes that GoFast's employees have been vetted and deemed trustworthy.

6.2.2 Evidence from Standards

Evidence of effective cyber security engineering can be assembled by leveraging security standards that the organization has chosen to follow. NIST Special Publication 800-53 [NIST 2013] provides a wide range of security and privacy controls. These controls are widely used as implementation mechanisms to meet security requirements. NIST 800-53A [NIST 2014a] is a companion document to NIST 800-53 that describes how an audit could be conducted to collect evidence about the controls. The audit focuses on determining the extent to which the organization has chosen to implement the controls. Information is not provided for determining how well the implementation is performing. NIST 800-55 [NIST 2008], as noted earlier, has a range of specific security measures that can be applied across the lifecycle.

Alberts, Allen, & Stoddard [Alberts 2012b] provide a description of measures derived from the security controls described in NIST 800-53 [NIST 2013] that could be assembled to evaluate the effectiveness of a control. Another useful standard, detailed in *Practical Measurement Framework for Software Assurance and Information Security* [Bartol 2008], is ISO/IEC 227002, which contains a controls catalog, an ISO equivalent of NIST 800-53.[8]

Product Evidence

Combining the process perspective with a product focus would assemble stronger evidence to support confidence that cyber security requirements are met. *Practical Measurement Framework for Software Assurance and Information Security* [Bartol 2008] provides an approach for measuring how effectively an organization can achieve software assurance goals and objectives at an organizational, program, or project level. This framework incorporates existing measurement methodologies and is intended to help organizations and projects integrate SwA measurement into their existing programs. (Refer to Chapter 3, "Secure Software Development Management and Organizational Models.")

---

8. www.iso27001security.com/html/27004.html

More recent engineering projects described by Woody, Ellison, and Nichols [Woody 2014] demonstrate that a disciplined lifecycle approach with quality defect identification and removal practices combined with code analysis tooling provide the strongest results for building security into software and systems. Defect prediction models are typically informed by measures of the software product at a specific time, longitudinal measures of the product, or measures of the development process used to build the product. Metrics typically used to analyze quality problems can include the following:

- Static software metrics, such as new and changed LOC, cyclomatic complexity,[9] counts of attributes, parameters, methods and classes, and interactions among modules

- Defect counts, usually found during testing or in production, often normalized to size, effort, or time in operation

- Software change metrics, including frequency of changes, LOC changed, or longitudinal product change data, such as number of revisions, frequency of revisions, numbers of modules changed, or counts of bug fixes over time

- Process data, such as activities performed or effort applied to activities or development phases

Many models currently in use rely on static or longitudinal product measures, such as code churn. Other approaches use historic performance or experience based on defect injection and removal (generally described using a "tank and filter" metaphor), as shown in Figure 6.2, to monitor and model the defect levels during the development process. The connections between defects, which are typically related to quality and security vulnerabilities, is still an active area of research. Many of the common weakness enumerations (CWEs) cited as the primary reasons for security failures are closely tied to recognized quality issues. Data shows vulnerabilities to be 1% to 5% of reported defects [Woody 2014]. There is wide agreement that quality problems are strong evidence for security problems.

However, focusing just on a product to assure that it has few defects is also insufficient. Removal of defects depends on assuring our capability to find them. Positive results from security testing and static code analysis are often provided as evidence that security vulnerabilities have been reduced, but it is a mistake to rely on them as the primary means for identifying defects. The omission of quality practices, such as inspections, can lead to defects exceeding the capabilities of existing code analysis tools [Woody 2014].

---

9. http://en.wikipedia.org/wiki/Cyclomatic_complexity

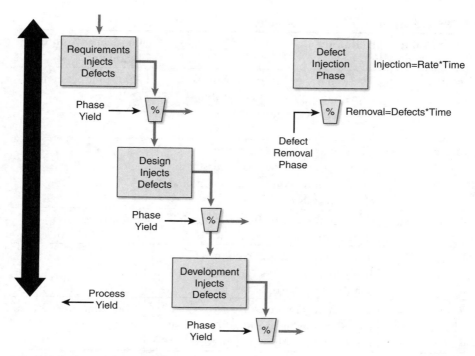

Figure 6.2 *"Tank and Filter" Quality Tracking Model*

Organizations must establish product relevance before applying the metrics to cyber security. In the research described above, the product was a medical device, and the security requirements being evaluated were assigned to the whole device. These same measures could be performed on a single software application running on this device. The relationship of the component to the whole must be determined before it is possible to observe the utility of applying metrics collected on a component to the composition. For example, a component that handles of the data input and output for the device represents a critical part of the cyber security concern for the device. Measures collected on a USB device driver on the device are not representative of the composition.

Evaluating the Evidence

Next, we need to be sufficiently specific about the definitions of the words we use to provide consistent and repeatable usage. As an example, consider the word *often*. In some contexts, this word may mean daily or weekly and in others it may mean multiple times per second. Table 6.5 provides an example of structuring terms related to frequency to establish consistency.

Table 6.5 *Example Frequency Structure*

Term (Value)	Definition	Guidelines/Context/ Examples
Frequent (5)	The scenario occurs on numerous occasions or in quick succession. It tends to occur quite often or at close intervals.	≥ one time per month (≥ 12 / year)
Likely (4)	The scenario occurs on multiple occasions. It tends to occur reasonably often but not in quick succession or at close intervals.	
Occasional (3)	The scenario occurs from time to time. It tends to occur "once in a while."	~ one time per 6 months (~ 2 / year)
Remote (2)	The scenario can occur, but it is not likely to occur. It has "an outside chance" of occurring.	
Rare (1)	The scenario infrequently occurs and is considered to be uncommon or unusual. It is not frequently experienced.	≤ one time every 3 years (≤ .33 / year)

Measures can be qualitative or quantitative; both are useful, but the assigned value (shown in parentheses in Table 6.5) depends on the question being asked and how well the measures support the decision.[10] Is it sufficient to have a relative frequency of occurrence, or does the decision demand a specific count? There are trade-offs to consider in making this determination: The more exact the information, the more costly it is to gather.[11]

10. NIST 800-55 [NIST 2008] also provides a terminology structure to help clarify terms like *sufficient* that can be easily interpreted many ways.

11. In his book *Engineering Safe and Secure Software Systems*, Axelrod provides an interesting comparison of qualitative and quantitative measurements for an automobile in Table 7.1 [Axelrod 2012].

Case Study: Risk Management for Wireless Emergency Alerts
(see Chapter 1, section 1.5.1)

Consider the following example of evaluating risk from the Wireless Emergency Alert (WEA) case study, using the terminology from Table 6.5:

Risk Statement

IF an outside actor with malicious intent obtains a valid certificate through social engineering and uses it to send an illegitimate Common Alerting Protocol (CAP)–compliant message by spoofing an Alert Originating System (AOS), THEN health, safety, legal, financial, and reputation consequences could result.

Probability Value

Rare

Rationale

This risk requires that a complex sequence of events occurs.

The actor has to be highly motivated.

The attack needs to coincide with an event where a large crowd is gathered.

Impact Value

Maximum

Rationale

The impact ultimately depends on whether people trust the WEA service and take the action recommended in the illegitimate WEA alert.

Health and safety damages could be severe, leading to potentially large legal liabilities.

The reputation of WEA could be severely damaged beyond repair.

Figure 6.3 Shows the Risk.

(*continued*)

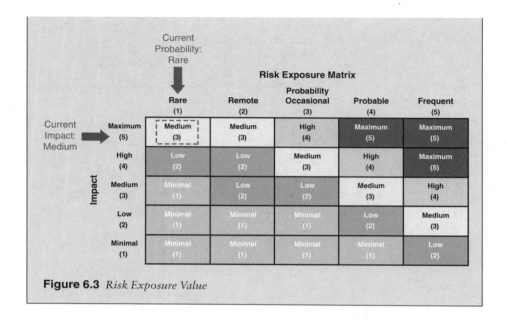

Figure 6.3 *Risk Exposure Value*

6.2.3 Measurement Management[12]

Because software is not created once and left unchanged, we cannot make measurements once and assume that they are sufficient for all ongoing needs. The same is true of cyber security information for the software. If we want to show change over time, we must collect and assemble measurements and structure them for future use. *Measurement management* ensures that suitable measures are created and applied as needed in the lifecycle of the software or system. Measurement management requires the formulation of coherent baselines of measures that accurately reflect product characteristics and lifecycle management needs. Measurement baselines must be capable of being revised as needed to track the evolving product throughout its lifecycle and evaluate relationships with similar products. Using the appropriate set of baselines, the measurement management process ensures that the right set of metrics is always in place to produce the desired measurement outcomes. This approach is consistent with existing international security measurement standards, such as ISO/IEC 27004 and

---

12. This section is drawn from *Measures for Managing Operational Resilience* [Allen 2011].

ISO/IEC 15939, and security measurement guidance, such as *Practical Measurement Framework for Software Assurance and Information Security* [Bartol 2008].

The measurement management process collects data about discrete aspects of a product and/or process functioning to support operational and strategic decision making about the product. The measurement management process should provide data-driven feedback in real time or near real time to project managers, development managers, and technical staff. The National Vulnerability Database[13] is one of the resource baselines publically available for cyber security. This database contains standards-based vulnerability data that can be used by automated tools to verify compliance of software product implementations.

Managing Through Measurement Baselines

Management control is typically enforced through measurement baselines. A *measurement baseline* is a collection of discrete metrics that characterize an item of interest for a target of measurement. Using a measurement baseline, it is possible to make meaningful comparisons of product and process performance to support management and operational decision making. Such comparisons can be vital to improving products and processes over time through the use of predictive and stochastic assurance models for decision making. Potential metrics for supporting such an effort might include basic measures such as defect data, productivity data, and threat/vulnerability data. An evolving baseline model provides managers with the necessary assurance insight, cost controls, and business information for any process or product, and it allows value tracking for the assurance process.

Formulating a measurement baseline involves four steps:

1. The organization identifies and defines the target of measurement (the goal aspect of the GQM model, as noted earlier).

2. The organization establishes the requisite questions that define needed metrics to assure the desired measurement objectives; the organization assembles the relevant measures in a formally structured and controlled baseline.

3. The organization establishes the comparative criteria for tracking performance. Those criteria establish what will be learned from analyzing the data from each metric over time.

4. The organization carries out the routine measurement data collection and analysis activities, using the baseline metrics.

---

13. www.nist.gov/itl/csd/stvm/nvd.cfm

Examples showing the results of this approach for operational resilience can be found in *Measures for Managing Operational Resilience* [Allen 2011],[14] which defines 10 strategic measures to support organizational strategic objectives. The following is an example of an organizational objective along with the measures that support it:

> **Objective:** In the face of realized risk, the *operational resilience management* (ORM) system ensures the continuity of essential operations of high-value services and their associated assets. Realized risk may include an incident, a break in service continuity, or a human-made or disaster or crisis.
>
> **Measure 9:** Probability of delivered service through a disruptive event
>
> **Measure 10:** For disrupted, high-value services with a service continuity plan, percentage of services that did not deliver service as intended throughout the disruptive event

Consider using "near misses" and "incidents avoided" as predictors of successful disruptions in the future.

---

14. This report and others in the SEI's Resilience Measurement and Analysis collection can be found at http://resources.sei.cmu.edu/library/asset-view.cfm?assetid=434555.

Chapter 7

Special Topics in Cyber Security Engineering

with Julia Allen, Warren Axelrod, Stephany Bellomo, and Jose Morales

In This Chapter

7.1 Introduction

Earlier chapters mention some special topics for readers who want to dig a little deeper in specific areas. Those topics are presented here:

- This chapter starts with a discussion of governance, recognizing that security is more than just a technical issue, and describes how organizations can set clear expectations for business conduct and then follow through to ensure that the organization fulfills those expectations.

- Then this chapter describes some findings on cyber security standards, an important area that is still evolving.

- Organizations that perform acquisition—rather than development—can achieve an emphasis on security requirements by using Security Quality

Requirements Engineering for Acquisition (A-SQUARE). All too often, cyber security is left to contractors, with little attention from acquisition organizations until systems are delivered or operational. We hope to see organizations address cyber security much earlier in the acquisition lifecycle, and security requirements are a good place to start.

• Next, this chapter discusses DevOps. In the field we are finally seeing recognition of the synergy of development and operations, after years of seeing them treated as disparate activities in a stovepiped project environment.

• Finally, this chapter discusses some recent research work that seeks to identify ways organizations can use malware analysis to identify security requirements that have led to vulnerabilities in earlier systems. These overlooked requirements can then be incorporated into the security requirements for future systems.

Each of these topics is unique, and you may not be interested in all of them. We offer them as a deeper exploration in specific areas of cyber security engineering.

7.2 Security: Not Just a Technical Issue[1]

7.2.1 Introduction

This section defines the scope of governance concern as it applies to security. It describes some of the top-level considerations and characteristics to use as indicators of a security-conscious culture and to determine whether an effective program is in place.

Security's days as just a technical issue are over. Security is becoming a central concern for leaders at the highest levels of many organizations and governments, and it transcends national borders. Today's organizations face constant high-impact security incidents that can disrupt operations and lead to disclosure of sensitive information. Customers are demanding greater security as evidence suggests that violations of personal privacy, the disclosure of personally identifiable information, and identity theft are on the rise. Business partners, suppliers, and vendors are requiring greater security from one another, particularly when providing mutual network and information access. Networked efforts to steal competitive intelligence and engage in extortion are becoming more prevalent. Security breaches and data disclosure increasingly arise from criminal behavior motivated by financial gain as well as state-sponsored actions motivated by national strategies.

Current and former employees and contractors who have or had authorized access to their organization's system and networks are familiar with internal policies,

---

1. This section was contributed by Julia Allen.

procedures, and technology and can exploit that knowledge to facilitate attacks and even collude with external attackers. Organizations must mitigate malicious insider acts such as sabotage, fraud, theft of confidential or proprietary information, and potential threats to our nation's critical infrastructure. Recent CERT research documents cases of successful malicious insider incidents even during the software development lifecycle.[2]

In the United States, managing cyber security risk is becoming a national imperative. In February 2013, the U.S. president issued an executive order[3] to enhance the security of the nation's critical infrastructure, resulting in the development of the National Institute of Standards and Technology (NIST) Cybersecurity Framework [NIST 2014]. According to the IT Governance Institute, "boards of directors will increasingly be expected to make information security an intrinsic part of governance, integrated with processes they already have in place to govern other critical organizational resources" [ITGI 2006]. The National Association of Corporate Directors (NACD) states that the cyber security battle is being waged on two levels—protecting a corporation's most valuable assets and the implications and consequences of disclosure in response to legal and regulatory requirements [Warner 2014]. According to an article in *NACD Magazine*, "Cybersecurity is the responsibility of senior leaders who are responsible for creating an enterprise-wide culture of security" [Warner 2014]. At an international level, the Internet Governance Forum (IGF)[4] provides a venue for discussion of public policy issues, including security, as they relate to the Internet. Ultimately, directors and senior executives set the direction for how enterprise security—including software security—is perceived, prioritized, managed, and implemented. This is governance in action.

The Business Roundtable (an association of chief executive officers of leading U.S. companies) recommends the following in its report *More Intelligent, More Effective Cybersecurity Protection* [Business Roundtable 2013]:

> CEOs should develop the capabilities required to integrate cybersecurity threat and risk information into CEO risk management.
>
> Boards of directors, as part of their risk oversight functions, continue to periodically review management's business resiliency plans, including cybersecurity, and oversee risk assessment and risk management processes, including those applicable to cybersecurity.

---

2. Refer to the CERT Insider Threat website (www.cert.org/insider-threat/publications) for presentations and podcasts on this subject.

3. www.whitehouse.gov/the-press-office/2013/02/12/executive-order-improving-critical-infrastructure-cybersecurity

4. www.intgovforum.org/cms/home-36966

As additional evidence of this growing trend, the Deloitte *2014 Board Practices Report: Perspective from the Boardroom* states the following [Deloitte 2014]:

> Cybersecurity has quickly become an important topic for companies and boards, particularly in light of recent data breaches. According to survey results, the level of board awareness on cybersecurity is moderate (32%) to high (49%) across all companies surveyed, with the exception of small cap companies. Most often the full board or the audit committee is responsible for the oversight of cybersecurity matters.

According to the Building Security In Maturity Model [McGraw 2015],

> Executives and middle management, including line of business owners and product managers, must understand how early investment in security design and security analysis affects the degree to which users will trust their products. Business requirements should explicitly address security needs. Any sizeable business today depends on software to work. Software security is a business necessity.

While growing evidence suggests that senior leaders are paying more attention to the risks and business implications associated with poor or inadequate security governance, a recent Carnegie Mellon University survey indicates that there is still a lot of room for improvement [Westby 2012]:

- Boards are still not undertaking key oversight activities related to cyber risks, such as reviewing budgets, security program assessments, and top-level policies; assigning roles and responsibilities for privacy and security; and receiving regular reports on breaches and IT risks.

- 57% of respondents are not analyzing the adequacy of cyber insurance coverage or undertaking key activities related to cyber risk management to help them manage reputational and financial risks associated with the theft of confidential and proprietary data and security breaches.

Governance and Security

Governance means setting clear expectations for business conduct and then following through to ensure that the organization fulfills those expectations. Governance action flows from the top of the organization to all of its business units and projects. Done right, governance augments an organization's approach to nearly any business problem, including security. National and international regulations call for organizations—and their leaders—to demonstrate due care with respect to security. This is where governance can help.

Moreover, organizations are not the only entities that benefit from strengthening enterprise[5] security through clear, consistent governance. Ultimately, entire nations benefit. "The national and economic security of the United States depends on the reliable functioning of critical infrastructure. Cybersecurity threats exploit the increased complexity and connectivity of critical infrastructure systems, placing the nation's security, economy, and public safety and health at risk" [NIST 2014].

Definitions of Security Governance

The term *governance* applied to any subject can have a wide range of interpretations and definitions. For the purpose of this chapter, we define *governing* for enterprise security[6] as follows [Allen 2005]:

- Directing and controlling an organization to establish and sustain a culture of security in the organization's conduct (values, beliefs, principles, behaviors, capabilities, and actions)
- Treating adequate security as a non-negotiable requirement of being in business

The NIST Cybersecurity Framework defines information security governance as follows: "The policies, procedures, and processes to manage and monitor the organization's regulatory, legal, risk environmental, and operational requirements are understood and inform the management of cybersecurity risk" [NIST 2014].

In the context of security, governance incorporates a strong focus on risk management. Governance is an expression of responsible risk management, and effective risk management requires efficient governance. One way governance addresses risk is to specify a framework for decision making. It makes clear who is authorized to make decisions, what the decision-making rights are, and who is accountable for decisions. Consistency in decision making across an enterprise, a business unit, or a project boosts confidence and reduces risk.

---

5. We use the terms *organization* and *enterprise* to convey the same meaning.

6. As used here, *security* includes software security, information security, application security, cyber security, network security, and information assurance. It does not include disciplines typically considered within the domain of physical security such as facilities, executive protection, and criminal investigations.

Duty of Care

In the absence of some type of meaningful governance structure and way of managing and measuring enterprise security, the following questions naturally arise (and in all of them, *organization* can include an entire enterprise, a business or operating unit, a project, and all of the entities participating in a software supply chain):

- How can an organization know what its greatest security risk exposures are?
- How can an organization know if it is secure enough to do the following:
  - Detect and prevent security events that require business-continuity, crisis-management, and disaster-recovery actions?
  - Protect stakeholder interests and meet stakeholder expectations?
  - Comply with regulatory and legal requirements?
  - Develop, acquire, deploy, operate, and use application software and software-intensive systems?
  - Ensure enterprise viability?

ANSI has the following to say with respect to an organization's fiduciary duty of care [ANSI 2008]:

> The key to understanding the financial risks of cybersecurity is to fully embrace its multidisciplinary nature. Cyber risk is not just a technical problem to be solved by the company's chief technology officer. Nor is it just a legal problem to be handed over to the company's chief legal counsel; a customer relationship problem to be solved by the company's communications director; a compliance issue for the regulatory guru; or a crisis management problem. Rather, it is all of these and more.

As a result, director and officer oversight of information and cyber security (including software security) is embedded within the duty of care owed to enterprise shareholders and stakeholders. Leaders who hold equivalent roles in government, non-profit, and educational institutions must view their responsibilities similarly.

Leading by Example

Demonstrating duty of care with respect to security is a tall order, but leaders must be up to the challenge. Their behaviors and actions with respect to security influence the rest of the organization. When staff members see the board and executive team giving time and attention to security, they know that security is worth their own time and attention. In this way, a security-conscious culture can grow.

It seems clear that boards of directors, senior executives, business unit and operating unit leaders, and project managers all must play roles in making and reinforcing the business case for effective enterprise security. Trust, reputation, brand, stakeholder value, customer retention, and operational costs are all at stake if security governance and management are performed poorly. Organizations are much more competent in using security to mitigate risk if their leaders treat it as essential to the business and are aware of and knowledgeable about security issues.

Characteristics of Effective Security Governance and Management

One of the best indications that an organization is addressing security as a governance and management concern is a consistent and reinforcing set of values, beliefs, principles, behaviors, capabilities, and actions that are consistent with security best practices and standards. These measures aid in building a security-conscious culture [Coles 2015]. These measures can be expressed as statements about the organization's current behavior and condition.[7]

Leaders who are committed to dealing with security at a governance level can use the following list to determine the extent to which a security-conscious culture is present (or needs to be present) in their organizations:

- The organization manages security as an enterprise issue, horizontally, vertically, and cross-functionally throughout the organization and in its relationships with partners, vendors, and suppliers. Executive leaders understand their accountability and responsibility with respect to security for the organization, their stakeholders, the communities they serve including the Internet community, and the protection of critical national infrastructures and economic and national security interests.

- The organization treats security as a business requirement. The organization sees security as a cost of doing business and an investment rather than an expense or discretionary budget-line item. Leaders at the top of the organization set security policy with input from key stakeholders. Business units and staff are not allowed to decide unilaterally how much security they want. Adequate and sustained funding and allocation of adequate security resources are given.

---

7. See also "Characteristics of Effective Security Governance" [Allen 2007] for a table of 11 characteristics that compares and contrasts an organization with effective governance practices and one where these practices are missing.

- The organization considers security as an integral part of normal strategic, capital, project, and operational planning cycles. Strategic and project plans include achievable, measurable security objectives and effective controls and metrics for implementing those objectives. Reviews and audits of plans identify security weaknesses and deficiencies as well as requirements for the continuity of operations. They measure progress against plans of action and milestones. Determining how much security is enough relates directly to how much risk exposure an organization can tolerate.

- The organization addresses security as part of any new project initiation, acquisition, or relationship and as part of ongoing project management. The organization addresses security requirements throughout all system/software development lifecycle phases, including acquisition, initiation, requirements engineering, system architecture and design, development, testing, release, operations/production, maintenance, and retirement.

- Managers across the organization understand how security serves as a business enabler (versus an inhibitor). They view security as one of their responsibilities and understand that their team's performance with respect to security is measured as part of their overall performance.

- All personnel who have access to digital assets and enterprise networks understand their individual responsibilities with respect to protecting and preserving the organization's security, including the systems and software that it uses and develops. Awareness, motivation, and compliance are the accepted, expected cultural norm. The organization consistently applies and reinforces security policy compliance through rewards, recognition, and consequences.

The relative importance of each of these statements depends on the organization's culture and business context. For those who are accustomed to using ISO/IEC 27001 [ISO/IEC 2013], similar topics can be found at a higher level.

7.2.2 Two Examples of Security Governance

Payment Card Industry

The development, stewardship, and enforcement of the Payment Card Industry (PCI) Data Security Standard (DSS) [PCI Security Standards Council 2015] represent a demonstrable act of governance by the PCI over its members and merchants. This standard presents a comprehensive set of 12 requirements for enhancing payment account data security and "was developed to facilitate the broad adoption of consist-ent data security measures globally." It "applies to all entities involved in payment card processing—including merchants, processors, acquirers, issuers, and service providers" [PCI Security Standards Council 2015].

An additional standard that is part of the PCI DSS standards suite is the Payment Application Data Security Standard (PA-DSS) [PCI Security Standards Council 2013]. PA-DSS specifically addresses software security. Its purpose is to assist software ven-dors of payment applications to develop and deploy products that are more secure, that protect cardholder data, and that comply with the broader PCI standard. All 14 PA-DSS practice descriptions include detailed subpractices and testing procedures for verifying that the practice is in place. The PCI Standards Council maintains a list of validated payment applications that meet this standard. Payment card merchants can use it to select applications that ensure better protection of cardholder data.

U.S. Energy Sector

In response to the U.S. 2013 executive order, the U.S. Department of Energy (DOE) developed the Electricity Subsector Cybersecurity Capability Maturity Model (ES-C2M2) to improve and understand the cyber security posture of the U.S. energy sec-tor. The 10 domains that compose the model and the companion self-assessment method "provide a mechanism that helps organizations evaluate, prioritize, and improve cybersecurity capabilities" [DoE 2014a]. U.S. energy sector owners and oper-ators are using the model to improve their ability to detect, respond to, and recover from cyber security incidents. As a result of the successful use of ES-C2M2, the DOE developed an equivalent model [DoE 2014b], with which the U.S. oil and natural gas subsector concurred, that is experiencing active adoption and use. The development, use, and stewardship of these models are strong examples of security governance for two national critical infrastructure sectors.

7.2.3 Conclusion

Most senior executives and managers understand governance and their responsibili-ties with respect to it. The intent here is to help leaders expand their perspectives to include security and incorporate enterprise-wide security thinking into their own—and their organizations'—governance and management actions. An organization's ability to achieve and sustain adequate security starts with executive sponsorship and commitment. Standards such as ISO 27001 [ISO/IEC 2013] reinforce and supple-ment industry initiatives.

7.3 Cyber Security Standards

7.3.1 The Need for More Cyber Security Standards[8]

To be able to certify compliance with security standards, we clearly first need to have a set of generally accepted standards. Although there have been quite a number of attempts to achieve acceptable information security standards, no overarching set is being consistently followed.

Governments around the globe favor the Common Criteria for Information Technology Security Evaluation, also known as ISO/IEC 15408. The PCI DSS [PCI Security Standards Council 2015] and the PA-DSS [PCI Security Standards Council 2013] apply to those handling payment card information and the vendors of software that process this information, respectively.

A subset of software systems need to be certified according to the Common Criteria or PCI standards in order for their acquisition and/or use to be permitted. It is noteworthy that, in both these cases, the standard-setting authorities (i.e., various government agencies and payments processing companies) are relatively powerful in terms of purchasing power (governments) or scope of influence (PCI).

Other compliance or certification reviews—such as auditing against International Organization for Standardization (ISO) or International Electrotechnical Commission (IEC) standards in general as well as specific audit reviews in particular—usually target specific departments and processes within an organization, and the certifications mostly apply only to an examined process at a specific point in time (for example, SSAE 16 reviews, which replaced SAS 70 Type 1 and Type 2 reviews). Such reviews usually do not dig deeply into the particular technologies in operation, nor do they determine whether these technologies meet a certain quality level. However, certain types of technical audits examine program code, platforms, networks, and the like.

Some regulators require broader "policy and procedures" compliance reviews. For example, the National Association of Securities Dealers Regulations (NASDR) requires securities firms in the U.S. to perform and report on extensive reviews of back-office and IT policy and procedures to ensure that they actually exist, are fully documented, and meet certain governance requirements. This situation suggests that we must better understand what standards are and how they relate to directives, policy, guidelines, procedures, etc. Table 7.1 provides a comparison among these various categories.

Table 7.1 includes descriptions from a variety of sources. It is interesting to note that they are not all definitions, and though some descriptions are similar, they are

---

8. This section was contributed by Warren Axelrod.

Table 7.1 *Descriptions and Characteristics of Principles, Policies, Standards, etc.*

Category	Descriptions	Characteristics/Examples
Directive	An expression of expectations by executive management	A directive is general, brief, and to the point; it is seldom modified.
Principle	Standards, conventions, and mechanisms [ISSA 2004] An enabler of governance and management; comprises the values and fundamental assumptions held by the enterprise, the beliefs that guide and put boundaries around the enterprise's decision making, communication within and outside the enterprise, and stewardship—caring for assets owned by another [ISACA 2014]	Principles address computer security from a very high-level viewpoint. Enterprises should use principles when developing computer security programs and policy, and when creating new systems, practices, or policies [Swanson 1996]. Principles are expressed at a high level, encompassing broad areas (e.g., accountability, cost-effectiveness, and integration) [Swanson 1996]. In *GAISP V3.0* [ISSA 2004], principles are organized in a three-level hierarchy: • Pervasive principles • Broad functional principles • Detailed principles
Policy	The rules and regulations set by the organization and laid down by management in compliance with applicable law, industry regulations, and the decisions of enterprise leaders [Bosworth 2002] In the case of computer security policy, senior management's directives to create a computer security program, establish its goals, and assign responsibilities [Swanson 1996]	Policies are mandatory; they are expressed in definite language and require compliance. Failure to conform to policy can result in disciplinary action [Bosworth 2002]. A policy may pertain to a specific operational environment [CCRA 2012]. Policies are mandatory and use the word *must* [Wood 1999]. Policies are higher-level requirements than standards and provide general instructions [Wood 1999]. Policies are intended to last up to five years [Wood 1999].

(Continued)

Table 7.1 *Continued*

Category	Descriptions	Characteristics/Examples
	Typically, a document that outlines specific requirements or rules [SANS 2015] Generally, a document that records a high–level principle or course of action that has been decided on; the intended purpose is to influence and guide both present and future decision making to be in line with the philosophy, objectives, and strategic plans established by the enterprise's management teams [ISACA 2014] High-level statements to provide guidance to workers making present and future decisions [Wood 1999] Overall intention and direction as formally expressed by management [ISACA 2014] A set of security rules, procedures, or guidelines for an organization [CCRA 2012]	Examples include the following [SANS 2015; Axelrod 2004]: • Application security policy • Electronic mail and messaging policy • Internet use policy • Remote access policy • Network security policy • Server security policy
Standard	Typically, a collection of system-specific or procedure-specific requirements [SANS 2015] A published statement on a topic specifying characteristics, usually measurable, that must be satisfied or achieved [Kissel 2013] A mandatory requirement, code of practice, or specification approved by a recognized standards organization (e.g., ISO) [ISACA 2014]	Standards are meant to last a few years due to changes in manual procedures, organizational structures, business processes, and information systems technologies. Following a standard somewhat ensures that an organization can maintain control over how software and hardware are configured, which facilitates changes and emergency updates [Axelrod 2004].

Category	Descriptions	Characteristics/Examples
Baseline	A specific implementation of a standard that is expected to be followed closely [Axelrod 2004]	Baselines are more technical than standards and are specific to a particular environment and version of software [Axelrod 2004].
	In terms of a "security baseline," a set of basic objectives that must be met by a given service or system [CERN 2010]	Baselines may have to be updated frequently as vendors modify software and release new versions [Axelrod 2004].
	Hardware, software, databases, and relevant documentation for an information system at a given point in time [Kissel 2013]	The set of basic objectives is chosen to be pragmatic and complete and does not impose technical guidance [CERN 2010].
Guideline	A suggested way to follow a standard, proposed as a good approach but not enforced	Guidelines are optional and recommended and use the word *should* [Wood 1999].
	A particular way of accomplishing something that is less prescriptive than a procedure [ISACA 2014]	
Process	Relatively high-level series of tasks designed to enable those within the organization to comply with policy [Axelrod 2004]	None
	Generally, a collection of activities influenced by the enterprise's policies and procedures that takes inputs from a number of sources (including other processes), manipulates the inputs, and produces outputs [ISACA 2014]	

(Continued)

Table 7.1 *Continued*

Category	Descriptions	Characteristics/Examples
Practice	A technique or methodology that, through experience and research, has proven to reliably lead to a desired result [TechTarget 2015] Guidance for organizations that describes the types of controls, objectives, and procedures that comprise an effective IT security program [Swanson 1996]	Practices show what should be done to enhance or measure an existing computer security program or aid in the development of a new program, and provide a common ground for determining the security of an organization [Swanson 1996].
Procedure	A lower-level process that generally captures a particular aspect or component of a process [Axelrod 2004] A document containing a detailed description of the steps necessary to perform specific operations in conformance with applicable standards; procedures are defined as parts of processes [ISACA 2014]	None

not entirely consistent. Nonetheless, our intent is to show the range of descriptions—where they are the same and where they differ. Inconsistencies might result in the misuse of definitions and terms, confusion about the meaning of terms, and consequent misdirection. These problems could account in large part for the inconsistent use of information security standards.[9]

The main result of this disparity of descriptions is a hierarchy of rules, some of which are mandatory ("must") and some of which are optional ("should"). These rules are set at different levels within an organization, usually apply to lower-level groups, and are enforced and audited by other parties.

We need accepted standards and a rich compendium of baselines in order to support universal measures of software cyber security assurance. When standards are not used, the fallback is usually to substitute common, essential, or "best" practices, with the argument that an organization cannot be faulted if it is as protective as or more protective than its peers in applying available tools and technologies.[10]

This logic is somewhat questionable since it frequently leads to compliance with mediocrity: If one organization is vulnerable, then other organizations that applied the same level of security are vulnerable also. We see this phenomenon in action when similar organizations fall victim to similar successful attacks.

Experts have argued that software monocultures lead to less secure systems environments. We can consider this argument in the context of software cyber security assurance processes: When many organizations in the same industries use similar systems *and* observe similar security measures, those organizations become more vulnerable. Organizations could benefit from varying their approaches to cyber security assurance.

7.3.2 A More Optimistic View of Cyber Security Standards

We are starting to see the emergence of cyber security standards that provide more cause for optimism than the earlier work referred to in Section 7.3.1. For example, a recent interview[11] highlighted the following cyber security standards:

---

9. A similar lack of focus and specificity exists in attempts to define policy standards and procedures for cyber warfare, which can have much graver outcomes. Nevertheless, the lack of cyber security standards, despite the proliferation of policies, is extremely costly in financial, economic, and social terms.

10. Donn Parker asserts that it is impossible to calculate cyber security risk, so metrics are meaningless [Parker 2009]. Steven Lipner claims that a metric for software quality does not exist [Lipner 2015]. Parker suggests implementing the best practices of peer organizations. Peter Tippett, who claims to have invented the first antivirus product, stated that there is no such thing as a "best practice" and instead uses the term "essential practice" to refer to a generally accepted approach [Tippett 2002].

11. www.forbes.com/sites/peterhigh/2015/12/07/a-conversation-with-the-most-influential-cybersecurity-guru-to-the-u-s-government/

- NIST SP 800-160: System Security Engineering: An Integrated Approach to Building Trustworthy Resilient Systems
- IEEE/ISO 15288: Systems and Software Engineering—System Life Cycle Processes
- The NIST TACIT approach for system security engineering: Threat, Assets, Complexity, Integration, Trustworthiness[12]

Another important document is NIST SP 800-53: Recommended Security Controls for Federal Information Systems and Organizations. This document has undergone several revisions in recent years and is being used extensively in government software systems acquisition and development. In addition, standards such as ISO/IEC 27001, ISO/IEC 27002, ISO/IEC 27034, and ISO/IEC 27036 all provide useful support, and NIST Special Publication 800-161 addresses supply chain risk.

7.4 Security Requirements Engineering for Acquisition

Although much work in security requirements engineering research has been aimed at in-house development, many organizations acquire software from other sources rather than develop it in-house. These organizations are faced with the same security concerns as organizations doing in-house development, but they usually have less control over the development process. Acquirers therefore need a way to assure themselves that security requirements are being addressed, regardless of the development process.

There have been some efforts related to acquisition of secure software. The Open Web Application Security Project (OWASP) group provides guidance for contract language that can be used in acquisition; the guidance includes a brief discussion of requirements [OWASP 2016]. An SEI method is available to assist in selecting COTS software [Comella-Dorda 2004]. The Common Criteria approach provides detailed guidance on how to evaluate a system for security [Common Criteria 2016]. In addition, there are security requirements engineering methods, such as SQUARE [Mead 2005], SREP [Mellado 2007], and Secure Tropos [Giorgini 2006]; some of these methods address the acquisition of secure software. The recent NIST Special Publication 800-53, Revision 4 provides guidance for selecting security controls [NIST 2013], and NIST Special Publication 800-161 addresses supply chain risk [NIST 2015].

We next examine various acquisition cases for security requirements engineering, using the SQUARE process model as a baseline.

---

12. Summarized in slide form at http://csrc.nist.gov/groups/SMA/fisma/documents/joint-conference_12-04-2013.pdf.

7.4.1 SQUARE for New Development

The SQUARE process for new development is shown in Table 7.2. This process has been documented [Mead 2005]; described in various books, papers, and websites [Allen 2008]; and used on a number of projects [Chung 2006]. This is the process that was used as the basis for SQUARE for Acquisition (A-SQUARE).

7.4.2 SQUARE for Acquisition

We next present various acquisition cases and the associated SQUARE adaptations.

Case 1: The Acquisition Organization Has the Typical Client Role for Newly Developed Software

In this example, the contractor is responsible for identifying requirements. We use SQUARE as the underlying method, but the contractor could use another method to identify the security requirements. If SQUARE is used throughout, steps 3–9 (highlighted in italics in Table 7.3) are performed by the contractor. This case presumes that the contract award has been made, and the contractor is on board. The acquisition organization has the typical client role in this example. It's important to note the client involvement in steps 1, 2, and 10. Also note that if the acquisition organization works side by side with the contractor, the separate review in step 10 can be eliminated, as the client inputs are considered in the earlier steps.

In the event that the contractor's security requirements engineering process is unspecified, the resulting compressed process looks as shown in Table 7.4.

Case 2: The Acquisition Organization Specifies the Requirements as Part of the RFP for Newly Developed Software

If an acquisition organization specifies requirements as part of an RFP, then the original SQUARE for development should be used (refer to Table 7.2). Note that relatively high-level security requirements may result from this exercise, since the acquisition organization may be developing the requirements in the absence of a broader system context. Also, the acquisition organization should avoid identifying requirements at a granularity that overly constrains the contractor.

Case 3: Acquisition of COTS Software

In acquiring COTS software, an organization should develop a list of requirements for the software and compare those requirements with the software packages under consideration (see Table 7.5). The organization may need to prioritize security

Table 7.2 *SQUARE Steps*

Step	Input	Techniques	Participants	Output
1 Agree on definitions	Candidate definitions from IEEE and other standards	Structured interviews, focus group	Stakeholders, requirements team	Agreed-to definitions
2 Identify assets and security goals	Definitions, candidate goals, business drivers, policies and procedures, examples	Facilitated work session, surveys, interviews	Stakeholders, requirements engineer	Assets and goals
3 Develop artifacts to support security requirements definition	Potential artifacts (e.g., scenarios, misuse cases, templates, forms)	Work session	Requirements engineer	Needed artifacts: scenarios, misuse cases, models, templates, forms
4 Perform risk assessment	Misuse cases, scenarios, security goals	Risk assessment method, analysis of anticipated risk against organizational risk tolerance, including threat analysis	Requirements engineer, risk expert, stakeholders	Risk assessment results
5 Select elicitation techniques	Goals, definitions, candidate techniques, expertise of stakeholders, organizational style, culture, level of security needed, cost–benefit analysis, etc.	Work session	Requirements engineer	Selected elicitation techniques

Step		Input	Techniques	Participants	Output
6	Elicit security requirements	Artifacts, risk assessment results, selected techniques	Joint Application Development (JAD), interviews, surveys, model-based analysis, checklists, lists of reusable requirements types, document reviews	Stakeholders facilitated by requirements engineer	Initial cut at security requirements
7	Categorize requirements as to level (system, software, etc.) and whether they are requirements or other kinds of constraints	Initial requirements, architecture	Work session using a standard set of categories	Requirements engineer, other specialists as needed	Categorized requirements
8	Prioritize requirements	Categorized requirements and risk assessment results	Prioritization methods, such as Triage, Win-Win	Stakeholders facilitated by requirements engineer	Prioritized requirements
9	Inspect requirements	Prioritized requirements, candidate formal inspection technique	Inspection method such as Fagan, peer reviews	Inspection team	Initial selected requirements, documentation of decision making process and rationale

Table 7.3 *Process When an Acquisition Organization Has a Typical Client Role for New Software*

Step	Input	Techniques	Organizational Responsibility	Output
1 Agree on definitions	Candidate definitions from IEEE and other standards	Structured interviews, focus group	Acquisition organization, contractor	Agreed-to definitions
2 Identify assets and security goals	Definitions, candidate goals, business drivers, policies and procedures, examples	Facilitated work session, surveys, interviews	Acquisition organization, contractor	Assets and goals
3 *Develop artifacts to support security requirements definition*	*Potential artifacts (e.g., scenarios, misuse cases, templates, forms)*	*Work session*	*Contractor*	*Needed artifacts: scenarios, misuse cases, models, templates, forms*
4 *Perform risk assessment*	*Misuse cases, scenarios, security goals*	*Risk assessment method, analysis of anticipated risk against organizational risk tolerance, including threat analysis*	*Contractor*	*Risk assessment results*
5 *Select elicitation techniques*	*Goals, definitions, candidate techniques, expertise of stakeholders, organizational style, culture, level of security needed, cost–benefit analysis, etc.*	*Work session*	*Contractor*	*Selected elicitation techniques*

Step	Input	Techniques	Organizational Responsibility	Output
6	Elicit security requirements	Artifacts, risk assessment results, selected techniques	Joint Application Development (JAD), interviews, surveys, model-based analysis, checklists, lists of reusable requirements types, document reviews	Contractor	Initial cut at security requirements
7	Categorize requirements as to level (system, software, etc.) and whether they are requirements or other kinds of constraints	Initial requirements, architecture	Work session using a standard set of categories	Contractor	Categorized requirements
8	Prioritize requirements	Categorized requirements and risk assessment results	Prioritization methods, such as triage, Win-Win	Contractor	Prioritized requirements
9	Review and inspect requirements	Prioritized requirements, candidate formal inspection technique	Inspection method such as Fagan, peer reviews	Contractor	Initial selected requirements, documentation of decision making process and rationale
10	Review of requirements by acquisition organization	Initial selected requirements	Traditional review	Acquisition organization, contractor	Final requirements

Table 7.4 *Compressed Process if Security Requirements Engineering Process Is Unknown*

Step		Input	Techniques	Organizational Responsibility	Output
1	Agree on definitions	Candidate definitions from IEEE and other standards	Structured interviews, focus group	Acquisition organization, contractor	Agreed-to definitions
2	Identify assets and security goals	Definitions, candidate goals, business drivers, policies and procedures, examples	Facilitated work session, surveys, interviews	Acquisition organization, contractor	Assets and goals
3	*Contractor identifies security requirements*	*Assets and goals*	*Requirements engineering approach selected by contractor*	*Contractor*	*Initial selected requirements, documentation of decision making process and rationale*
4	Review of requirements by acquisition organization	Initial selected requirements	Traditional review	Acquisition organization, contractor	Final requirements

Table 7.5 *Process for Acquiring COTS Software*

Step	Input	Techniques	Participants	Output
1 Agree on definitions	Candidate definitions from IEEE and other standards	Structured interviews, focus group	Acquisition organization: stakeholders, security specialists	Agreed-to definitions
2 Identify assets and security goals	Definitions, candidate goals, business drivers, policies and procedures, examples	Facilitated work session, surveys, interviews	Acquisition organization: stakeholders, security specialists	Assets and goals
3 Identify preliminary security requirements	Assets and goals	Work session	Acquisition organization: security specialists	Preliminary security requirements
4 Review COTS software package information and specifications	Assets, goals, preliminary security requirements	Study security features of various packages and documents them, in a spreadsheet, for example	Acquisition organization: security specialists, COTS vendors	Spreadsheet of security features of various packages

(Continued)

Table 7.5 *Continued*

Step	Input	Techniques	Participants	Output
5 Finalize security requirements	Preliminary security requirements, features of various packages	Work session: use the spreadsheet to refine and modify the preliminary security requirements to arrive at a final set	Acquisition organization: security specialists	Final security requirements
6 Perform trade-off analysis	Final security requirements, spreadsheet of security features	Trade-off analysis of COTS products relative to final security requirements	Acquisition organization: stakeholders, security specialists	Prioritized list of COTS products relative to security requirements
7 Final product selection	Prioritized list of COTS products relative to security, other important COTS product features	Trade-off analysis	Acquisition organization: stakeholders	Final COTS product selection

requirements together with other requirements [Comella-Dorda 2004]. Compromises and trade-offs may need to be made, and the organization may have to figure out how to satisfy some security requirements outside the software itself—for example, with system-level requirements, security policy, or physical security. The requirements themselves are likely to be high-level requirements that map to security goals rather than detailed requirements used in software development.

Note that in acquiring COTS software, organizations often do minimal trade-off analysis and may not consider security requirements at all, even when they do such trade-off analysis. The acquiring organization should consider "must have" versus "nice to have" security requirements. In addition, reviewing the security features of specific offerings may help the acquiring organization identify the security requirements that are important.

7.4.3 Summary

The original SQUARE method has been documented extensively and has been used in a number of case studies and pilots. In addition, a number of associated robust tools exist. Academic course materials and workshops are also available for SQUARE. SQUARE for Acquisition is not quite as mature, as it was developed more recently. Here we have presented alternative versions of SQUARE for use in acquisition. It has been taught in university and government settings, and there is a prototype tool for A-SQUARE. Organizations that use SQUARE or A-SQUARE will succeed in addressing security requirements early and will avoid the pitfalls of operational security flaws that result from overlooked security requirements.

It is important to note that A-SQUARE is just one approach for identifying security requirements during acquisition. We suggest exploring other existing methods before making a decision on which one to use.

7.5 Operational Competencies (DevOps)[13]

7.5.1 What Is DevOps?

DevOps is a synergistic convergence of emerging concerns that stem from two separate communities: the software development community and the operations community (release engineers and system administrators). Prior to the birth of the DevOps

---

13. This section was contributed by Stephany Bellomo.

movement, both communities suffered from the inability to rapidly and reliably deploy software, and each felt the effects in different ways. From the software development perspective, Agile teams found progress on delivery of new features grinding to a halt as they entered the integration, certification, and deployment phases of the software lifecycle. From the operations perspective, the release engineers suffered from unstable production software and painful releases. Symptoms of dysfunction included a culture of finger pointing between development (Dev) and operations (Ops) teams, delays due to late discovery of security or resiliency issues, and error-prone/human-intensive release processes.

Problems such as these drove a handful of practitioners to talk openly about practices they apply on their own projects to address similar problems. This discussion ultimately led to the birth of the DevOps movement. In 2009, Flickr's John Allspaw and Paul Hammond gave a cornerstone talk at Velocity, titled "10+ Deploys Per Day"[14] that got the attention of the operations community. They described several practices for reducing deployment cycle time while maintaining a high degree of operational stability/resiliency. In 2009, Patrick Debois from Belgium and Andrew "Clay" Shafer from the United States coined the term *DevOps*. Debois held the first DevOpsDays event in Ghent in 2010. Today, DevOpsDays conferences are held in cities all over the world. The initial scope of the DevOps movement focused primarily on cloud-based information technology (IT) systems; however, the scope has since broadened. There is general agreement that the specific DevOps practices used on each project can and should be evaluated for suitability and tailored for each project context. We are seeing some DevOps practices applied to non-IT-based systems, including embedded and real-time safety-critical systems, such as avionics, automobiles, and weapons systems [Regan 2014].

DevOps is essentially a term for a group of concepts that catalyzed into a movement. At a high level, DevOps can be characterized by two major themes: (1) collaboration between development and operations staff and (2) a focus on improving operational work efficiency and effectiveness. We discuss these themes in the next sections.

Collaboration Between Development and Operations Staff

The focus of DevOps is to break down artificial walls between development and operations teams that have evolved due to organizational separation of these groups. We refer to this separation as "stovepiping." The idea is to change the culture from one in which development teams "throw the software over the fence" to the operations teams to a more collaborative, integrated culture. Examples of suggested DevOps practices to break down these barriers from both sides of the fence include earlier involvement of release engineers in the software design and assignment of

---

14. www.youtube.com/watch?v=LdOe18KhtT4

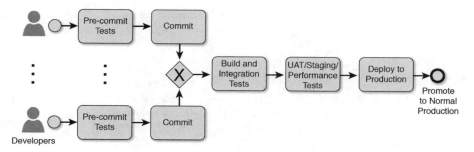

Figure 7.1 *Example of a Deployment Pipeline [Bass 2015]*

production support "pager duty" to the software developers after a new feature release to instill a sense of post-development ownership.

Focus on Improvement in Operational Work Efficiency and Effectiveness

The focus of the trend toward improved efficiency is based on Lean principles [Nord 2012] and is about improving efficiency and effectiveness of the end-to-end deployment lifecycle. Lean objectives adopted by the DevOps community include reducing waste, removing bottlenecks, and speeding up feedback cycle time. This effort requires team members to have the ability to reason about the various stages features go through during a DevOps deployment cycle. The popular book by Humble and Farley, *Continuous Delivery*, introduces the concept of deployment pipeline for this purpose (shown in Figure 7.1). The deployment pipeline provides a mental model for reasoning where bottlenecks and inefficiencies occur as features make their way from development through testing and, finally, to production.

For many projects, software releases were high-risk events; because of this, many software projects bundled various features together, delaying delivery of completed functionality to users. Continuous delivery suggests a paradigm shift in which features/development changes are individually deployed after the software has passed a series of automated tests/pre-deployment checks. We revisit the deployment pipeline in the next section.

7.5.2 DevOps Practices That Contribute to Improving Software Assurance

The previous section provides background on the emergence of the DevOps movement and a brief discussion of related trends and concepts. In this section, we turn our attention to emerging DevOps practices that contribute to improving software

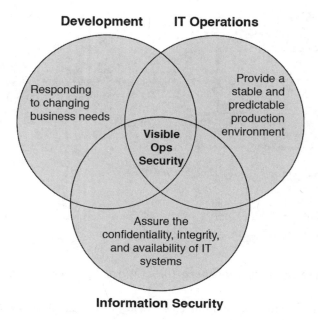

Figure 7.2 *Visible Ops Security Focuses on the Point Where IT Operations, Development, and Information Security Objectives Overlap [Kim 2008]*

assurance (which is defined in Chapter 1, "Cyber Security Engineering: Lifecycle Assurance of Systems and Software"). In this section, we focus primarily on software assurance as it relates to cyber security.

In the popular book *Visible Ops Security*, the authors describe competing objectives between development and operations groups that cause natural tension [Kim 2008]. Development teams are pressured to make changes faster to respond to business needs. On the other hand, operations teams are incentivized to reduce risk and minimize change because they are responsible for maintaining stable, secure, and reliable IT service. The idea behind *Visible Ops Security* is that integrating information security (InfoSec) staff on DevOps projects helps alleviate this conflict (see Figure 7.2).

The process of integrating InfoSec into the DevOps project context is described in four phases in *Visible Ops Security* [Kim 2008]. In the next sections, we use these four phases to structure the discussion of security-related DevOps practices. The term *DevOpsSec* refers to extending the concept of DevOps by integrating InfoSec.

Phase 1: Integration of InfoSec Experts

The long-term goal of integrating InfoSec professionals into DevOps projects is to gain visibility into potential software assurance risks. In Phase 1, InfoSec experts gain situational awareness by analyzing processes supporting daily operations such as change management, access control, and incident handling procedures. This analysis requires establishing an ongoing and trusting relationship between InfoSec professionals and the rest of the project team (developer and operations staff) and balancing the concerns shown in Figure 7.2. In addition, the team must establish an integration strategy. Integration strategies may involve co-locating InfoSec personnel with the project team for the life of the project or having a cross-functional, matrixed integration. Regardless of the integration strategy, InfoSec teams should resist the urge to create a new stand-alone DevOpsSec team, which can result in a new stovepipe within the organization.

Phase 2: Business-Driven Risk Analysis

Phase 2 focuses first on understanding what matters most to the business (thus the business-driven part of the phase title). Once the team understands business priorities and key business processes, it identifies IT controls required to protect critical resources. The team can apply several practices in this phase to address security concerns; examples include threat modeling and analysis and DevOpsSec requirements and design analysis. We discuss these practices in the next sections.

Threat Modeling and Analysis

Risk analysis approaches, such as those described in the Resilience Management Model analysis method [Caralli 2011b], may be applied in this phase to identify critical resources. Critical resources may be people, processes, facilities, or system artifacts, such as databases, software processes, configuration files, etc. After identifying critical resources, the team applies a structured analysis method to identify ways to protect those assets. In the spirit of Lean, threat modeling and analysis activities should give special consideration to protecting resources related to the business processes that provide the highest value to the organization. (Value depends on the business objectives and may take many forms, such as monetary assets, user satisfaction, mission goal achievement, etc.)

DevOpsSec Requirements and Design Analysis

Because architectural design decisions can have broad implications, InfoSec should factor into early reviews of emerging requirements and architectural design decisions. Context-specific design choices, in the form of architecture design tactics, can have a significant impact on resiliency and/or security posture. For example, a recent research study of architecture tactics used on real software projects to enable deployability revealed the use of several security-related design tactics, including fault detection, failover, replication, and module encapsulation/localization tactics [Bellomo 2014]. InfoSec professionals can leverage feasibility prototypes—in addition to document-driven analysis—to experiment with options for high-risk architectural changes and to analyze potential runtime threat exposure for new design concepts.

Phase 3: Integration and Automation of Information Security Standards/Controls

In Phase 3, the objective is to improve the quality of releases by integrating and automating information security standards compliance checks into projects and builds. In the spirit of improving efficiency, teams should use automation to replace manual and/or error-prone tasks as much as possible. There are several opportunities for automation at each stage throughout the deployment pipeline. The earlier a deficiency is detected in the deployment pipeline, the less costly (and painful) it is to address. For example, a secure coding error found at build or check-in time can usually be fixed by the developer quickly with little impact to others, whereas that same coding change made in a later stage could impact other components using that code. Automated tests may be executed against a variety of software and environmental artifacts such as code files, runtime software components, configuration files, etc. Many types of tests can be automated; for our purposes, we focus on automated tests that teams can leverage for security analysis and detection purposes. Test artifacts become available at different stages in the deployment pipeline; therefore, we have organized the discussion of the following information security automation tests according to the stages shown in Figure 7.1.

Pre-Commit Tests

For code-level security conformance checking, teams can run static analysis tests against code or other artifacts prior to checking in code. (Figure 7.1 refers to checking in code as "committing code.") Common static analysis approaches used in the DevOps context include code complexity analysis, secure coding standards conformance checking, IT/web secure coding best practices conformance checking, and code-level certification control/policy violations checking. The results of these tests can provide greater insight into the overall health of the system for risk analysis. In practice, some project teams also integrate static analysis tests into the continuous build and integration cycle.

Build and Integration Tests

In addition to static analysis, an increasingly common DevOps best practice involves integrating security compliance tests into the continuous integration build cycle. These automated compliance tests run every time the developer checks in code or initiates a new build of the software. If a violation is detected, the build fails and the offending developer is notified immediately. Ideally, work does not continue until the build is fixed to avoid pushing the problem downstream.

The following Twitter case study provides an example of a success story about an InfoSec team that successfully integrated a suite of security tests into the continuous build and integration lifecycle.

Case Study: Put Your Robots to Work: Security Automation at Twitter[15]

The birth of the Twitter InfoSec program was triggered by the hacking of the @barackobama account, which resulted in an FTC injunction requiring Twitter to be secure for the next 15 years. Hence, successful Twitter InfoSec was born.

Even though they were using automated tools when they started, team members were still doing a lot of manual work. For example, the static code analysis step was "automated," but InfoSec team members still had to do a lot of waiting—waiting for a scan to complete, get back the big stack of reports, interpret the reports, and then find the person responsible for fixing it. And when the code changed, they had to do it all over again!

Team members wanted to put their robots to work, so they built static code analysis into the Jenkins continuous integration process and, after that was done, they set out to build the Security Automation Dashboard (SADB—the logo is, of course, a sad bee). SADB takes input from several tools, such as Brakeman, Phantom Gang, CSP, ThreatDeck, and Roshambo, and produces outputs such as email alerts to developers. In typical Twitter development, Brakeman runs on each code commit (i.e., git push), and when vulnerabilities are found, SADB emails the developer about how to fix it. Better yet, when the fix is committed, SADB emails the developer again, congratulating him or her for fixing it!

By taking this approach, Twitter InfoSec enforces the practice of continuous feedback by testing the code early and often. The team members characterized their journey as follows:

- From manual to automated

- From low visibility to trending/reports

- From late discovery of issues to auto notification

- From constant emergency mode to operating more strategically

---

15. Summarized from the article "Here's How the Amazing Twitter InfoSec Team Helps DevOps," by Gene Kim. http://itrevolution.com/heres-how-the-amazing-twitter-infosec-team-helps-devops/.

User Acceptance Testing/Staging/Performance Tests

User acceptance tests and performance tests can provide a variety of InfoSec insights. During user acceptance testing (UAT), InfoSec team members can observe live usage patterns to see if they reveal any new security concerns. Because the staging environment (ideally) reflects the configuration of the production environment, the InfoSec team can analyze the runtime configuration for vulnerabilities that are hard to detect in design documents (staging is a pre-production testing environment). Results of nonfunctional tests (e.g., resiliency, performance, or scalability tests) may provide new insights into how well the system responds or performs under strenuous circumstances. In addition, the DevOps community advocates complete—or as complete as possible—test coverage to maintain confidence as the system evolves.

Deploy to Production

Several DevOps practices improve assurance posture while code is in the process of being deployed. However, before we discuss these practices, let's first visit some of the practices that should be applied before the deployment stage. For example, Infrastructure as Code (IaC) is a recommended practice. IaC refers to use of automated scripts and tooling for provisioning of infrastructure and environment setup. A benefit of the IaC approach to building infrastructure is that the InfoSec team can examine the automation scripts to ensure conformance to security controls rather than manually evaluating disparate individual environments for configuration violations. The practice of building infrastructure from scripts also helps enforce configuration parity across all environments (e.g., development, staging, production), which helps to minimize vulnerabilities introduced by manual configuration changes. Regular checks should done to ensure that open source software patches are up to date and known vulnerabilities are addressed prior to release.

Once the pre-deployment environment conformance checks are clean and all tests have passed, it is time to deploy code into production. We highly recommend using automated scripts for releasing code into production. These automated scripts, and associated configuration files, are also useful artifacts for InfoSec analysis. They can be used by InfoSec team members to validate that the software deployment configuration conforms to the approved design document.

Phase 4: Continuous Monitoring and Improvement

Visible Ops Security primarily focuses on the need for the operations community to embrace continuous process improvement and monitoring. In the following sections we discuss those needs as well as two other dimensions, deployment pipeline metrics and system health and resiliency metrics, which have received a lot of attention in the DevOps community in recent years.

DevOpsSec and Process Improvement

Continuous monitoring and improvement is a fairly well-accepted practice in the software community; however, according to some practitioners, a move in this direction poses some challenge for the operations community. During a roundtable interview for a 2015 *IEEE Software Magazine Release Engineering* special issues article, we interviewed release engineers from Google, Facebook, and Mozilla. They explained that the shift toward organizational process improvement requires a mindset change for release engineers to move from a triage/checklist mentality (rewarded by managers for years) toward institutionalized processes [Adams 2015]. From an InfoSec perspective, this shift is useful and necessary. It is very difficult, if not impossible, for InfoSec personnel to determine whether operational processes are secure when they are executed in an ad hoc manner.

Use of Deployment Pipeline Metrics to Minimize Security Bottlenecks

Another key concept behind DevOps is the idea of monitoring end-to-end deployment pipeline cycle time and individual stage feedback cycle time. The development, operations, and security stakeholders (shown on the left side of Figure 7.3) gain insight about the quality at each stage of the deployment pipeline by monitoring feedback results. Some examples of metrics for each stage are shown in Figure 7.3. At the Pre-commit Tests stage, DevOpsSec stakeholders get feedback from static analysis or code-level secure coding results; at the Commit stage, stakeholders get feedback on commit failures; at the Build and Integration stage and at the Testing stages, stakeholders get feedback on automated compliance tests; at the Deploy to Production stage, stakeholders get feedback on deployment cycle time (or deployment failures and rollbacks); and at the Production stage, stakeholders get feedback on performance, outages, audit logs, etc. If any of these feedback loops break down or become bottlenecks that slow down deployment, teams must perform analysis to address the issue. In this way, DevOpsSec teams have targeted metrics and insight to continuously improve deployment cycle time, focusing attention where the real problems are.

System Health and Resiliency Metrics

Because of the emphasis on improving workflow efficiency, a key DevOps practice area is monitoring and metrics. These capabilities benefit InfoSec professionals in two ways: (1) They provide additional data to improve "situational awareness" during early risk analysis and (2) once the software is in production, the metrics and logs produced through DevOps processes can be used for cyber-threat analysis. DevOps metrics are commonly used for purposes such as reducing end-to-end deployment cycle time and improving system performance/resiliency. The interest in metrics such as these has led to the emergence of tools and techniques to make operational

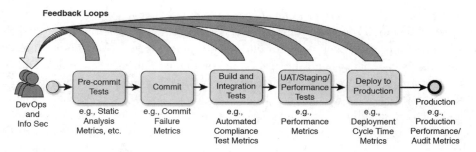

Figure 7.3 *Deployment Pipeline Feedback Loops and Metrics*

metrics more visible and useful. A popular mechanism for improving data visibility, bolstered by the DevOps vendor community, is the DevOps dashboard. DevOps dashboards are tools that usually come configured with a set of canned metrics and a way to implement custom metrics. Most dashboards can also be programmed to send alerts to administrators when a threshold is exceeded; some dashboards also suggest threshold boundaries based on normal historic system usage.

A key source of input for DevOps dashboards and alerts is log files (e.g., audit, error, and status logs). As with traditional system development, log data is typically routed to a common location, where it can be accessed for dashboard display and other analysis purposes. As with traditional projects, audit logs—particularly information about changing privileges or roles—continue to be useful artifacts for InfoSec analysis. These logs can also be used to support anomaly detection analysis, which involves monitoring for deviation from normal usage patterns. Operations staff use approaches such as anomaly detection analysis to monitor for issues ranging from software responsiveness to cyberattack. In fact, at DevOps DC in June 2015, there was much talk of work that focused on developing complex algorithms leveraging metrics generated from various DevOps tools to identify patterns of deviation and malicious behavior.

7.5.3 DevOpsSec Competencies

The previous section describes several DevOps practices that promote software assurance. This section describes several InfoSec competencies needed to support these DevOps practices. Traditional InfoSec competencies are still necessary to provide a strong foundation for supporting DevOps projects. However, due to the focus on automation and rapid feature delivery, some additional skills (or, in some cases, refreshing of skills) are required. In the sections that follow, we list examples of DevOpsSec-specific competencies; for consistency, we organize these skills around the four phases for integrating InfoSec into DevOps projects.

Phase 1: Integrating InfoSec Experts

People Skills

Successful DevOps InfoSec professionals must be capable of establishing and maintaining an ongoing trusting relationship between developers and operations groups. They must also be able to balance competing goals, as shown in Figure 7.2.

DevOpsSec Integration Strategy

It is not always easy to change the mindset of an organization that has lived with a stovepiped information security operating model for many years. Successful InfoSec professionals need to understand the organizational context, including opportunities and limitations, and must be able to formulate successful integration strategies. Depending on the situation, they may also need creativity and a positive attitude to devise and implement integration strategies that can work in their environment.

Security Analysis for Daily Operations

To obtain situational awareness with respect to daily operations, DevOps InfoSec professionals need skills to analyze processes and identify risks related to daily operational support. These skills and processes address topics such as security risks in current change management, access control, and incident handling procedures.

Phase 2: Business-Driven Risk and Security Process Analysis

Business-Aligned Threat Modeling

InfoSec professionals must have the skills to apply risk/threat-based analysis approaches (e.g., RMM) to identify and protect critical resources. This requirement is not new; however, there are several new challenges with respect to DevOps. Functionality may be delivered more frequently (e.g., multiple times per day), so InfoSec professionals must perform risk analysis faster and more efficiently than ever before. Constantly changing software means InfoSec professionals are working with a moving target. There is little tolerance for big, lengthy risk assessments, so risk analysis methods must be tailored to fit within this operating context. In addition, the deployment pipeline itself is a set of integrated tools that must be operationally resilient and protected from cyberattack. The virtualized environments on which many of the software systems developed by DevOps projects are deployed are increasingly software intensive (e.g., virtual machines, container technology). So, the scope of a risk assessment may need to extend beyond the software to be deployed. The deployment pipeline and the visualized infrastructure the software is running on may need to be included in risk assessments.

DevOpsSec Requirements and Design Analysis
InfoSec professionals need skills to rapidly and competently review architectural designs for potential vulnerabilities in a fast-paced environment. Ideally, InfoSec professionals integrated with DevOps teams have technical skills to provide guidance to developers as they consider design options. For example, design tactics should be considered to promote security and resiliency.

Phase 3: Integration and Automation of Information Security Standards/Controls

Security Tool Automation
As described in the Twitter case study, successful DevOps InfoSec professionals have strong technical capabilities that allow them to develop, or at least interpret, results from security automation tools. Opportunities exist at all stage of the development pipeline for InfoSec professionals to help develop and/or set up automation tools. As shown in Figure 7.3, examples of security-related automation tools include build and integration tests; UAT, staging, and performance tests; pre-deployment tests; and post-deployment anomaly detection and monitoring.

Enforcing Environment Conformance
With the advent of virtual machine technology, infrastructure has migrated from being primarily hardware intensive to being largely software intensive. This change has enabled the creation of the infrastructure environment through automation (generally using scripts). DevOps InfoSec professionals should have sufficient technical skills and depth to understand the risks related to using these technologies as well as the benefits. A benefit of the move toward IaC and script-driven provisioning is that environment configuration and policy conformance checking can be more easily automated. This benefit is possible because conformance-checking tools can run the verification tests against the automated scripts. Leveraging capabilities such as these speeds up the certification process and reduces the risk of vulnerabilities related to environment inconsistency/nonconformance.

Patches and Open Source
At this writing, the majority of DevOps projects are still IT projects and typically use a significant amount of COTS (e.g., virtual machine software, containers, middleware, databases, and libraries) as well as open source components. Consequently, InfoSec professionals should be capable of verifying that all necessary security patches are applied and that known vulnerabilities in third-party software are mitigated.

Phase 4: Continuous Monitoring and Improvement of Competencies

Process Institutionalization and Continuous Measurement/Monitoring
DevOps InfoSec professionals should have sufficient skills to evaluate process effectiveness and provide guidance and assistance when needed. They should also be capable of measuring process deviation and interpreting results.

Deployment Process Streamlining to Minimize Security Bottlenecks
InfoSec professionals must be able to analyze end-to-end deployment pipeline processes with an eye toward minimizing information security process-related bottlenecks. They must have the creativity to bring new options to the table for streamlining and improving efficiency of traditional information security tasks (e.g., automating manual tasks) as well as willingness to challenge the status quo. For this analysis, InfoSec professionals (shown on the left side of Figure 7.3) should understand what metrics are generated as a natural byproduct of the deployment lifecycle and be capable of proposing data-driven improvements.

DevOps Metrics for Security Analysis (e.g., Dashboards and Logs)
InfoSec professionals should be capable of using data from mining of dashboards and logs to gain a better sense of situational awareness with respect to the overall health and resiliency of the system. They should also understand what production metrics are available, or can be easily made available, for ongoing cyber-threat analysis. For example, audit logs are useful artifacts for monitoring privilege or role-escalation attacks.

7.6 Using Malware Analysis[16]

Hundreds of vulnerabilities are publicly disclosed each month [NIST 2016]. Exploitable vulnerabilities typically emerge from one of two types of core flaws: code flaws and design flaws. In the past, both types of flaws have facilitated several cyberattacks, a subset of which manifested globally.

We define a *code flaw* as a vulnerability in a code base that requires a highly technical, crafted exploit to compromise a system; examples are buffer overflows and command injections. *Design flaws* are weaknesses in a system that may not require a high level of technical skill to craft exploits to compromise the system. Examples include failure to validate certificates, non-authenticated access, automatic granting

---

16. This section was written by Nancy Mead with Jose Morales and Greg Alice.

of root privileges to non-root accounts, lack of encryption, and weak single-factor authentication. A *malware exploit* is an attack on a system that takes advantage of a particular vulnerability.

A *use case* [Jacobson 1992] describes a scenario conducted by a legitimate user of the system. Use cases have corresponding requirements, including security requirements. A *misuse case* [Alexander 2003] describes use by an attacker and highlights a security risk to be mitigated. A misuse case describes a sequence of actions that can be performed by any person or entity to harm the system. Exploitation scenarios are often documented more formally as misuse cases. In terms of documentation, misuse cases can be documented in diagrams alongside use cases and/or in a text format similar to that of a use case.

Several approaches for incorporating security into the software development lifecycle (SDLC) have been documented. Most of these enhancements have focused on defining enforceable security policies in the requirements gathering phase and defining secure coding practices in the design phase. Although these practices are helpful, cyberattacks based on core flaws have persisted.

Major corporations, such as Microsoft, Adobe, Oracle, and Google, have made their security lifecycle practices public [Lipner 2005; Oracle 2014; Adobe 2014; Google 2012]. Collaborative efforts, such as the Software Assurance Forum for Excellence in Code (SAFECode) [Bitz 2008], have also documented recommended practices. These practices have become de facto standards for incorporating security into the SDLC.

These security approaches are limited by their reliance on security policies, such as access control, read/write permissions, and memory protection, as well as on standard secure code writing practices, such as bounded memory allocations and buffer overflow avoidance. These processes are helpful in developing secure software products, but—given the number of successful exploits that occur—they fall short. For example, techniques such as design reviews, risk analysis, and threat modeling typically do not incorporate lessons learned from the vast landscape of known successful cyberattacks and their associated malware.

The extensive and well-documented history of known cyberattacks can be used to enhance current SDLC models. More specifically, a known malware sample can be analyzed to determine whether it exploits a vulnerability. The vulnerability can be studied to determine whether it results from a code flaw or a design flaw.

For design flaws, we can attempt to determine the overlooked requirements that resulted in the vulnerability. We make this determination by documenting the misuse case corresponding to the exploit scenario and creating the corresponding use case. Such use cases represent overlooked security requirements that should be applied to future development and thereby avoid similar design flaws leading to exploitable vulnerabilities. This process of applying malware analysis to ultimately create new use cases and their corresponding security requirements can help enhance the security of future systems.

7.6.1 Code and Design Flaw Vulnerabilities

Two types of flaws lead to exploitable vulnerabilities: code flaws and design flaws. A *code flaw* is a weakness in a code base that requires specifically crafted code-based exploits to compromise a system; examples are buffer overflows and command injections. More specifically, code flaws result from source code being written without the implementation of secure coding techniques.

Design flaws result from weaknesses that do not necessarily require code-based exploits to compromise the system. More specifically, a design flaw can result from overlooked security requirements. Examples are failure to validate certificates, non-authenticated access, root privileges granted to non-root accounts, lack of encryption, and weak single-factor authentication. Some design flaws can be exploited with minimal technical skill, leading to more probable system compromise. The process leading to a vulnerability exploit or remediation via software update is shown in Figure 7.4 [Mead 2014]. We focus on vulnerabilities resulting from a design flaw. In these cases, the overlooked requirements can be converted to a use case applicable to future SDLC cycles.

A large body of well-documented and studied cyberattacks is available to the public via multiple sources. In this section, we describe some publicly disclosed cases of exploited vulnerabilities that facilitated cyberattacks and arose from design flaws. For each case, we describe the vulnerability and the exploit used by malware. We also

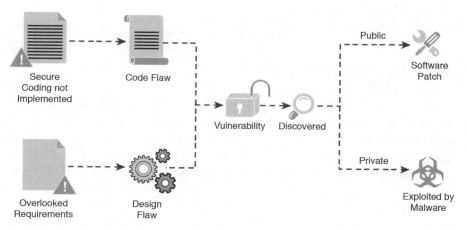

Figure 7.4 *Creation of a Vulnerability*

present the overlooked requirement(s) that led to the design flaw that created the vulnerability. By learning from these cases and analyzing associated malware, we can create use cases that can be included in SDLC models.

Case 1: D-Link Routers

In October 2013, a vulnerability was discovered that granted unauthenticated access to a backdoor of the administrative panel of several D-Link routers [Shywriter 2013; Craig 2013]. Each router runs as a web server, and a username and password are required for access. The router's firmware was reverse engineered, and the web server's authentication logic code revealed that a string comparison with "xmlset_roodkcableoj28840ybtide" granted access to the administration panel.

A user could be granted access by simply changing his or her web browser's user-agent string to "xmlset_roodkcableoj28840ybtide." Interestingly, the string in reverse partially reads "editby04882joelbackdoor." It was later determined that this string was used to automatically authenticate configuration utilities stored within the router.

The utilities needed to automatically reconfigure various settings and required a username and password (which could be changed by a user) to access the administration panel. The hardcoded string comparison was implemented to ensure that these utilities accessed and reconfigured the router via the web server whenever needed, without requiring a username and password.

The internally stored configuration utilities should not have been required to access the administration panels via the router's web server, which is typically used to grant access to external users. A non-web-server-based communication channel between internally stored proprietary configuration utilities and the router's firmware could have avoided the specific exploit described here, although further analysis could have led to a more general solution.

Case 2: Android Operating System

In 2014, Xing et al. [Xing 2014] discovered critical vulnerabilities in the Android operating system (OS) that allowed an unprivileged malicious application to acquire privileges and attributes without user awareness. The vulnerabilities were discovered in the Android Package Manager and were automatically exploited when the operating system was upgraded to a newer version.

A malicious application already installed in a lower version of Android OS would claim specific privileges and attributes that were available only in a higher version of the Android OS. When the OS was upgraded to the higher version, the claimed privileges and attributes were automatically granted to the application without user awareness.

The overlooked requirement in this case was to specify that during an upgrade of the Android OS, previously installed applications should not be granted privileges and attributes introduced in the higher OS without user authorization.

Case 3: Digital Certificates

In March 2013, analysts discovered that malware authors were creating legitimate companies for the sole purpose of acquiring verifiable digital certificates [Kitten 2013]. These certificates are used by malware to be authenticated and allowed to execute on a system since they each possess a valid digital signature.

When an executable file starts running on an operating system such as Windows, a check for a valid digital signature is performed. If the signature is invalid, the user receives a warning that advises him or her not to allow the program to execute on the system. By possessing a valid digital signature, malware can execute on a system without generating any warnings to the user.

The reliance on a digital signature to allow execution of binaries on a system is no longer sufficient to avoid malware infection. The overlooked requirement in this case was to, along with verifying the digital signature, carry out multiple security checks before granting execution privilege to a file, such as the following:

- Scanning the file for known malware
- Querying whether the file has ever been executed in the system before
- Checking whether the digital signature was seen previously in other legitimate files executed on this system

Examining the Cases

In each of the cyberattack cases described here, the vulnerabilities could have been avoided had they been identified during requirements elicitation. Using risk analysis and/or good software engineering techniques, teams can identify all circumstances of use and craft appropriate responses for each case. These cases can also be generalized and applied as needed.

The following abstracts can lead to requirements statements:

- **Case 1: Identify all possible communication channels**—Designate valid communication channels and do not permit other communication channels to gain privileges.
- **Case 2: Do not automatically transfer privileges during an upgrade**—Request validation from the user that the application or additional user should be granted privileges.

- **Case 3: Require multiple methods of validation on executable files**—In addition, as a default, consider asking for user confirmation prior to running an executable file.

In addition to the specific cases of exploited vulnerabilities discussed above, there have been several other cyberattacks on software systems that used one or more exploited vulnerabilities resulting from either a code flaw or a design flaw. These vulnerabilities are defined in a hierarchical structure using the Common Weakness Enumeration (CWE) [Kitten 2013; MITRE 2014].

The CWE provides a common language to discuss, identify, and handle causes of software security vulnerabilities. These vulnerabilities can be found in source code, system design, or system architecture. An individual CWE represents a single vulnerability type. A subset of CWEs can be attributed to design flaws resulting from overlooked requirements; some of the design flaw CWEs pertinent to the cases above are listed in Table 7.6.

The lessons learned from previous cyberattacks and the underlying CWEs can be used to better understand overlooked requirements and resulting security implications. Analyzed and publicly disclosed cyberattacks provide details about how attackers implemented an exploit on a specific vulnerability. CWEs provide a better understanding of security vulnerabilities underlying a cyberattack. Combining information from these two sources facilitates the creation and inclusion of use cases that capture the overlooked requirements that lead to design flaws.

7.6.2 Malware-Analysis–Driven Use Cases

Malware exploits vulnerabilities to compromise a system. Vulnerabilities are normally identified by analyzing a software system or a malware sample. When a vulnerability is identified in a software system, it is documented and remedied via a software update.

Vendors inform the public of vulnerabilities that are considered critical and that impact a large user base; the OpenSSL Heartbleed vulnerability is an example of

Table 7.6 *Sampling of Design Flaw CWEs [Mead 2014]*

CWE Identifier	Description
CWE-306	Missing Authentication for Critical Function
CWE-654	Reliance on Single Factor in Security Decision
CWE-295	Improper Certificate Validation
CWE-326	Inadequate Encryption Strength
CWE-357	Insufficient UI Warning of Dangerous Operations

such a vulnerability [Wikipedia 2014a]. A vulnerability is usually identified via malware analysis after the malware has entered the wild and compromised systems. Sometimes the discovered exploited vulnerability in the analyzed malware is a zero-day vulnerability.

Zero-day [Wikipedia 2014b] vulnerabilities are some of the biggest threats to cyber security today because they are discovered in private. They are typically kept private and exploited by malware for long periods of time. "Zero-days" afford malware authors time to craft exploits. Zero-days are not guaranteed to be detected by conventional security measures, making their threat even more serious.

One approach to avoid creating vulnerabilities is to implement secure lifecycle models. These models can be enhanced with the inclusion of use cases that are derived from previously discovered vulnerabilities that resulted from design flaws. Analyzing malware that exploits a vulnerability provides details of the vulnerability itself and, more importantly, provides details of the exploit implementation. The exploit details can offer additional insight into the vulnerability and the underlying design flaw.

The previous examples indicate that standard secure lifecycle practices may not be adequate to identify all avenues for potential attacks. Potential attacks must be addressed at requirements collection time (and at every subsequent phase of the lifecycle).

The selected case studies illustrate that malware analysis can reveal needed security requirements that may not be identified in the normal course of development, even when secure lifecycle practices are used. At present, malware discovery is often used to develop patches or address coding errors but not necessarily to inform future security requirements specification. We believe that failure to exercise this feedback loop is a serious flaw in security requirements engineering, which tends to start with a blank slate rather than use lessons learned from prior successful attacks. We recommend that secure lifecycle practices be modified to benefit from malware analysis.

Examining techniques that are focused on early security development lifecycle activities can reveal how malware analysis might be applied. We recommend a process for creating malware-analysis–driven use cases that incorporates malware analysis into a feedback loop for security requirements engineering on future projects and not just into patch development for current systems [Mead 2014]. Such a process can be implemented using the following steps (also illustrated in Figure 7.5 [Mead 2014]:

1. A malicious code sample is analyzed both statically and dynamically.

2. The analysis reveals that the malware is exploiting a vulnerability that results from either a code flaw or a design flaw.

3. In the case of a design flaw, the exploitation scenario corresponds to a misuse case that should be described. The misuse is analyzed to determine the overlooked use case.

4. The overlooked use case corresponds to an overlooked security requirement.

5. The use case and corresponding requirements statement is added to a requirements database.

6. The requirements database is used in future software development projects.

Steps 1 and 2 include standard approaches to analyzing a malicious code sample. The specific analysis techniques used in steps 1 and 2 are beyond the scope of this paper. In step 2, the analysis is used to determine whether the exploited vulnerability is the result of a code flaw or a design flaw. Typically, the source of the vulnerability can be determined through detailed analysis of the exploit code. Of course, these steps presume that the malware is detected, which in itself is a challenge.

Step 2 illustrates the advantage of malware analysis by leveraging the exploit code to determine the flaw type. Standard vulnerability discovery and analysis without malware analysis excludes exploit code and may make flaw type identification less straightforward.

Step 3 details how the exploit was carried out in the form of a misuse case, which provides the needed information to determine the overlooked use case that led to the design flaw.

In step 4, the overlooked use case is the basis for deciding what may have been the overlooked requirement(s) at the time the software system was created that led to the design flaw. These are the requirements that should have been included in the original SDLC of the software system, which would have prevented creation of the design flaw that led to the exploited vulnerability.

Steps 5 and 6 record the overlooked use case and corresponding requirement(s) for use in future SDLC cycles. This process is meant to enhance future SDLC cycles in a simplified manner by providing known overlooked requirements that led to exploited vulnerabilities. By including these requirements in future SDLC cycles, the

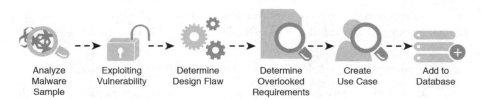

Analyze Malware Sample   Exploiting Vulnerability   Determine Design Flaw   Determine Overlooked Requirements   Create Use Case   Add to Database

Figure 7.5 *Malware-Analysis–Driven Use Case Creation*

resulting software systems can be made more secure by helping to avoid the creation of exploitable vulnerabilities.

7.6.3 Current Status and Future Research

We recommend incorporating the feedback loop described in this chapter into the secure software development process as a standard practice. We have described the process steps to support such a feedback loop. Researchers have studied Security Quality Requirements Engineering (SQUARE) [Mead 2005] and proposed modifications to incorporate malware analysis. In one pilot study, researchers found that requirements developed to mitigate a successful prior attack on an existing system in the same domain were given higher priority by the customer of the new system under development.

As mentioned earlier in this chapter, an extended case study explored the proposed process of analyzing a malware sample. Using a sample of malware that steals data from Android mobile devices, we determined the exploitation scenario that was used by the malware exploit. Our investigation into the consequences of this malware exploit revealed a design flaw in a mobile application that could compromise user data. We studied the design flaw to determine the applicable misuse cases and used those misuse cases to ascertain the missing security requirements to be used on future mobile applications for the Android platform [Alice 2014; Mead 2015].

A prototype tool has been developed to support the process of enhancing exploit reports to include misuse cases, use cases for mitigation, and overlooked security requirements. These enhanced reports are then stored in a database that can be used by requirements engineers on future systems. The source code for the MORE tool (Malware Analysis Leading to Overlooked Security Requirements) is available for free download from www.cert.org/cybersecurity-engineering/research/security-requirements-elicitation.cfm.

Exploit kits [McGraw 2015] are often used by malware in a plug-and-play fashion to infect a system. An exploit kit is a piece of software that contains working exploits for several vulnerabilities. It is designed to run primarily on a server (an exploit server) to which victim machines are redirected after a user clicks a malicious link, either in a webpage or an email. The victim machine is scanned for vulnerabilities. If a vulnerability is identified, the exploit kit automatically executes any applicable exploit to compromise the machine and infect it with malware. In general, malware either has exploits built into its binary or relies on exploit kits to initially compromise a machine. The implications of exploit kits is another area of exploration that may provide code samples for use in the process.

An open question for consideration: Do specific types of malware exist that are likely to occur in specific kinds of critical systems, such as control systems? Analysis of historical and current malware incidents may help to identify exploits that target specific types of applications. Knowing these exploit types in advance could help requirements engineers identify standard misuse cases and the needed countermeasures for their specific application types.

These misuse cases would again lead to corresponding use cases and security requirements. It may be wishful thinking to expect all developers of future systems to give priority to security requirements and apply the methods that we are postulating. However, developers of mission-critical systems, financial systems, and other essential systems, such as critical infrastructure systems, recognize the importance of security and should be willing to invest in it throughout the development process.

7.7 Summary

At this point this book has discussed a sequence of activities, starting with risk analysis, proceeding through management/organizational models, engineering/competency models, gap analysis, and ultimately metrics. Here in Chapter 7, we have additionally provided special topics that are worth consideration. This leaves us in a good position to consider how to develop an action plan to address cyber security in Chapter 8.

Chapter 8

Summary and Plan for Improvements in Cyber Security Engineering Performance

In This Chapter

- 8.1 Introduction
- 8.2 Getting Started on an Improvement Plan
- 8.3 Summary

8.1 Introduction

The following topics exhibit varying levels of maturity and use differing terminology, but they all play a role in building assured systems:

Effective cyber security engineering requires the integration of security into the software acquisition and development lifecycle. For engineering to address security effectively, requirements that establish the target goal for security must be in place. Risk management must include identification of possible threats and vulnerabilities within the system, along with ways to accept or address them. There will always be cyber security risk, but an engineer needs to be able to plan for the ways in which a system should avoid as well as recognize, resist, and recover from an attack.

Mechanisms that ensure correctness and compliance can be excellent tools if they are applied by teams and individuals with cyber security expertise and linked to appropriate and complete cyber security requirements.

Throughout this book, we have provided ways in which practitioners, managers, faculty, and students can address cyber security engineering throughout the lifecycle. In addition, we provide mechanisms for addressing each of the key principles introduced in Chapter 1, "Cyber Security Engineering: Lifecycle Assurance of Systems and Software": *risk, trusted dependencies, interactions, attacker, coordination and education, well planned and dynamic, and measurable.* Risk considerations should be part of each decision made throughout the lifecycle, and cyber security risk modeling can be addressed using methodologies such as the Security Risk Assurance Methodology (SERA) discussed in Chapter 2, "Risk Analysis—Identifying and Prioritizing Needs." Interactions among the technologies that support a mission must be monitored and managed for effective cyber security. Just because technology elements can be connected does not mean they should be, and effective cyber security engineering supports appropriate choices.

The various chapters provide support for the underlying principles. Developing an understanding of mission *risk* (see Chapter 2) and addressing cyber security engineering (see Chapters 2 and 7, "Special Topics in Cyber Security Engineering") provide mechanisms for addressing this area of concern. Means for defining, evaluating, and managing dependencies; linking integration choices with protection needs; and mechanisms for managing *interactions* are provided (see Chapter 3, "Secure Software Development Management and Organizational Models"). *Education* underlies all of our work and is specifically part of the basis for Chapters 3, 4, "Engineering Competencies," and 5, "Performing Gap Analysis." *Planning* is discussed throughout but forms an integral part of methods discussed in Chapters 3, 4, and 5. *Measurement* is the focus of Chapter 6, "Metrics." *Attacker considerations* are proposed throughout but most specifically when developing requirements that drive technology choices early in the lifecycle. The A-SQUARE methodology introduced in Chapter 7 is particularly valuable in supporting the development of good security requirements during acquisition.

It's not enough to write about cyber security engineering, however. We want to see good cyber security engineering models and methods put into practice. We recognize that each organization or project may be at a different point when it comes to improvement plans. Some organizations are already doing a lot in terms of implementing cyber security engineering strategy. Others may just be starting to think about it. Either way, the material presented in this book can help in developing a new cyber security engineering strategy or refining an existing one. As noted earlier, for purchasers of this book, we are providing free access to our online course: Software Assurance for Executives. This course provides an excellent overview of software assurance topics for busy managers and executives. To obtain access to Software Assurance for Executives, please send an email to:

stepfwd-support@cert.org

RE: SwA Executive Course

In addition, the resources on our accompanying website, and the reference material we have provided all will contribute to developing a strategy.

Website for Cyber Security Engineering http://www.cert.org/cybersecurity-engineering/

The order of the chapters provides the suggested order of implementation of a cyber security engineering strategy and program:

- **Risk analysis (Chapter 2)**—The first step toward lifecycle assurance, cyber security risk analysis can be performed using techniques such as the Mission Risk Diagnostic (MRD) and SERA.

- **Organizational competencies (Chapter 3)**—Next comes the identification and development of competencies that support management (this includes the organization's ability to address cyber security).

- **Engineering competencies (Chapter 4)**—Identification and development of competencies from an engineering perspective form the next step.

- **Methods (Chapter 5)**—Models can be used for benchmarking cyber security capabilities and performing gap analysis; the SEI's Software Assurance Competency Model and the Building Security In Maturity Model (BSIMM) are two examples.

- **Measurement (Chapter 6)**—Measurement involves the methods and mechanisms needed not only to evaluate cyber security but to properly balance it with other operational needs such as performance and reliability.

- **Special topics (Chapter 7)**—Topics such as governance and other organizational and engineering capabilities may be needed to provide a well-planned and dynamic approach to cyber security engineering.

8.2 Getting Started on an Improvement Plan

In Chapter 3, we discussed maturity levels that we developed for use in our earlier work [Allen 2008]. In this chapter, we show how these maturity levels can be used to categorize the approaches presented in this book:

- **L1**—The approach provides guidance for how to think about a topic for which there is no proven or widely accepted approach. The intent of the area is to raise awareness and aid the reader in thinking about the problem and candidate solutions. The area may also describe promising research results that may have been demonstrated in a constrained setting.

- **L2**—The approach describes practices that are in early pilot use and that demonstrate some successful results.

- **L3**—The approach describes practices that have been successfully deployed (i.e., they are mature) but are in limited use in industry or government organizations. They may be more broadly deployed in a particular market sector.

- **L4**—The approach describes practices that have been successfully deployed and are in widespread use. Readers can start using these practices today with confidence. Experience reports and case studies are typically available.

When an organization is developing an improvement plan, the maturity levels can help assess whether to play it safe with approaches at higher maturity levels or whether to take the risk of using less mature approaches. For a less mature approach, say at maturity level 1 or 2, we suggest initially trying the approach on a less critical pilot project rather than adopting it across the organization. Tables 8.1 through 8.6 show the approaches presented in each chapter and their maturity levels.

Table 8.1 *Risk Analysis (Chapter 2)*

Approach	Description	Maturity Level
Mission Risk Diagnostic (MRD)	Can be used to analyze how organizational risks, which can include lack of capability in risk management, impact the ability of a system to meet its objectives	3
Operational Risk Analysis	Compares planned to actual	4
Security Engineering Risk Analysis (SERA)	Provides a view for each system of the security risks it may be contributing that can negatively affect a mission	2

Table 8.2 *Management and Organizational Models (Chapter 3)*

Approach	Description	Maturity Level(s)
Building Security In Maturity Model (BSIMM)	Quantifies the activities carried out by real software security initiatives	4

CERT Resilience Management Model Resilient Technical Solution Engineering Process Area	Defines what is required to develop resilient software and systems	4 when derivative models such as Cybersecurity Capability Maturity Model (C2M2) and DHS Cyber Resilience Review (CRR) are included
CMMI for Acquisition (CMMI-ACQ)	Enables organizations to avoid or eliminate barriers in the acquisition process through practices and terminology that transcend the interests of individual departments or groups	3
CMMI Assurance Process Reference Model	Recommends additions to CMMI-DEV v1.2 to address software assurance	2
CMMI for Development (CMMI-DEV)	Consists of best practices that address development activities applied to products and services	4
CMMI for Services (CMMI-SVC)	Provides guidance on developing and improving mature service practices	4
DHS SwA Measurement Work by Bartol and Moss	Provides an approach for measuring the effectiveness of achieving software assurance goals and objectives at an organizational, program, or project level	1
International Process Research Consortium (IPRC) Roadmap	Consists of research nodes and research questions for security as a product quality	1
Microsoft Security Development Lifecycle (SDL)	Introduces security and privacy early and throughout all phases of the development process	4
Open Web Application Security Project (OWASP) Software Assurance Maturity Model (SAMM)	Provides an open framework to help organizations formulate and implement a strategy for software security that is tailored to the specific risks facing the organization	3

(*continued*)

Table 8.2 *Continued*

Approach	Description	Maturity Level(s)
SEI Framework for Building Assured Systems	Addresses the customer and researcher challenges of selecting security methods and research approaches for building assured systems	1
SEI Research in Relation to the Microsoft SDL	Examines the linkages between CERT research and the Microsoft SDL	2 and 3

Table 8.3 *Engineering Competencies (Chapter 4)*

Approach	Description	Maturity Level
DHS Competency Model	Provides insight into how competency models can differ from one another	2
SEI Software Assurance Competency Model	Provides a foundation for assessing and advancing the capability of software assurance professionals	2

Table 8.4 *Gap Analysis (Chapter 5)*

Approach	Description	Maturity Level
Building Security In Maturity Model	Benchmarks and quantifies the activities carried out by real software security initiatives	4
SEI Software Assurance Competency Model	Provides a foundation for assessing and advancing the capability of software assurance professionals	2

Table 8.5 *Metrics (Chapter 6)*

Approach	Description	Maturity Level
Implementing a metrics program	Collects data about discrete aspects of a product and/or process functioning to support operational and strategic decision making about the product	4
Metrics for cyber security engineering	Provides additional data to improve "situational awareness" during early risk analysis and can also be used for cyber-threat analysis	1

Table 8.6 *Special Topics in Cyber Security Engineering (Chapter 7)*

Approach	Description	Maturity Level
DevOps	Synergizes emerging concerns that stem from two separate communities: the software development community and the operations community	4
Governance	Sets clear expectations for business conduct and then following through to ensure that the organization fulfills those expectations	4
Malware Analysis to Identify Overlooked Security Requirements (MORE)	Identifies ways organizations can use malware analysis to identify security requirements that have led to vulnerabilities in earlier systems; allows overlooked requirements to be incorporated into the security requirements for future systems	1
SQUARE for Acquisition (A-SQUARE)	Provides a way for organizations that perform acquisition—rather than development—to achieve an emphasis on security requirements	2
Standards	Ensures that an organization can maintain control over how software and hardware are configured, which facilitates changes and emergency updates	Varies, depending on the standard

8.3 Summary

The choice is not whether to develop a cyber security engineering strategy but rather when and how to implement it. In our connected world, it is vital for organizations and projects to come up with their own tailored plans to address cyber security engineering. As professionals, each of us should have our own plan to improve our cyber security engineering competencies. This book, along with the associated website, executive overview course, and reference material, provide you with the tools to get started.

References

[Abran 2004]

Abran, Alain, Moore, James W., Bourque, Pierre, & Tripp, Leonard L., eds. *Guide to the Software Engineering Body of Knowledge*. IEEE Computer Society. 2004. www.computer.org/web/swebok/index.

[Adams 2015]

Adams, Bram, Bellomo, Stephany, Bird, Christian, Marshall-Keim, Tamara, Khomh, Foutse, & Moir, Kim. The Practice and Future of Release Engineering: A Round-table with Three Release Engineers. *IEEE Software: Special Issue on Release Engineering*. Volume 32. Number 2. March/April 2015. Pages 42–49.

[Adobe 2014]

Adobe Systems, Inc. *Proactive Security | Adobe Security*. 2014. www.adobe.com/security/proactive-efforts.html.

[Alberts 2002]

Alberts, Christopher, & Dorofee, Audrey. *Managing Information Security Risks: The OCTAVE Approach*. Addison-Wesley. 2002. http://resources.sei.cmu.edu/library/asset-view.cfm?assetID=30678.

[Alberts 2006]

Alberts, Christopher. *Common Elements of Risk*. CMU/SEI-2006-TN-014. Software Engineering Institute, Carnegie Mellon University. 2006. http://resources.sei.cmu.edu/library/asset-view.cfm?assetID=7899.

[Alberts 2010]

Alberts, Christopher J., Allen, Julia H., & Stoddard, Robert W. *Integrated Measurement and Analysis Framework for Software Security*. CMU/SEI-2010-TN-025. Software Engineering Institute, Carnegie Mellon University. 2010. http://resources.sei.cmu.edu/library/asset-view.cfm?AssetID=9369.

[Alberts 2012a]

Alberts, Christopher & Dorofee, Audrey. *Mission Risk Diagnostic (MRD) Method Description.* CMU/SEI-2012-TN-005. Software Engineering Institute, Carnegie Mellon University. 2012. http://resources.sei.cmu.edu/library/asset-view.cfm? AssetID=10075.

[Alberts 2012b]

Alberts, Christopher J. Allen, Julia H., & Stoddard, Robert W. *Deriving Software Security Measures from Information Security Standards of Practice.* Software Engineering Institute, Carnegie Mellon University. 2012. http://resources.sei.cmu. edu/library/asset-view.cfm?assetID=28784.

[Alberts 2014]

Alberts, Christopher, Woody, Carol, & Dorofee, Audrey. *Introduction to the Security Engineering Risk Analysis (SERA) Framework.* CMU/SEI-2014-TN-025. Software Engineering Institute, Carnegie Mellon University. 2014. http://resources. sei.cmu.edu/library/asset-view.cfm?AssetID=427321.

[Alexander 2003]

Alexander, Ian. Misuse Cases: Use Cases with Hostile Intent. *IEEE Software.* Volume 20. Number 1. January–February 2003. Pages 58–66.

[Alice 2014]

Alice, Gregory Paul, & Mead, Nancy R. *Using Malware Analysis to Tailor SQUARE for Mobile Platforms.* CMU/SEI-2014-TN-018. Software Engineering Institute, Carnegie Mellon University. 2014. http://resources.sei.cmu.edu/library/ asset-view.cfm?assetID=425994.

[Allen 2005]

Allen, Julia. *Governing for Enterprise Security.* CMU/SEI-2005-TN-023. Software Engineering Institute, Carnegie Mellon University. 2005. http://resources.sei.cmu. edu/library/asset-view.cfm?assetid=7453.

[Allen 2007]

Allen, Julia, & Westby, Jody R. *Governing for Enterprise Security (GES) Implementation Guide.* CMU/SEI-2007-TN-020. Software Engineering Institute, Carnegie Mellon University. 2007. http://resources.sei.cmu.edu/library/asset-view. cfm?assetid=8251.

[Allen 2008]

Allen, Julia H., Barnum, Sean, Ellison, Robert J., McGraw, Gary, & Mead, Nancy R. *Software Security Engineering: A Guide for Project Managers*. Addison-Wesley Professional. 2008.

[Allen 2011]

Allen, Julia H., & Curtis, Pamela D. *Measures for Managing Operational Resilience*. Software Engineering Institute, Carnegie Mellon University. CMU/SEI-2011-TR-019. http://resources.sei.cmu.edu/library/asset-view.cfm?AssetID=10017.

[ANSI 2008]

American National Standards Institute (ANSI) & Internet Security Alliance (ISA). *The Financial Impact of Cyber Risk: 50 Questions Every CFO Should Ask*. 2008. www.isalliance.org/publications/.

[Axelrod 2004]

Axelrod, C. Warren. *Outsourcing Information Security*. Artech House. 2004.

[Axelrod 2012]

Axelrod, C. Warren. *Engineering Safe and Secure Software Systems*. Artech House. 2012.

[Babylon 2009]

Babylon, Ltd. *Definition of Framework*. June 15, 2016 [accessed]. http://dictionary.babylon-software.com/framework/.

[Backus 1957]

Backus, J. W., Beeber, R. J., Best, S., Goldberg, R., Haibt, L. M., Herrick, H. L., Nelson, R. A., Sayre, D., Sheridan, P. B., Stern, H., Ziller, I., Hughes, R. A., & Nutt, R. *The FORTRAN Automatic Coding System*. 1957. http://archive.computerhistory.org/resources/text/Fortran/102663113.05.01.acc.pdf.

[Bartol 2008]

Bartol, Nadya. *Practical Measurement Framework for Software Assurance and Information Security, Version 1.0*. Practical Software & Systems Measurement (PSM). 2008. www.psmsc.com/Prod_TechPapers.asp.

[Bartol 2009]

Bartol, Nadya, Bates, Bryan, Goertzel, Karen M., & Winograd, Theodore. *Measuring Cyber Security and Information Assurance, State-of-the-Art Report (SOAR)*. Department of Defense—Information Assurance Technology and Assurance Center (IATAC). 2009. https://buildsecurityin.us-cert.gov/sites/default/files/MeasuringCybersecurityIA.PDF.

[Basili 1984]

Basili, Victor R., & Weiss, David M. A Methodology for Collecting Valid Software Engineering Data. *IEEE Transactions on Software Engineering*. Volume SE-10. Number 6. November 1984. Pages 728–738.

[Basili 1988]

Basili, Victor R., & Rombach, H. Dieter. The TAME Project: Towards Improvement-Oriented Software Environments. *IEEE Transactions on Software Engineering*. Volume 14. Number 6. June 1988. Pages 758–773.

[Bass 2015]

Bass, Len, Ingo Weber, & Liming Zhu. *DevOps: A Software Architect's Perspective*. Addison-Wesley Professional, 2015.

[Behrens 2012]

Behrens, Sandra, Alberts, Christopher J., & Ruefle, Robin. *Competency Lifecycle Roadmap: Toward Performance Readiness*. CMU/SEI-2012-TN-020. Software Engineering Institute, Carnegie Mellon University. 2012. http://resources.sei.cmu.edu/library/asset-view.cfm?assetid=28053.

[Bellomo 2014]

Bellomo, Stephany, Ernst, Neil, Nord, Robert, & Kazman, Rick. Toward Design Decisions to Enable Deployability—Empirical Study of Three Projects Reaching for the Continuous Delivery Holy Grail. Dependability and Security of System Operation (DSSO) Workshop. Atlanta, Georgia. June 2014. http://resources.sei.cmu.edu/asset_files/conferencepaper/2014_021_001_424904.pdf.

[Bitz 2008]

Bitz, Gunter, et al. Edited by Stacy Simpson. *Fundamental Practices for Secure Software Development—A Guide to the Most Effective Secure Development*

Practices in Use Today. SAFECode. 2008. www.safecode.org/publications/SAFE-Code_Dev_Practices1108.pdf.

[Bosworth 2002]

Bosworth, Seymour, & Kabay, Michel E. *Computer Security Handbook*, 4th ed. John Wiley and Sons. 2002.

[Business Roundtable 2013]

Business Roundtable. *More Intelligent, More Effective Cybersecurity Protection*. 2013. http://businessroundtable.org/resources/more-intelligent-more-effective-cybersecurity-protection.

[Caralli 2016]

Caralli, Richard A., Allen, Julia H., Curtis, Pamela D., White, David W., & Young, Lisa R. *CERT Resilience Management Model, Version 1.0: Resilient Technical Solution Engineering (RTSE)*. 2011. www.cert.org/resilience/products-services/cert-rmm/index.cfm.

[Caralli 2011]

Caralli, Richard A., Allen, Julia H., & White, David W. *CERT Resilience Management Model (CERT-RMM): A Maturity Model for Managing Operational Resilience*. Addison-Wesley Professional, 2010.

[CCRA 2012]

Common Criteria Recognition Arrangement (CCRA). *Common Criteria for Information Technology Security Evaluation—Part 1: Introduction and General Model, Version 3.1, Revision 4*. CCMB-2012-09-001. 2012. www.commoncriteriaportal.org/files/ccfiles/CCPART1V3.1R4_marked_changes.pdf.

[CERN 2010]

European Council for Nuclear Research (CERN). Computer Security: Mandatory Security Baselines. *CERN Computer Security Information*. 2010. https://security.web.cern.ch/security/rules/en/baselines.shtml.

[Charette 1990]

Charette, Robert N. *Application Strategies for Risk Analysis*. McGraw-Hill Book Company. 1990.

[Chew 2008]

Chew, Elizabeth, Swanson, Marianne, Stine, Kevin, Bartol, Nadya, Brown, Anthony, & Robinson, Will. *Performance Measurement Guide for Information Security*. National Institute of Standards and Technology. NIST SP 800-55 Rev 1. 2008. http://csrc.nist.gov/publications/nistpubs/800-55-Rev1/SP800-55-rev1.pdf.

[Chung 2006]

Chung, Lydia, Hung, Frank, Hough, Eric, Ojoko-Adams, Don, & Mead, Nancy. *Security Quality Requirements Engineering (SQUARE): Case Study Phase III*. CMU/SEI-2006-SR-003. Software Engineering Institute, Carnegie Mellon University. 2006. http://resources.sei.cmu.edu/library/asset-view.cfm?assetid=7799.

[CMMI Institute 2015]

CMMI Institute. *CMMI Institute*. July 2015 [accessed]. http://cmmiinstitute.com.

[CMMI Product Team 2010a]

CMMI Product Team. *CMMI for Acquisition, Version 1.3*. CMU/SEI-2010-TR-032. Software Engineering Institute, Carnegie Mellon University. 2010. http://resources.sei.cmu.edu/library/asset-view.cfm?AssetID=9657.

[CMMI Product Team 2010b]

CMMI Product Team. *CMMI for Development, Version 1.3*. CMU/SEI-2010-TR-033. Software Engineering Institute, Carnegie Mellon University. 2010. http://resources.sei.cmu.edu/library/asset-view.cfm?AssetID=9661.

[CMMI Product Team 2010c]

CMMI Product Team. *CMMI for Services, Version 1.3*. CMU/SEI-2010-TR-034. Software Engineering Institute, Carnegie Mellon University. 2010. http://resources.sei.cmu.edu/library/asset-view.cfm?AssetID=9665.

[CMMI Product Team 2013]

CMMI Product Team. *Security by Design with CMMI® for Development, Version 1.3*. (CMMI-DEV, V1.3) [SEI 2010 a]. Software Engineering Institute, Carnegie Mellon University. 2013. http://cmmiinstitute.com/resources/security-design-cmmi-development-version-13.

[CNSS 2015]

Committee on National Security Systems (CNSS). *Committee on National Security Systems (CNSS) Glossary*. CNSSI Number 4009. Revised April 2015. www.cnss.gov/CNSS/issuances/Instructions.cfm.

[Coles 2015]

Coles, Robert, Barsade, Sigal, & Mehta, Sheetal. *Embedding a "Culture of Security" Is the Best Defense*. Knowledge@Wharton. 2015. http://knowledge.wharton.upenn.edu/article/embedding-culture-security-best-defense/.

[Comella-Dorda 2004]

Comella-Dorda, Santiago, Dean, John, Lewis, Grace, Morris, Edwin J., Oberndorf, Patricia, & Harper, Erin. *A Process for COTS Software Product Evaluation*. CMU/SEI-2003-TR-017. Software Engineering Institute, Carnegie Mellon University. 2004. http://resources.sei.cmu.edu/library/asset-view.cfm?AssetID=6701.

[Common Criteria 2016]

Common Criteria. *Common Criteria for Information Technology Security Evaluation*. June 24, 2016 [accessed]. www.commoncriteriaportal.org.

[Craig 2013]

Craig. Reverse Engineering a D-Link Backdoor [blog post]. */DEV/TTYS0*. October 12, 2013. www.devttys0.com/2013/10/reverse-engineering-a-d-link-backdoor/.

[Curtis 2002]

Curtis, Bill, Hefley, William E., & Miller, Sally A. *The People Capability Maturity Model: Guidelines for Improving the Workforce*. Addison-Wesley Professional, 2001.

[Deloitte 2014]

Deloitte. *2014 Board Practices Report: Perspective from the Boardroom*. 2014. www2.deloitte.com/us/en/pages/regulatory/board-practices-report-perspectives-boardroom-governance.html.

[DHS 2008]

U.S. Department of Homeland Security (DHS). *Software Assurance (SwA) Processes and Practices Working Group—Process Reference Model for Assurance Mapping to CMMI-DEV V1.2.* 2008. https://buildsecurityin.us-cert.gov/swa/procwg.html.

[DHS 2010]

U.S. Department of Homeland Security (DHS). *Software Assurance (SwA) Measurement Working Group.* 2010. https://buildsecurityin.us-cert.gov/swa/measwg.html.

[DHS 2012]

U.S. Department of Homeland Security (DHS). *Software Assurance Professional Competency Model.* 2012. https://buildsecurityin.us-cert.gov/sites/default/files/Competency%20Model_Software%20Assurance%20Professional_%2010_05_2012%20final.pdf.

[DoD 2012]

U.S. Department of Defense (DoD). Department *of Defense Instruction Number 5200.44—Protection of Mission Critical Functions to Achieve Trusted Systems and Networks (TSN).* DoD Instruction Number 5200.44. 2012. www.dtic.mil/whs/directives/corres/pdf/520044p.pdf.

[DoE 2014a]

U.S. Department of Energy (DoE). *Electricity Subsector Cybersecurity Capability Maturity Model (ES-C2M2), Version 1.1.* 2014. http://energy.gov/oe/downloads/electricity-subsector-cybersecurity-capability-maturity-model-v-11-february-2014.

[DoE 2014b]

U.S. Department of Energy (DoE). *Oil and Natural Gas Subsector Cybersecurity Capability Maturity Model (ONG-C2M2), Version 1.1.* 2014. http://energy.gov/oe/downloads/oil-and-natural-gas-subsector-cybersecurity-capability-maturity-model-february-2014.

[DoLETA 2012]

U.S. Department of Labor—Employment and Training Administration (DoLETA). *Information Technology Competency Model.* 2012. www.careeronestop.org/CompetencyModel/competency-models/information-technology.aspx.

[Giorgini 2006]

Giorgini, Paolo, Mouratidis, Haralambos, & Zannone, Nicola. Modelling Security and Trust with Secure Tropos. *Integrating Security and Software Engineering: Advances and Future Visions.* IGI Global. 2006. Pages 160–189. www.igi-global.com/chapter/modelling-security-trust-secure-tropos/24055.

[Google 2012]

Google. *Google's Approach to IT Security: A Google White Paper.* 2012. https://cloud.google.com/files/Google-CommonSecurity-WhitePaper-v1.4.pdf.

[Hadfield 2011]

Hadfield, Steve, Schweitzer, Dino, Gibson, David, Fagin, Barry, Carlisle, Martin, Boleng, Jeff, & Bibighaus, Dave. *Defining, Integrating, and Assessing a Purposeful Progression of Cross-Curricular Initiatives into a Computer Science Program.* Frontiers in Education Conference. Rapid City, South Dakota. October 2011. http://archive.fie-conference.org/fie2011/papers/1545.pdf.

[Hadfield 2012]

Hadfield, Steve. *Integrating Software Assurance and Secure Programming Concepts and Mindsets into an Undergraduate Computer Science Program.* Department of Homeland Security Semi-Annual Software Assurance Forum. McLean, Virginia. March 2012. https://buildsecurityin.us-cert.gov/sites/default/files/Integrating%20Software%20Assurance%20and%20Secure%20Programming%20Concep.pdf.

[Hilburn 2013a]

Hilburn, Thomas B., Ardis, Mark A., Johnson, Glenn, Kornecki, Andrew J., & Mead, Nancy R. *Software Assurance Competency Model.* CMU/SEI-2013-TN-004. Software Engineering Institute, Carnegie Mellon University. 2013. http://resources.sei.cmu.edu/library/asset-view.cfm?assetid=47953.

[Hilburn 2013b]

Hilburn, Tom B., & Mead, Nancy R. Building Security In: A Road to Competency. *IEEE Security & Privacy*. Volume 11. Number 5. September/October 2013. Pages 89–92. http://ieeexplore.ieee.org/xpl/articleDetails.jsp?reload=true&arnumber=6630006.

[Howard 2006]

Howard, Michael, & Lipner, Steve. *The Security Development Lifecycle*. Microsoft Press. 2006.

[Humphrey 1989]

Humphrey, Watts S. *Managing the Software Process*. Addison-Wesley Professional. 1989.

[IEEE 2000]

Institute of Electrical and Electronics Engineers (IEEE). *The Authoritative Dictionary of IEEE Standards Terms*, 7th ed. http://ieeexplore.ieee.org/servlet/opac?punumber=4116785.

[IEEE-CS 2014]

Institute of Electrical and Electronics Engineers (IEEE) Computer Society. *Software Engineering Competency Model, Version 1.0 (SWECOM)*. 2014. www.computer.org/web/peb/swecom.

[IPRC 2006]

International Process Research Consortium (IPRC). *A Process Research Framework*. Software Engineering Institute, Carnegie Mellon University. 2006. http://resources.sei.cmu.edu/library/asset-view.cfm?assetid=30501.

[ISACA 2014]

Information Systems Audit and Control Association (ISACA). *Cybersecurity Fundamentals Glossary*. 2014. www.isaca.org/pages/glossary.aspx.

[ISO/IEC 2007]

International Organization for Standardization & International Electrotechnical Commission. *Systems and Software Engineering—Measurement Process*. ISO/IEC 15939. 2007.

[ISO/IEC 2008a]

International Organization for Standardization & International Electrotechnical Commission (ISO/IEC). *Information Technology—Security Techniques—Evaluation Criteria for IT Security—Part 2: Security Functional Components.* ISO/IEC 15408-2. 2008.

[ISO/IEC 2008b]

International Organization for Standardization & International Electrotechnical Commission (ISO/IEC). *Information Technology—Security Techniques—Evaluation Criteria for IT Security—Part 3: Security Assurance Components.* ISO/IEC 15408-3. 2008.

[ISO/IEC 2009]

International Organization for Standardization & International Electrotechnical Commission (ISO/IEC). *Information Technology—Security Techniques—Evaluation Criteria for IT Security—Part 1: Introduction and General Model.* ISO/IEC 15408-1. 2009.

[ISO/IEC 2011]

International Organization for Standardization & International Electrotechnical Commission (ISO/IEC). *Information Technology—Security Techniques—Application Security—Part 1: Overview and Concepts.* ISO/IEC 27034-1. 2011.

[ISO/IEC 2013]

International Organization for Standardization & International Electrotechnical Commission (ISO/IEC). *Information Technology—Security Techniques—Information Security Management Systems—Requirements.* ISO/IEC 27001. 2013.

[ISO/IEC 2015]

International Organization for Standardization & International Electrotechnical Commission (ISO/IEC). *Information Technology—Security Techniques—Application Security—Part 2: Organization Normative Framework.* ISO/IEC 27034-2. 2015.

[ISSA 2004]

Information Systems Security Association (ISSA). *Generally Accepted Information Security Principles, GAISP V3.0, Update Draft.* 2004. https://citadel-information.

com/wp-content/uploads/2010/12/issa-generally-accepted-information-security-practices-v3-2004.pdf.

[ITGI 2006]

IT Governance Institute (ITGI). *Information Security Governance: Guidance for Boards of Directors and Executive Management*, 2nd ed. 2006. www.isaca.org/ knowledge-center/research/documents/information-security-govenance-for-board-of-directors-and-executive-management_res_eng_0510.pdf.

[Jacobson 2008]

Jacobson, Ivar. *Object-Oriented Software Engineering: A Use Case Driven Approach*. Addison-Wesley Professional, 2008.

[Jaquith 2007]

Jaquith, Andrew. *Security Metrics: Replacing Fear, Uncertainty, and Doubt*. Addison-Wesley Professional, 2007.

[Kelly 1998]

Kelly, Tim P. *Arguing Safety—A Systematic Approach to Managing Safety Cases* [Doctoral Diss.]. University of York. 1998. www-users.cs.york.ac.uk/tpk/ tpkthesis.pdf.

[Kelly 2004]

Kelly, Tim, & Weaver, Rob. The Goal Structuring Notation: A Safety Argument Notation. *Proceedings of the Dependable Systems and Networks 2004 Workshop on Assurance Cases*. Florence, Italy. July 2004. www-users.cs.york.ac.uk/tpk/ dsn2004.pdf.

[Khajenoori 1998]

Khajenoori, S., Hilburn, T., Hirmanpour, I., Turner, R., & Qasem, A. *Software Engineering Competency Study: Final Report*. ERAU-FAA Project, Federal Aviation Administration. December 1998.

[Kim 2008]

Kim, Gene, Love, Paul, & Spafford, George. *Visible Ops Security*. IT Process Institute, Inc. 2008.

[Kissel 2013]

Kissel, Richard, ed. *Glossary of Key Information Security Terms, NISTIR 7298, Revision 2*. U.S. Department of Commerce. 2013. www.nist.gov/manuscript-publication-search.cfm?pub_id=913810.

[Kitten 2013]

Kitten, Tracy. Digital Certificates Hide Malware—Fraudsters' Fake Companies Fool Cert Authorities. *BankInfoSecurity.com*. March 11, 2013. www.bankinfosecurity.com/digital-certificates-hide-malware-a-5592/op-1.

[Leveson 2004]

Leveson, Nancy. A New Accident Model for Engineering Safer Systems. *Safety Science*. Volume 42. Number 4. April 2004. Pages 237–270. http://sunnyday.mit.edu/accidents/safetyscience-single.pdf.

[Lipner 2005]

Lipner, Steve, & Howard, Michael. *The Trustworthy Computing Security Development Lifecycle*. March 2005. http://msdn.microsoft.com/en-us/library/ms995349.aspx.

[Lipner 2015]

Lipner, Steven B. Privacy and Security—Security Assurance—How Can Customers Tell They Are Getting It? *Communications of the ACM*. Volume 58. Number 11. November 2015. Pages 24–26.

[McGraw 2015]

McGraw, Gary, Migues, Sammy, & West, Jacob. *Building Security In Maturity Model, Version 6 (BSIMM6)*. 2015. www.bsimm.com/download/.

[Mead 2005]

Mead, Nancy, Hough, Eric, & Stehney, Ted, II. *Security Quality Requirements Engineering*. Software Engineering Institute, Carnegie Mellon University. 2005. http://resources.sei.cmu.edu/library/asset-view.cfm?AssetID=7657.

[Mead 2010a]

Mead, Nancy R., Allen, Julia H., Ardis, Mark A., Hilburn, Thomas B., Kornecki, Andrew J., Linger, Richard C., & McDonald, James. *Software Assurance*

Curriculum Project Volume I: Master of Software Assurance Reference Curriculum. CMU/SEI-2010-TR-005. Software Engineering Institute, Carnegie Mellon University. 2010. http://resources.sei.cmu.edu/library/asset-view.cfm?assetid=9415.

[Mead 2010b]

Mead, Nancy, & Allen, Julia. *Building Assured Systems Framework.* CMU/SEI-2010-TR-025. Software Engineering Institute, Carnegie Mellon University. 2010. http://resources.sei.cmu.edu/library/asset-view.cfm?AssetID=9611.

[Mead 2010c]

Mead, Nancy R., Hilburn, Thomas B., & Linger, Richard C. *Software Assurance Curriculum Project, Volume II: Undergraduate Course Outlines.* CMU/SEI-2010-TR-019. Software Engineering Institute, Carnegie Mellon University. 2010. http://resources.sei.cmu.edu/library/asset-view.cfm?assetid=9543.

[Mead 2011a]

Mead, Nancy R., Allen, Julia H., Ardis, Mark A., Hilburn, Thomas B., Kornecki, Andrew J., & Linger, Richard C. *Software Assurance Curriculum Project Volume III: Master of Software Assurance Course Syllabi.* CMU/SEI-2011-TR-013. Software Engineering Institute, Carnegie Mellon University. 2011.

[Mead 2011b]

Mead, Nancy R., Hawthorne, Elizabeth K., & Ardis, Mark A. *Software Assurance Curriculum Project, Volume IV: Community College Education.* CMU/SEI-2011-TR-017. Software Engineering Institute, Carnegie Mellon University. 2011.

[Mead 2013a]

Mead, Nancy R., & Shoemaker, Dan. *The Software Assurance Competency Model: A Roadmap to Enhance Individual Professional Capability.* CERT. 2013. http://resources.sei.cmu.edu/library/asset-view.cfm?assetid=299147.

[Mead 2013b]

Mead, Nancy R., Shoemaker, Dan, & Woody, Carol. Principles and Measurement Models for Software Assurance. *International Journal of Secure Software Engineering.* Volume 4. Number 1. April 2013. www.igi-global.com/article/principles-measurement-models-software-assurance/76352.

[Mead 2014]

Mead, Nancy R., & Morales, Jose Andre. Using Malware Analysis to Improve Security Requirements on Future Systems. *Evolving Security & Privacy Requirements Engineering (ESPRE) Workshop, IEEE International Requirements Engineering Conference Proceedings*. August 2014. Pages 37–42. http://ieeexplore.ieee.org/xpl/articleDetails.jsp?reload=true&arnumber=6890526.

[Mead 2015]

Mead, Nancy R., Morales, Jose Andre, & Alice, Gregory Paul. A Method and Case Study for Using Malware Analysis to Improve Security Requirements. *International Journal of Secure Software Engineering*. Volume 6. Number 1. January–March 2015. Pages 1–23. www.igi-global.com/article/a-method-and-case-study-for-using-malware-analysis-to-improve-security-requirements/123452.

[Mellado 2007]

Mellado, Daniel, Fernández-Medina, Eduardo, & Piattini, Mario. A Common Criteria Based Security Requirements Engineering Process for the Development of Secure Information Systems. *Computer Standards & Interfaces*. Volume 29. Number 2. February 2007. Pages 244–253.

[Microsoft 2010a]

Microsoft. *Microsoft Security Development Lifecycle*. 2010. www.microsoft.com/security/sdl/about/process.aspx.

[Microsoft 2010b]

Microsoft. *Microsoft Security Development Lifecycle Version 5.0*. 2010. http://download.microsoft.com/download/F/2/0/F205C451-C59C-4DC7-8377-9535D0A208EC/Microsoft%20SDL_Version%205.0.docx.

[NIST 2008]

National Institute of Standards and Technology (NIST). *Performance Measurement Guide for Information Security*. 2008. http://nvlpubs.nist.gov/nistpubs/Legacy/SP/nistspecialpublication800-55r1.pdf.

[NIST 2014a]

National Institute of Standards and Technology (NIST). *Assessing Security and Privacy Controls in Federal Information Systems and Organizations: Building*

Effective Assessment Plans. Special Publication 800-53A. December 2014. http://nvlpubs.nist.gov/nistpubs/SpecialPublications/NIST.SP.800-53Ar4.pdf.

[MITRE 2014]

MITRE. *Common Weakness Enumeration: A Community-Developed Dictionary of Software Weakness Types.* 2014 [accessed]. http://cwe.mitre.org.

[MITRE 2016]

MITRE. *Making Security Measurable.* June 14, 2016 [accessed]. http://measurablesecurity.mitre.org.

[Moreno 2012]

Moreno, Ana M., Sanchez-Segura, Maria-Isabel, Medina-Dominguez, Fuensanta, & Carvajal, Laura. Balancing Software Engineering Education and Industrial Needs. *The Journal of Systems and Software.* Volume 85. Issue 7. July 2012. Pages 1607–1620.

[NASA 2004]

National Aeronautics and Space Administration (NASA). *Software Assurance Standard.* NASA-STD-8739.8. 2004. www.hq.nasa.gov/office/codeq/doctree/87398.htm.

[NASA 2016]

National Aeronautics and Space Administration (NASA). *Systems Engineering Competencies.* June 20, 2016 [accessed]. http://appel.nasa.gov/developmental-programs/seldp/program/se_competencies-html/.

[NDIA 1999]

National Defense Industrial Association Test and Evaluation Division (NDIA). *Test and Evaluation Public-Private Partnership Study.* 1999. www.ndia.org/resources/pages/publication_catalog.aspx.

[NIST 2013]

National Institute of Standards and Technology (NIST). *Recommended Security Controls for Federal Information Systems and Organizations.* Special Publication 800-53, Revision 4. 2013. http://csrc.nist.gov/publications/PubsSPs.html#800-53.

[NIST 2014]

National Institute of Standards and Technology (NIST). *Framework for Improving Critical Infrastructure Cybersecurity Version 1.0.* February 2014. www.nist.gov/cyberframework/index.cfm.

[NIST 2015]

National Institute of Standards and Technology (NIST). *Supply Chain Risk Management Practices for Federal Information Systems and Organizations.* Special Publication 800-161. 2015. http://csrc.nist.gov/publications/PubsSPs.html#800-161.

[NIST 2016]

NIST. *National Vulnerability Database.* June 24, 2016 [accessed]. https://nvd.nist.gov.

[Nord 2012]

Nord, Robert L., Ozkaya, Ipek, & Raghvinder, S. Sangwan. Making Architecture Visible to Improve Flow Management in Lean Software Development. *IEEE Software.* Volume 29. Number 5. September–October 2012. Pages 33–39.

[OMG 2013]

Object Management Group (OMG). *How to Deliver Resilient, Secure, Efficient, and Easily Changed IT Systems in Line with CISQ Recommendations.* 2013. www.omg.org/CISQ_compliant_IT_Systemsv.4-3.pdf.

[Oracle 2014]

Oracle. *Importance of Software Security Assurance.* 2014. www.oracle.com/us/support/assurance/development/secure-coding-standards/index.html.

[Oracle 2016]

Oracle. *Security Solutions.* June 6, 2016 [accessed]. www.oracle.com/us/technologies/security/overview/index.html.

[OWASP 2015]

OWASP. OWASP SAMM Project. *Open Web Application Security Project (OWASP).* 2015 [accessed]. www.owasp.org/index.php/OWASP_SAMM_Project.

[OWASP 2016]

Open Web Application Security Project (OWASP). *OWASP Secure Software Contract Annex*. March 2, 2016. www.owasp.org/index.php/OWASP_Secure_Software_Contract_Annex.

[Parker 2009]

Parker, Donn B. Making the Case for Replacing Risk-Based Security. *Enterprise Information Security and Privacy*. Artech House. 2009. Pages 91–101.

[PCI Security Standards Council 2013]

Payment Card Industry (PCI) Security Standards Council. *Payment Card Industry (PCI) Payment Application Data Security Standard, Requirements and Security Assessment Procedures, Version 3.0*. 2013. www.pcisecuritystandards.org/document_library.

[PCI Security Standards Council 2015]

Payment Card Industry (PCI) Security Standards Council. *Payment Card Industry (PCI) Data Security Standard, Version 3.1*. 2015. www.pcisecuritystandards.org/document_library.

[Regan 2014]

Regan, Colleen, Lapham, Mary Ann, Wrubel, Eileen, Beck, Stephen, & Bandor, Michael. *Agile Methods in Air Force Sustainment: Status and Outlook*. CMU/SEI-2014-TN-009. Software Engineering Institute, Carnegie Mellon University. 2014. http://resources.sei.cmu.edu/library/asset-view.cfm?assetid=312754.

[Royce 1970]

Royce, Winston. Managing the Development of Large Software Systems. Pages 1–9. In *Proceedings, IEEE WESCON*. Los Angeles, California. August 1970. Not publicly available. Reprinted in *ICSE '87 Proceedings of the 9th International Conference on Software Engineering*. IEEE Computer Society Press. March 1987, pp 328–338.

[SAE 2004]

SAE International. *Software Reliability Program Standard*. JA1002_200401. 2004. http://standards.sae.org/ja1002_200401/.

[SAFECode 2010]

SAFECode. *Software Assurance Forum for Excellence in Code (SAFECode)*. June 15, 2016 [accessed]. www.safecode.org.

[Saltzer 1974]

Saltzer, Jerome H., & Schroeder, Michael D. The Protection of Information in Computer Systems. *Communications of the ACM*. Volume 17. Issue 7. 1974.

[SANS 2015]

SANS. Information Security Policy Templates. *SANS Information Security Training*. November 8, 2015 [accessed]. www.sans.org/security-resources/policies.

[Shoemaker 2013]

Shoemaker, Dan, & Mead, Nancy R. *Software Assurance Measurement—State of the Practice*. CMU/SEI-2013-TN-019. Software Engineering Institute, Carnegie Mellon University. 2013. http://resources.sei.cmu.edu/library/asset-view.cfm?AssetID=72885.

[Shunn 2013]

Shunn, Arjuna, Woody, Carol, Seacord, Robert, & Householder, Allen. *Strengths in Security Solutions*. Software Engineering Institute, Carnegie Mellon University. 2013. http://resources.sei.cmu.edu/library/asset-view.cfm?assetid=77878.

[Shywriter 2013]

ShyWriter. SECURITY ALERT: Back Door Found in D-Link Routers. *Malwarebytes Forums*. October 14, 2013. https://forums.malwarebytes.org/index.php?showtopic=134875.

[Stevens Institute of Technology 2009]

Stevens Institute of Technology. *Graduate Software Engineering 2009 (GSwE2009)—Curriculum Guidelines for Graduate Degree Programs in Software Engineering*. 2009. www.acm.org/binaries/content/assets/education/gsew2009.pdf.

[Swanson 1996]

Swanson, Marianne, & Guttman, Barbara. *NIST Special Publication 800-14, Generally Accepted Principles and Practices for Securing Information Technology*

Systems. National Institute of Standards and Technology. 1996. http://csrc.nist.gov/publications/nistpubs/800-14/800-14.pdf.

[TechTarget 2015]

TechTarget. What Is Best Practice? *TechTarget SearchSoftwareQuality*. November 8, 2015 [accessed]. http://searchsoftwarequality.techtarget.com/definition/best-practice.

[Tippett 2002]

Tippett, Peter. Viewpoint Discussion—Calculating Your Security Risk. *The Washington Post*. December 4, 2002. www.washingtonpost.com/wp-srv/liveonline/advertisers/viewpoint_tru120402.htm.

[TSI 2014]

Trustworthy Software Initiative & British Standards Institution. *Software Trustworthiness—Governance and Management—Specification*. PAS 754. British Standards Institution. 2009.

[Veracode 2012]

Veracode. Study of Software Related Cybersecurity Risks in Public Companies, Feature Supplement of Veracode's State of Software Security Report. 2012. https://info.veracode.com/state-of-software-security-volume-4-supplement.html.

[Warner 2014]

Warner, Judy, & Epstein, Adam J. Playing for Keeps: Keeping Your Cyber Issues in Check. *NACD Magazine*. September 25, 2014. www.nacdonline.org/Magazine/Article.cfm?ItemNumber=11730.

[Westby 2012]

Westby, Jody R. *Governance of Enterprise Security Survey: CyLab 2012 Report—How Boards & Senior Executives Are Managing Cyber Risks*. Carnegie Mellon University. 2012. www.cylab.cmu.edu/education/governance.html.

[White House 2013]

White House. *Improving Critical Infrastructure Cybersecurity*. Executive Order 13636. February 12, 2013. www.whitehouse.gov/the-press-office/2013/02/12/executive-order-improving-critical-infrastructure-cybersecurity.

[Wikipedia 2011a]

Wikipedia. *Morris Worm*. June 2011 [accessed]. http://en.wikipedia.org/wiki/Morris_worm.

[Wikipedia 2011b]

Wikipedia. *IBM System/370*. June 2011 [accessed]. http://en.wikipedia.org/wiki/System/370.

[Wikipedia 2014a]

Wikipedia. *Heartbleed*. April 2014 [accessed]. http://en.wikipedia.org/wiki/Heartbleed.

[Wikipedia 2014b]

Wikipedia. *Zero-Day Attack*. April 2014 [accessed]. http://en.wikipedia.org/wiki/Zero-day_attack.

[Wood 1999]

Wood, Charles Cresson. *Information Security Policies Made Easy: Version 7*. Baseline Software. 1999.

[Woody 2014]

Woody, Carol, Ellison, Robert J., & Nichols, William. *Predicting Software Assurance Using Quality and Reliability Measures*. CMU/SEI-2014-TN-026. Software Engineering Institute, Carnegie Mellon University. 2014. http://resources.sei.cmu.edu/library/asset-view.cfm?AssetID=428589.

[Xing 2014]

Xing, Luyi, Pan, Xiaorui, Wang, Rui, Yuan, Kan, & Wang, XiaoFeng. *Upgrading Your Android, Elevating My Malware: Privilege Escalation Through Mobile OS Updating*. Presented at 2014 IEEE Symposium on Security and Privacy. May 2014. www.informatics.indiana.edu/xw7/papers/privilegescalationthroughandroidupdating.pdf.

Bibliography

Alberts, Christopher J., Dorofee, Audrey J., Higuera, Ron, Murphy, Richard L., Walker, Julie A., & Williams, Ray C. *Continuous Risk Management Guidebook.* Software Engineering Institute, Carnegie Mellon University. 1996. Pages 7–9. http://resources.sei.cmu.edu/library/asset-view.cfm?assetid=30856.

Body of Knowledge and Curriculum to Advance Systems Engineering (BKCASE). *BKCASE.* June 29, 2016 [accessed]. www.bkcase.org.

Chrissis, Mary Beth, Konrad, Mike, & Moss, Michele. Ensuring Your Development Processes Meet Today's Cyber Challenges. *CrossTalk.* Volume 26. Number 2. March/April 2013. Pages 29–33. www.crosstalkonline.org/issues/marchapril-2013.html.

Committee on National Security Systems (CNSS). *National Information Assurance (IA) Glossary.* CNSSI Number 4009. 2009. www.ncsc.gov/nittf/docs/CNSSI-4009_National_Information_Assurance.pdf.

Elahi, Golnaz, Yu, Eric, & Zannone, Nicola. A Vulnerability-Centric Requirements Engineering Framework: Analyzing Security Attacks, Countermeasures, and Requirements Based on Vulnerabilities. *Requirements Engineering Journal.* Volume 15. Number 1. March 2010. Pages 41–62. http://dl.acm.org/citation.cfm?id=1731695.

Ellison, Robert J., Goodenough, John B., Weinstock, Charles B., & Woody, Carol. *Evaluating and Mitigating Software Supply Chain Security Risks.* CMU/SEI-2010-TN-016. Software Engineering Institute, Carnegie Mellon University. 2010. http://resources.sei.cmu.edu/library/asset-view.cfm?assetid=9337.

Haley, Charles, Laney, Robin, Moffett, Jonathan, & Nuseibeh, Bashar. Security Requirements Engineering: A Framework for Representation and Analysis. *IEEE Transactions on Software Engineering.* Volume 34. Number 1. January–February 2008. Pages 133–153. http://ieeexplore.ieee.org/xpl/articleDetails.jsp?arnumber=4359475.

Humphrey, Watts S. *A Discipline for Software Engineering.* Addison-Wesley Professional, 1995.

Jacobson, Ivar, & Lawson, Harold Bud, eds. *Software Engineering in the Systems Context—Addressing Frontiers, Practice and Education.* College Publications, Kings College, London. 2016. www.collegepublications.co.uk/systems/?00007.

Krigsman, Michael. Six Types of IT Project Failure. *TechRepublic*. September 29, 2009. www.techrepublic.com/blog/tech-decision-maker/six-types-of-it-project-failure/.

Levinson, Meredith. Project Management: The 14 Most Common Mistakes IT Departments Make. *CIO*. July 23, 2008. www.cio.com/article/2434788/project-management/project-management--the-14-most-common-mistakes-it-departments-make.html.

Mead, Nancy R., & Hilburn, Thomas B. Building Security In: Preparing for a Software Security Career. *IEEE Security & Privacy*. Volume 11. Number 6. November–December 2013. Pages 80–83. http://ieeexplore.ieee.org/xpl/article Details.jsp?tp=&arnumber=6682937.

Merrell, Samuel A., Moore, Andrew P., & Stevens, James F. Goal-Based Assessment for the Cybersecurity of Critical Infrastructure. *2010 IEEE International Conference on Technologies for Homeland Security (HST)*. 2010. Pages 84–88. http://ieeexplore.ieee.org/stamp/stamp.jsp?tp=&arnumber=5655090.

MITRE. *Common Attack Pattern Enumeration and Classification*. June 29, 2016 [accessed]. http://capec.mitre.org.

Open Web Application Security Project (OWASP). *Software Assurance Maturity Model: A Guide to Building Security into Software Development*. June 29, 2016 [accessed]. www.opensamm.org.

Romero-Mariona, Jose. Secure and Usable Requirements Engineering. *24th IEEE/ACM International Conference on Automated Software Engineering, 2009*. Pages 703–706. http://ieeexplore.ieee.org/xpl/articleDetails.jsp?arnumber=5431703.

Sharp, Alec, & McDermott, Patrick. *Workflow Modeling: Tools for Process Improvement and Application Development*, 2nd ed. Artech House. 2008.

U.S. Department of Defense. *Information Assurance Workforce Improvement Program*. DoD 8570.01-M. 2005. http://dtic.mil/whs/directives/corres/pdf/857001m.pdf.

Appendix A

WEA Case Study: Evaluating Security Risks Using Mission Threads[1]

by Carol Woody, PhD, and Christopher Alberts

Importance of Systems of Systems

Everything we do these days involves system and software technology: Cars, planes, banks, restaurants, stores, telephones, appliances, and entertainment rely extensively on technology. Much of this capability is supported by systems of systems—independent heterogeneous systems that work together to address desired functionality through complex network, data, and software interactions. The Wireless Emergency Alerts (WEA) service is a good example of a system of systems.

WEA enables local, tribal, state, territorial, and federal public safety officials to send geographically targeted text alerts to the public. The U.S. Department of Homeland Security Science and Technology (DHS S&T) Directorate partners with the Federal Emergency Management Agency (FEMA), the Federal Communication Commission (FCC), and commercial mobile service providers (CMSPs) to enhance public safety through the deployment of WEA, which permits emergency management organizations nationwide to submit alerts for public distribution by mobile carriers [FEMA 2015]. Alert originators can send three types of messages:

- Presidential alerts, issued by the president of the United States to reach any region of the nation or the nation as a whole

- Imminent threat alerts

- AMBER (America's Missing: Broadcast Emergency Response) alerts

---

1. Originally published in *CrossTalk* September/October 2014.

CMSPs relay these alerts from FEMA's Integrated Public Alert and Warning System (IPAWS) to mobile phones using cell broadcast technology, which does not get backlogged during times of emergency, unlike wireless voice and data services. Customers who own WEA-capable mobile phones automatically receive these alerts during an emergency if they are located in the affected geographic area.

Alert originators already have extensive alert dissemination capability through the Emergency Alert System, highway signage systems, Internet websites, and telephone dialing systems, just to mention a few widely used alerting channels. The WEA system, shown in Figure A.1, expands these options to mobile devices. FEMA established the message structure along with the approvals needed to have the Alert Aggregator system disseminate messages to mobile devices. Many alert originators plan to integrate this capability with systems already in place for other dissemination channels.

The *Systems Engineering Handbook* describes the following challenges for the development (and sustainment) of systems of systems [Haskins 2010]:

- Each participating system operates independently.

- Each participating system has its own update, enhancement, and replacement cycle.

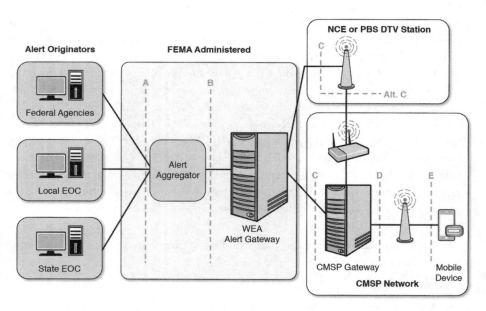

Figure A.1 *WEA System of Systems*

- Overall performance of the desired functionality depends on how the various participating systems can interact, which is not always known in advance.

- Missing or conflicting standards can make the design of data exchanges among the participating systems complex and difficult to sustain.

- Each participating system has its own management, and the coordination of requirements, budget constraints, schedules, interfaces, and upgrades can have a major impact on the expected capability of the system of systems.

- Fuzzy boundaries can cause confusion and error; no one really owns the interface, but one of the participants needs to take leadership to ensure some level of shared understanding.

- The system of systems is never finished because as each system grows, expands, and ages, there is a constant need for adjustment.

Public safety officials and alert recipients want to be able to rely on WEA capabilities and need to have confidence that the alerts are accurate and timely. Effective security is required to support this confidence. The risk that an attacker could create false alerts or cause valid alerts to be delayed, destroyed, or modified is a critical issue. Such actions could place the alert-originating organization's mission—and the lives and property of the citizens it serves—at risk.

DHS S&T asked a team of security experts at the Carnegie Mellon University's Software Engineering Institute (SEI) to research this problem and identify a means for evaluating WEA alert originator security concerns. The team selected mission thread analysis as a means for developing a view of the system of systems that could be used for evaluating security risks.

An analysis approach was needed to prepare alert originators to address the following critical security questions [Allen 2008]:

- What do alert originators need to protect? Why does it need to be protected? What happens if it is not protected?

- What potential adverse consequences do alert originators need to prevent? At what cost? How much disruption can they stand before they take action?

- How do alert originators determine and effectively manage the residual risk?

In addition, alert originators needed to consider the local, state, and federal compliance standards that the organization must address to ensure that the planned choices for security also meet other mandated standards.

Preparing for Mission Thread Analysis

Drawing on SEI security expertise, initial questions were assembled to assist the alert originator in gathering information about the current environment and preparing for WEA (or any new technology capability).

The alert-originating organization should compose answers to the following questions:

- What WEA capability do we plan to implement (types of alerts to issue, geographic regions to cover)?

- Can we expand existing capabilities to add WEA, or do we need new capabilities?

- Are good security practices in place for the current operational environment? Is there any history of security problems that can inform our planning?

- Will we use current resources (technology and people), or do we need to add resources?

Responses to these questions begin to frame the target operational context and the critical functionality that organizations must evaluate for operational security. Each organization has a different mix of acquired technology and services, in-house development components, and existing operational capability into which the WEA capability will be woven. With the use of mission threads, responses to these questions can be described in a visually compelling form that management, system architects, system and software engineers, and stakeholders can share and refine.

A mission thread is an end-to-end set of steps that illustrate the technology and people resources needed to deliver expected behavior under a set of conditions and provide a basis for identifying and analyzing potential problems that could represent risks. For each mission step, the expected actions, outcomes, and assets are assembled. Confirmation that the components appropriately respond to expected operational use increases confidence that the system will function as intended, even in the event of an attack [Ellison 2008].

Mission threads provide a means to identify and evaluate the ways, intentional or unintentional, that component system failures could occur and how such failures would impact the mission. Next, a WEA example is provided to demonstrate how the SEI used a mission thread to analyze security.

WEA Mission Thread Example

Mission thread analysis begins with the development of an operational mission thread. For WEA, typically 25 steps take place from the determination of the need for an alert to the receipt of that alert by cell phone owners:

1. First responder contacts local alerting authority via an approved device (cell phone, email, radio, etc.) to state that an event meets criteria for using WEA to issue, cancel, or update an alert and provides information for message.

2. Local alerting authority (person) determines that the call or email from the first responder is legitimate.

3. Local alerting authority instructs Alert Origination System (AOS) operator to issue, cancel, or update an alert using information provided by first responder.[2]

4. AOS operator logs on to the AOS.

5. AOS logon process activates auditing of the operator's session.

6. AOS operator enters alert, cancel, or update message.

7. AOS converts message to a format compliant with the Common Alerting Protocol (CAP, a WEA input standard).

8. CAP-compliant message is signed by a second person for local confirmation.

9. AOS transmits message to the IPAWS Open Platform for Emergency Networks (OPEN) Gateway.

10. IPAWS-OPEN Gateway verifies[3] message and returns status message to AOS.

11. AOS operator reads status message and responds as needed.

12. If the message was verified, IPAWS-OPEN Gateway sends message to WEA Alert Aggregator.

---

2. In some cases, the alerting authority and the AOS operator may be the same person.

3. In this list of steps, message verification includes authentication and ensuring that the message is correctly formatted.

13. WEA Alert Aggregator verifies message and returns status to IPAWS-OPEN Gateway.

14. IPAWS-OPEN Gateway processes status and responds as needed.

15. WEA Alert Aggregator performs additional message processing as needed.

16. If the message was verified, WEA Alert Aggregator transmits alert to Federal Alert Gateway.

17. Federal Alert Gateway verifies message and returns status to WEA Alert Aggregator.

18. WEA Alert Aggregator processes status and responds as needed.

19. If the message was verified, Federal Alert Gateway converts message to CMAC (Commercial Mobile Alert for Interface C) format.

20. Federal Alert Gateway transmits message to CMSP gateway.

21. CMSP Gateway returns status to Federal Alert Gateway.

22. Federal Alert Gateway processes status and responds as needed.

23. CMSP Gateway sends message to CMSP Infrastructure.

24. CMSP Infrastructure sends message via broadcast to mobile devices in the designated area(s).

25. Mobile device users (recipients) receive the message.

Although many of these steps do not involve technology, they can still represent security risks to the mission. Mission thread analysis, unlike other techniques such as Failure Mode and Effect Analysis [Stamatis 2003], allows consideration of the people and their interactions with technology in addition to the functioning of a system itself. Also, most security evaluations consider only individual system execution. However, effective operational execution of a mission must cross organizational and system boundaries to be complete. The use of mission thread analysis for security provides a way to confirm that each participating system is secure and does not represent a risk to all others involved in mission execution.

Figure A.2 provides a picture of the WEA mission thread and includes step numbers from the list to link each step to the appropriate system area. Successful completion requires flawless execution of four major system areas—alert originator, FEMA IPAWS system, CMSPs, and cell phone recipients—each shown in a row of the figure. Each area operates independently, and they are connected only through the transmission of an alert.

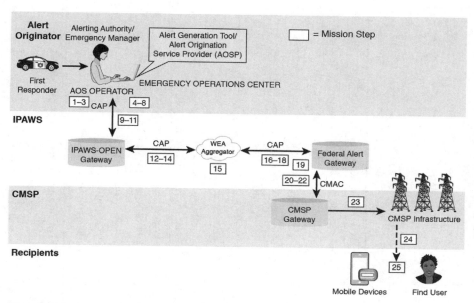

Figure A.2 *WEA Mission Thread Diagram*

WEA Security Analysis

Using the mission thread illustrated in Figure A.2, potential security concerns can be identified through possible security threats. For the WEA example, the SEI selected the STRIDE threat method for threat evaluation. STRIDE, developed by Microsoft, considers six typical categories of security concerns: spoofing, tampering with data, repudiations, information disclosure, denial of service, and elevation of privilege [Microsoft 2013]. The name of this threat method is derived from the first letter of each security concern [Howard 2006]. As an illustration of how STRIDE can be applied, focus on steps 4–9 of the mission thread, which represent the transition across two major system areas from the alert originator to the FEMA system and provide an opportunity for mission failure if interaction between the system areas is not secure. Table A.1 shows the result of the STRIDE analysis on the selected steps.

For each step, the team analyzed technology assets critical to step execution to determine ways that STRIDE threats can compromise each asset used in that step [Howard 2006]. Security and software experts as well as individuals familiar with the operational mission must participate in this portion of the analysis. The security and software experts have an understanding of what can go wrong and the potential

Table A.1 *STRIDE Analysis for Selected WEA Mission Thread Steps*

Step	Assets	STRIDE Threat Identification[a] Examples
4. AOS operator attempts to log on to the alert origination system.	• One person • Server (valid accounts/authentication information) • Logon procedure • Logon application • Username/password data in database • Communications between logon software, server, and AOS	S: Unidentified individual attempts to log on with AOS operator's information R: AOS operator denies having logged on I: Capture of logon info using key logger or packet sniffer D: AOS operator's account not registered or servers are down E: Successful logon by an unidentified and unauthorized individual
5. AOS logon activates auditing of the operator's session.	• Auditing application • Auditing procedure • Communications from accounts to auditing application • Local or remote storage	T: Logged entries added, deleted, or modified inappropriately I: Logged entries containing credential data are compromised D: Log full or server unavailable
6. AOS operator enters alert, cancel, or update message.	• One person • Alert scripts • Procedures for building scripts • GUI application • Communications between GUI application and alert generation software (including server and application)	T: Formatting errors produce incorrect message D: Scripts are unavailable or corrupted

7. AOS converts message to CAP-compliant format required by IPAWS.	• Conversion application	T: Data are changed between the AOS and the server D: Server is down
8. CAP-compliant message is signed by two people.	• Signature entry application • Signature validation application • Public/private key pair for every user	S: Digital signature is falsified R: User claims not to have signed D: Server goes down so keys cannot be distributed, or keys have expired and message cannot be sent
9. AOS transmits message to the IPAWS-OPEN Gateway.	• Application that securely connects to IPAWS • Information used to authenticate AOS and IPAWS	S: Falsified AOS CAP message or IPAWS gateway attacked and site is redirected T: Data within message are modified I: Message is not encrypted and credentials are visible D: IPAWS-OPEN Gateway is down

[a] S: spoofing; T: tampering with data; R: repudiation; I: information disclosure; D: denial of service; E: elevation of privilege.

impact of each possible failure on the analysis. Those knowledgeable about the operational execution can ensure that the scenarios are realistic and valid. Available documentation can provide a start for the development of the mission threads, but there is a tendency to document the desired operational environment and not the real one. Effective security risk analysis requires access to realistic operational information.

Based on this input, security experts (individuals with operational security training and experience) identified at least two security risks that could lead to mission failure:

- Authentication of the individual using the AOS in step 4
- Validation and protection of the digital signatures applied to the alert approved for submission to the Alert Aggregator in step 8

To analyze these risks in greater detail and help alert originators understand how a security risk could materialize, mission threads for each specific risk were assembled. Figure A.3 provides a picture of the risk scenario that describes the second security risk (validity of the digital signature) noted from the analysis of the WEA operational mission thread. The following paragraphs provide a dialogue that describes ways in which the security threat could materialize and why the alert origination organization should consider possible mitigations.

An outside attacker with malicious intent decides to obtain a valid certificate and use it to send an illegitimate CAP-compliant message. The attacker's goal is to send people to a dangerous location, hoping to inflict physical and emotional harm on them. The key to this attack is capturing a valid certificate from an alert originator. The attacker develops two strategies for capturing a valid certificate. The first strategy targets an alert originator directly. The second strategy focuses on AOS vendors. Targeting a vendor could be a particularly fruitful strategy for the attacker. The number of vendors that provide AOS software is small. As a result, each vendor controls a large number of certificates. A compromised vendor could provide an attacker with many potential organizations to target.

No matter which strategy is pursued, the attacker looks for vulnerabilities (i.e., weaknesses) in technologies or procedures that can be exploited. For example, the attacker tries to find vulnerabilities that expose certificates to exploit, such as the following:

- Unmonitored access to certificates
- Lack of encryption controls for certificates during transit and storage
- Lack of role-based access to certificates

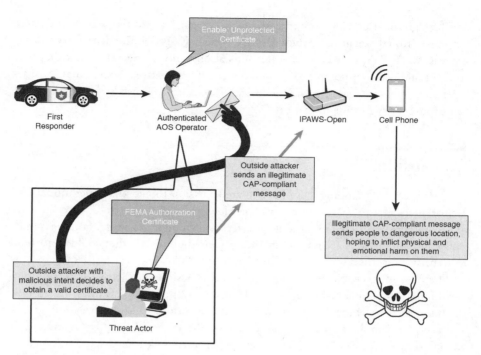

Figure A.3 *Security Risk Scenario*

The attacker might also explore social engineering techniques to obtain a certificate. Here, the attacker attempts to manipulate someone from the alert originator or vendor organization into providing access to a legitimate certificate or to get information that will be useful in the attacker's quest to get a certificate.

Obtaining a certificate is not a simple endeavor. The attacker must be sufficiently motivated and skilled to achieve this interim goal. However, once this part of the scenario is complete, the attacker is well positioned to send an illegitimate CAP-compliant message. The attacker has easy access to publicly documented information defining how to construct CAP-compliant messages.

The attacker's goal in this risk is to send people to a location that will put them in harm's way. To maximize the impact, the attacker takes advantage of an impending event (e.g., weather event, natural disaster). Because people tend to verify WEA messages through other channels, synchronizing the attack with an impending event makes it more likely that people will follow the attacker's instructions. This scenario could produce catastrophic consequences, depending on the severity of the event with which the attack is linked.

Through the use of mission thread analysis, security expertise can be integrated with operational execution to fully describe and analyze operational security risk situations. While there may be many variations of operational execution, an exhaustive study of all options is not necessary. Building a representative example that provides a detailed view of a real operational mission from start to finish has proven to be of value for security risk identification.

Conclusion

The process of developing a well-articulated mission thread that operational and security experts can share and analyze provides an opportunity to uncover missing or incomplete requirements as well as differences in understanding, faulty assumptions, and interactions across system and software boundaries that could contribute to security concerns and potential failure [Ellison 2008].

The mission thread analysis connects each mission step with the technology and human assets needed to execute that step and provides a framework to link potential security threats directly to mission execution. Mission thread diagrams and tables assemble information in a structure that can be readily reviewed and validated by operational and technology experts from various disciplines, including acquisition, development, and operational support. Mission thread security analysis can be an effective tool for improved identification of security risks to increase confidence that the system of systems will function with appropriate operational security.

References

[Allen 2008]

Allen, Julia; Barnum, Sean; Ellison, Robert J.; McGraw, Gary; & Mead, Nancy. *Software Security Engineering: A Guide for Project Managers*. Addison-Wesley. 2008.

[Ellison 2008]

Ellison, Robert J.; Goodenough, John B.; Weinstock, Charles B.; & Woody, Carol. *Survivability Assurance for System of Systems*. CMU/SEI-2008-TR-008. Software Engineering Institute, Carnegie Mellon University. 2008. http://resources.sei.cmu.edu/library/asset-view.cfm?assetID=8693.

[FEMA 2015]

Federal Emergency Management Agency. Wireless Emergency Alerts. *Federal Emergency Management Agency.* June 21, 2015. http://www.fema.gov/wireless-emergency-alerts.

[Haskins 2010]

Haskins, Cecilia, ed. *Systems Engineering Handbook: A Guide for System Life Cycle Processes and Activities,* version 3.2. Revised by Kevin Forsberg, M. Krueger, & R. Hamelin. International Council on Systems Engineering (INCOSE). 2010.

[Howard 2006]

Howard, Michael & Lipner, Steve. *The Security Development Life Cycle.* Microsoft Press. 2006.

[Microsoft 2013]

Microsoft. The STRIDE Threat Model. *Microsoft Developer Network.* 7 June 2013 [accessed]. http://msdn.microsoft.com/en-US/library/ee823878%28v=cs.20%29 .aspx.

[Stamatis 2003]

Stamatis, D. H. Failure Mode and Effect Analysis: FMEA from Theory to Execution. 2nd ed. ASQ Quality Press. 2003.

Appendix B

The MSwA Body of Knowledge with Maturity Levels Added

The following content comes from the *Master of Software Assurance Reference Curriculum* report [Mead 2010a], with maturity levels added for each BoK component.

1. **Assurance Across Life Cycles**
   Outcome: Graduates will have the ability to incorporate assurance technologies and methods into life-cycle processes and development models for new or evolutionary system development, and for system or service acquisition.

   1.1. Software Life-Cycle Processes

       1.1.1. New development [L4]
       Processes associated with the full development of a software system

       1.1.2. Integration, assembly, and deployment [L4]
       Processes concerned with the final phases of the development of a new or modified software system

       1.1.3. Operation and evolution [L4]
       Processes that guide the operation of the software product and its change over time

       1.1.4. Acquisition, supply, and service [L3]
       Processes that support acquisition, supply, or service of a software system

   1.2. Software Assurance Processes and Practices

       1.2.1. Process and practice assessment [L3]
       Methods, procedures, and tools used to assess assurance processes and practices

    1.2.2. Software assurance integration into SDLC phases [L2/3]
        Integration of assurance practices into typical life-cycle phases (for example, requirements engineering, architecture and design, coding, test, evolution, acquisition, and retirement)

2. Risk Management

Outcome: Graduates will have the ability to perform risk analysis and tradeoff assessment and to prioritize security measures.

  2.1. Risk Management Concepts

    2.1.1. Types and classification [L4]
        Different classes of risks (for example, business, project, technical)

    2.1.2. Probability, impact, severity [L4]
        Basic elements of risk analysis

    2.1.3. Models, processes, metrics [L4] [L3—metrics]
        Models, process, and metrics used in risk management

  2.2. Risk Management Process

    2.2.1. Identification [L4]
        Identification and classification of risks associated with a project

    2.2.2. Analysis [L4]
        Analysis of the likelihood, impact, and severity of each identified risk

    2.2.3. Planning [L4]
        Risk management plan covering risk avoidance and mitigation

    2.2.4. Monitoring and management [L4]
        Assessment and monitoring of risk occurrence and management of risk mitigation

  2.3. Software Assurance Risk Management

    2.3.1. Vulnerability and threat identification [L3]
        Application of risk analysis techniques to vulnerability and threat risks

    2.3.2. Analysis of software assurance risks [L3]
        Analysis of risks for both new and existing systems

    2.3.3. Software assurance risk mitigation [L3]
        Plan for and mitigation of software assurance risks

    2.3.4. Assessment of Software Assurance Processes and Practices [L2/3]
        As part of risk avoidance and mitigation, assessment of the identification and use of appropriate software assurance processes and practices

3. Assurance Assessment

Outcome: Graduates will have the ability to analyze and validate the effectiveness of assurance operations and create auditable evidence of security measures.

3.1. Assurance Assessment Concepts

　　3.1.1. Baseline level of assurance; allowable tolerances, if quantitative [L1]
　　　　Establishment and specification of the required or desired level of assurance for a specific software application, set of applications, or a software-reliant system (and tolerance for same)

　　3.1.2. Assessment methods [L2/3]
　　　　Validation of security requirements
　　　　Risk analysis
　　　　Threat analysis
　　　　Vulnerability assessments and scans [L4]
　　　　Assurance evidence
　　　　Knowledge of how various methods (such as those above) can be used to determine if the software or system being assessed is sufficiently secure within tolerances

3.2. Measurement for Assessing Assurance

　　3.2.1. Product and process measures by life-cycle phase [L1/2]
　　　　Definition and development of key product and process measurements that can be used to validate the required level of software assurance appropriate to a given life-cycle phase

　　3.2.2. Other performance indicators that test for the baseline as defined in 3.1.1, by life-cycle phase [L1/2]
　　　　Definition and development of additional performance indicators that can be used to validate the required level of software assurance appropriate to a given life-cycle phase

　　3.2.3. Measurement processes and frameworks [L2/3]
　　　　Knowledge of range of software assurance measurement processes and frameworks and how these might be used to accomplish software assurance integration into SDLC phases

　　3.2.4. Business survivability and operational continuity [L2]
　　　　Definition and development of performance indicators that can specifically address the software/system's ability to meet business survivability and operational continuity requirements, to the extent the software affects these

3.3. Assurance Assessment Process (collect and report measures that demonstrate the baseline as defined in 3.1.1.)

　　3.3.1. Comparison of selected measurements to the established baseline [L3]
　　　　Analysis of key product and process measures and performance indicators to determine if they are within tolerance when compared to the defined baseline

　　3.3.2. Identification of out-of-tolerance variances [L3]
　　　　Identification of measures that are out of tolerance when compared to the defined baselines and ability to develop actions to reduce the variance

4. Assurance Management

Outcome: Graduates will have the ability to make a business case for software assurance, lead assurance efforts, understand standards, comply with regulations, plan for business continuity, and keep current in security technologies.

4.1. Making the Business Case for Assurance

4.1.1. Valuation and cost/benefit models, cost and loss avoidance, return on investment [L3]
Application of financially-based approaches, methods, models, and tools to develop and communicate compelling cost/benefit arguments in support of deploying software assurance practices

4.1.2. Risk analysis [L3]
Knowledge of how risk analysis can be used to develop cost/benefit arguments in support of deploying software assurance practices

4.1.3. Compliance justification [L3]
Knowledge of how compliance with laws, regulations, standards, and policies can be used to develop cost/benefit arguments in support of deploying software assurance practices

4.1.4. Business impact/needs analysis [L3]
Knowledge of how business impact and needs analysis can be used to develop cost/benefit arguments in support of deploying software assurance practices, specifically in support of business continuity and survivability

4.2. Managing Assurance

4.2.1. Project management across the life cycle [L3]
Knowledge of how to lead software and system assurance efforts as an extension of normal software development (and acquisition) project management skills

4.2.2. Integration of other knowledge units [L2/3]
Identification, analysis, and selection of software assurance practices from any knowledge units that are relevant for a specific software development or acquisition project

4.3. Compliance Considerations for Assurance

4.3.1. Laws and regulations [L3]
Knowledge of the extent to which selected laws and regulations are relevant for a specific software development or acquisition project, and how compliance might be demonstrated

4.3.2. Standards [L3]
Knowledge of the extent to which selected standards are relevant for a specific software development or acquisition project, and how compliance might be demonstrated

4.3.3. Policies [L2/3]

Knowledge of how to develop, deploy, and use organizational policies to accelerate the adoption of software assurance practices, and how compliance might be demonstrated

5. System Security Assurance

Outcome: Graduates will have the ability to incorporate effective security technologies and methods into new and existing systems.

5.1. For Newly Developed and Acquired Software for Diverse Systems

5.1.1. Security and safety aspects of computer-intensive critical infrastructure [L2]

Knowledge of safety and security risks associated with critical infrastructure systems such as found, for example, in banking and finance, energy production and distribution, telecommunications, and transportation systems

5.1.2. Potential attack methods [L3]

Knowledge of the variety of methods by which attackers can damage software or data associated with that software by exploiting weaknesses in the system design or implementation

5.1.3. Analysis of threats to software [L3]

Analysis of the threats to which software is most likely to be vulnerable in specific operating environments and domains

5.1.4. Methods of defense [L3]

Familiarity with appropriate countermeasures such as layers, access controls, privileges, intrusion detection, encryption, and code review checklists

5.2. For Diverse Operational (Existing) Systems

5.2.1. Historic and potential operational attack methods [L4]

Knowledge of and ability to duplicate the attacks that have been used to interfere with an application's or system's operations

5.2.2. Analysis of threats to operational environments [L3]

Analysis of the threats to which software is most likely to be vulnerable in specific operating environments and domains

5.2.3. Designing of and plan for access control, privileges, and authentication [L3]

Design of and plan for access control and authentication

5.2.4. Security methods for physical and personnel environments [L4]

Knowledge of how physical access restrictions, guards, background checks, and personnel monitoring can address risks

5.3. Ethics and Integrity in Creation, Acquisition, and Operation of Software Systems

5.3.1. Overview of ethics, code of ethics, and legal constraints [L4]
Knowledge of how people who are knowledgeable about attack and prevention methods are obligated to use their abilities, both legally and ethically, referencing the Software Engineering Code of Ethical and Professional Conduct [ACM 2016]

5.3.2. Computer attack case studies [L3]
Knowledge of the legal and ethical considerations involved in analyzing a variety of historical events and investigations

6. **System Functionality Assurance**
Outcome: Graduates will have the ability to verify new and existing software system functionality for conformance to requirements and to help reveal malicious content.

6.1. Assurance Technology

6.1.1. Technology evaluation [L3]
Evaluation of capabilities and limitations of technical environments, languages, and tools with respect to creating assured software functionality and security

6.1.2. Technology improvement [L3]
Recommendation of improvements in technology as necessary within project constraints

6.2. Assured Software Development

6.2.1. Development methods [L2/3]
Rigorous methods for system requirements, specification, architecture, design, implementation, verification, and testing to develop assured software

6.2.2. Quality attributes [L3—depends on the property]
Software quality attributes and how to achieve them

6.2.3. Maintenance methods [L3]
Assurance aspects of software maintenance and evolution

6.3. Assured software analytics

6.3.1. Systems analysis [L2 architectures; L3/4 networks, databases (identity management, access control)]
Analysis of system architectures, networks, and databases for assurance properties

6.3.2. Structural analysis [L3]
Structuring the logic of existing software to improve understandability and modifiability

6.3.3. Functional analysis [L2/3]

Reverse engineering of existing software to determine functionality and security properties

6.3.4. Analysis of methods and tools [L3]
Capabilities and limitations of methods and tools for software analysis

6.3.5. Testing for assurance [L3]
Evaluation of testing methods, plans, and results for assuring software

6.3.6. Assurance evidence [L2]
Development of auditable assurance evidence

6.4. Assurance in acquisition

6.4.1. Assurance of acquired software [L2]
Assurance of software acquired through supply chains,[1] vendors, and open sources, including developing requirements and assuring delivered functionality and security

6.4.2. Assurance of software services [L3]
Development of service level agreements for functionality and security with service providers and monitoring compliance

7. System Operational Assurance

Outcome: Graduates will have the ability to monitor and assess system operational security and respond to new threats.

7.1. Operational Procedures

7.1.1. Business objectives [L3]
Role of business objectives and strategic planning in system assurance

7.1.2. Assurance procedures [L3]
Creation of security policies and procedures for system operations

7.1.3. Assurance training [L4]
Selection of training for users and system administrative personnel in secure system operations

7.2. Operational Monitoring

7.2.1. Monitoring technology [L4]
Capabilities and limitations of monitoring technologies, and installation and configuration or acquisition of monitors and controls for systems, services, and personnel

7.2.2. Operational evaluation [L4]
Evaluation of operational monitoring results with respect to system and service functionality and security

---

1. For more information about software security supply chain risk, download the SEI report *Evaluating and Mitigating Software Supply Chain Security Risks* [Ellison 2010].

7.2.3. Operational maintenance [L3]
Maintenance and evolution of operational systems while preserving assured functionality and security

7.2.4. Malware analysis [L2/3]
Evaluation of malicious content and application of countermeasures

7.3. System Control

7.3.1. Responses to adverse events [L3/4]
Plan for and execution of effective responses to operational system accidents, failures, and intrusions

7.3.2. Business survivability [L3]
Maintenance of business survivability and continuity of operations in adverse environments (See also Outcome 3, Assurance Assessment.)

References

[ACM 2016]

Association of Computing Machinery & Institute of Electrical and Electronics Engineers. Software Engineering Code of Ethics and Professional Practice. *Association of Computing Machinery*. June 9, 2016 [accessed]. http://www.acm.org/about/se-code.

[Ellison 2010]

Ellison, Robert J.; Goodenough, John B.; Weinstock, Charles B.; & Woody, Carol. *Evaluating and Mitigating Software Supply Chain Security Risks*. CMU/SEI-2010-TR-016. Software Engineering Institute, Carnegie Mellon University. 2010. http://resources.sei.cmu.edu/library/asset-view.cfm?assetid=9337.

[Mead 2010]

Mead, Nancy R.; Allen, Julia H.; Ardis, Mark A.; Hilburn, Thomas B.; Kornecki, Andrew J.; Linger, Richard C.; & McDonald, James. *Software Assurance Curriculum Project Volume I: Master of Software Assurance Reference Curriculum*. CMU/SEI-2010-TR-005. Software Engineering Institute, Carnegie Mellon University. 2010. http://resources.sei.cmu.edu/library/asset-view.cfm?assetid=9415.

Appendix C

The Software Assurance Curriculum Project

The SEI established the Software Assurance Curriculum Project in 2009. The project has developed four documents that correlate well with the objective to enhance SwA curriculum guidance (see Table C.1).

Table C.1 *Software Assurance Curriculum Project Documents*

Document	Description
Volume I: Master of Software Assurance Reference Curriculum	Provides material for establishing or revising a master of software assurance (MSwA) program: curriculum development guidelines, graduate-student outcomes, recommended student preparation, an SwA body of knowledge, a high-level MSwA curriculum architecture, and implementation guidelines.
Volume II: Undergraduate Course Outlines	Provides the syllabi for seven undergraduate SwA courses: Computer Science I and II, Introduction to Computer Security, Software Security Engineering, Software Quality Assurance, Software Assurance Analytics, and Software Assurance Capstone Project. Each syllabus contains a course description, prerequisite knowledge, a list of learning objectives and topics, sources for the course, course delivery features, and course assessment features.

(continued)

Table C.1 *Continued*

Document	Description
Volume III: Master of Software Assurance Course Syllabi	Provides the syllabi for nine graduate SwA courses: Assurance Management; System Operational Assurance; Assured Software Analytics; Assured Software Development 1, 2, and 3; Assurance Assessment; System Security Assurance; and Software Assurance Capstone Experience. The syllabi are organized similarly to those in Volume II but include a schedule of weekly in-class activities, suggested readings, and out-of-class assignments.
Volume IV: Community College Education	Provides the syllabi for six SwA courses appropriate for community college students: Computer Science I, II, and III; Introduction to Computer Security; Secure Coding; and Introduction to Assured Software Engineering.

The courses listed in Table C.1 go well beyond secure coding and SwA at the implementation level. They cover security issues throughout the life cycle, as part of requirements analysis, architecture and module design, implementation, testing, and operation and maintenance. The graduate level includes additional SwA topics in such traditional areas as management and process, requirements engineering, design, construction, testing, and sustainment. These areas include SwA topics such as security policy and security functionality requirements; attack methods to damage software; analysis of threats to software; appropriate countermeasures such as layers, access controls, privileges, intrusion detection, and encryption; and designing and planning for access control, privileges, and authentication.

Because no SwA body of knowledge existed, one of the project team's first tasks was to establish one. After extensively reviewing software security reports, books, and articles and after surveys of and discussions with industry and government SwA professionals, the curriculum team developed the SwA Core Body of Knowledge (CorBoK). The CorBoK covers the spectrum of SwA practices involved in software system acquisition, development, operation, and evolution. It's the source for the content of the courses listed for Volumes II, III, and IV in Table C.1. Table C.2 lists the CorBoK's principal components and knowledge areas (KAs) and describes the principal MSwA student outcomes associated with each KA.

Table C.2 *SwA CorBoK Knowledge Areas*

Knowledge Area	MSwA Student Outcomes
Assurance Across Lifecycles	The ability to incorporate assurance technologies and methods into lifecycle processes and development models for new or evolutionary system development and for system or service acquisition.
Risk Management	The ability to perform risk analysis and trade-off assessment and to prioritize security measures.
Assurance Assessment	The ability to analyze and validate the effectiveness of assurance operations and create auditable evidence of security measures.
Assurance Management	The ability to make a business case for software assurance, lead assurance efforts, understand standards, comply with regulations, plan for business continuity, and keep current in security technologies.
System Security Assurance	The ability to incorporate effective security technologies and methods into new and existing systems.
System Functionality Assurance	The ability to verify new and existing software system functionality for conformance to requirements and to help reveal malicious content.
System Operational Assurance	The ability to monitor and assess system operational security and respond to new threats.

Based on the KAs, the project team created the MSwA Curriculum Architecture (see Table C.3). This architecture is compatible with software engineering master's degree programs because software engineering courses can incorporate the SwA-specific topics. Note that the MSwA core and the capstone experience in Table C.3 list the courses in the Volume III document; in total, they cover all the knowledge areas listed in Table C.2. The architecture provides a structural basis for programs that deliver the outcomes described in Table C.2. Of course, programs may cover the SwA body of knowledge and the corresponding outcomes using a different organization and set of courses, as listed in Table C.3. Table C.3 also lists the three preparatory areas students need to pursue the MSwA: computing foundations, software engineering, and security engineering. Volume I describes these areas in detail.

Table C.3 *The Master in Software Assurance Curriculum Architecture*

Curriculum Elements	Knowledge Areas
Preparatory materials	Computing Foundations
	Software Engineering
	Security Engineering
MSwA core	Assurance Management
	System Operational Assurance
	Assured Software Analytics
	Assured Software Development 1, 2, and 3
	Assurance Assessment
	System Security Assurance
Electives	Courses related to assurance in selected domains
Capstone experience	Project

Appendix D

The Software Assurance Competency Model Designations[1]

Table D.1 presents the CorBoK knowledge areas and second-level units, along with a description of the appropriate knowledge and skills for each competency level and the effectiveness attributes. Each level builds on the previous one: a designation of L1 applies to L1 through L5, a designation of L2 applies to L2 through L5, and so on. The level descriptions indicate the competency activities that are demonstrated at each level.

---

1. This chapter includes major contributions to the SEI's Software Assurance Competency Model from our collaborators Mark Ardis, Glenn Johnson, and Andrew Kornecki.

Table D.1 *SwA Competency Designations*

KA	Unit	Knowledge/Skill/Effectiveness Competency Activities
Assurance Across Life Cycles	Software Life Cycle Processes	L1: Understand and execute the portions of a defined process applicable to their assigned tasks.
		L2: Manage the application of a defined life-cycle software process for a small internal project.
		L3: Lead and assess process application for small and medium-sized projects, over a variety of life-cycle phases, such as new development, acquisition, operation, and evolution.
		L4: Manage the application of a defined life-cycle software process for a large project, including selecting and adapting existing SwA practices by life-cycle phase.
		L5: Analyze, design, and evolve life-cycle processes that meet the special organizational or domain needs and constraints.
	Software Assurance Processes and Practices	L1: Possess general awareness of methods, procedures, and tools used to assess assurance processes and practices.
		L2: Apply methods, procedures, and tools to assess assurance processes and practices.
		L3: Manage integration of assurance practices into typical life-cycle phases.
		L4: Lead the selection and integration of life-cycle assurance processes and practices in all projects across an organization.
		L5: Analyze assurance assessment results to determine best practices for various life-cycle phases.

Risk Management	Risk Management Concepts	L1: Understand the basic elements of risk analysis.
		L2: Explain how risk analysis is performed.
		L3: Determine the models, process, and metrics to be used in risk management for small internal projects.
		L4: Develop the models, processes, and metrics to be used in risk management of any sized project.
		L5: Analyze the effectiveness of the use and application of risk management concepts across an organization.
	Risk Management Process	L1: Describe an organizational risk management process.
		L2: Identify and classify the risks associated with a project.
		L3: Analyze the likelihood, impact, and severity of each identified risk for a project. Plan and monitor risk management for small to medium-sized projects.
		L4: Plan and monitor risk management for a large project.
		L5: Develop a program for analyzing and enhancing risk management practices across an organization.
	Software Assurance Risk Management	L1: Describe risk analysis techniques for vulnerability and threat risks.
		L2: Apply risk analysis techniques to vulnerability and threat risks.
		L3: Analyze and plan for mitigation of software assurance risks for small systems.
		L4: Analyze and plan for mitigation of software assurance risks for both new and existing systems.
		L5: Assess software assurance processes and practices across an organization and propose improvements.

(continued)

Table D.1 *Continued*

KA	Unit	Knowledge/Skill/Effectiveness Competency Activities
Assurance Assessment	Assurance Assessment Concepts	L1: Provide tool and documentation support for assurance assessment activities.
		L2: Support assurance assessment activities.
		L3: Apply various assurance assessment methods (such as validation of security requirements, risk analysis, threat analysis, vulnerability assessments and scans, and assurance evidence) to determine if the software/system being assessed is sufficiently secure within tolerances.
		L4: Establish and specify the required or desired level of assurance for a specific software application, set of applications, or software-reliant system.
		L5: Research, analyze, and recommend best practices for assurance assessment methods and techniques.
	Measurement for Assessing Assurance	L1: Provide tool and documentation support for assurance assessment measurement.
		L2: Support assurance assessment measurement activities.
		L3: Implement assurance assessment measurement activities.
		L4: Determine and then analyze the key product and process measurements, and performance indicators that can be used to validate the required level of software assurance; determine which software assurance measurement processes and frameworks might be used to accomplish software assurance integration into lifecycle phases.
		L5: Research, analyze, and recommend best practices for assurance assessment measurement.

Assurance Management	Making the Business Case for Assurance	L1: Understand the need for business case analysis.
		L2: Apply a business case tradeoff analysis to existing data and determine the validity of the case.
		L3: Identify and gather data needed, and produce the business case.
		L4: Perform sophisticated business case analysis.
		L5: Perform research to develop new business case analysis approaches.
	Managing Assurance	L1: Understand the importance of assurance in the lifecycle.
		L2: Support software assurance management tasks.
		L3: Manage small software assurance projects, building in software assurance practices and measurement.
		L4: Manage medium-sized to large projects, building in software assurance practices and measurement.
		L5: Develop new methods for managing assurance.
	Compliance Considerations for Assurance	L1: Understand the importance of compliance and possess awareness of laws and regulations.
		L2: Apply known compliance considerations, laws, and policies to a project.
		L3: Lead compliance activities for a conventional project.
		L4: Lead compliance activities for a complex project, and participate in standards and policy activities.
		L5: Lead standard and policy development activities. Propose new standards and policies.

(continued)

Table D.1 *Continued*

		Knowledge/Skill/Effectiveness
KA	Unit	Competency Activities
System Security Assurance	For Newly Developed and Acquired Software for Diverse Applications	L1: Possess knowledge of safety and security risks associated with critical infrastructure systems (e.g., banking and finance, energy production and distribution, telecommunications, and transportation systems). L2: Describe the variety of methods by which attackers can damage software or data associated with that software by exploiting weaknesses in the system design or implementation. L3: Apply software assurance countermeasures such as layers, access controls, privileges, intrusion detection, encryption, and code review checklists. L4: Analyze the threats to which software is most likely to be vulnerable in specific operating environments and domains. L5: Perform research on security risks and attack methods, and use it to support modification or creation of techniques used to counter such risks and attacks.
	For Diverse Operational (Existing) Systems	L1: Possess knowledge of the attacks that have been used to interfere with an application's or system's operations. L2: Possess knowledge of how gates, locks, guards, and background checks can address risks. L3: Design and plan for access control and authentication. L4: Analyze the threats to which software is most likely to be vulnerable in specific operating environments and domains. L5: Perform research on security risks and attack methods, and use it to support modification or creation of techniques used to counter such risks and attacks.

Ethics and Integrity in Creation, Acquisition, and Operation of Software Systems	L1: Possess knowledge of how people who are knowledgeable about attack and prevention methods are obligated to use their abilities, both legally and ethically.	
	L2: Possess knowledge of the legal and ethical considerations involved in analyzing a variety of historical events and investigations.	
	L3: Follow legal and ethical guidelines in the creation and maintenance of software systems.	
	L4: Play a leadership role in the practice of ethical behavior for software security.	
	L5: Create new case studies for use in education about ethical and legal issues.	
System Functionality Assurance	Assurance Technology	L1: Possess general awareness of technologies used for system functionality assurance.
		L2: Apply assurance technology to determine system functionality assurance.
		L3: Manage integration of selected technology in the functionality assurance process.
		L4: Select and guide decisions on the use of selected technologies for specific projects.
		L5: Analyze assurance technologies and contribute to the development of new ones.
	Assured Software Development	L1: Understand the importance of assurance in the development process.
		L2: Engage in the development tasks contributing to functionality assurance.
		L3: Lead the development of a functionality assurance process in small projects.
		L4: Select and guide decisions on the use of a specific assurance process in large projects.
		L5: Analyze assured development processes and contribute to the development of new ones.

(continued)

Table D.1 *Continued*

	Knowledge/Skill/Effectiveness	
KA	Unit	Competency Activities
System Functionality Assurance	Assured Software Analytics	L1: Understand the need for using an analytical approach to software development and the use of supporting tools.
		L2: Apply specific selected methods for structured and functional analysis "in the small."
		L3: Lead projects applying specific selected methods for structured and functional analysis "in the large."
		L4: Lead development teams in testing assurance and developing auditable assurance evidence.
		L5: Develop new methods and techniques allowing for testing assurance, and develop auditable assurance evidence.
	Assurance in Acquisition	L1: Understand the need to identify risks in internal software, contracted software, commercial off-the-shelf (COTS) software, and software as a service (SaaS).
		L2: Define and analyze risks in the acquisition of contracted software, COTS software, and SaaS; use mitigation tactics to test; and identify risks prior to integration.
		L3: Manage multiple supply chains and use measures to reduce risk in acquisition; require vendors to use security measures equal to or greater than internal policy.
		L4: Lead acquisition teams by providing policy, process, tools, and language to prevent the acquisition of insecure software.
		L5: Establish comprehensive policies, plans, and education to L1–L4 personnel, all software development lifecycle stakeholders, and procurement teams to protect against the acquisition of insecure software.

System Operational Assurance	Operational Procedures	L1: Understand the role of business objectives and strategic planning in system assurance.
		L2: Support the creation of security policies and procedures for system operations.
		L3: Create security policies and procedures for the operation of a designated system.
		L4: Define the process and procedures for creating security policies and procedures for the operation of a designated system.
		L5: Research, analyze, and recommend best practices for determining security policies and procedures for system operations.
	Operational Monitoring	L1: Provide support for the installation and use of tools for monitoring and controlling system operation.
		L2: Support the installation and configuration or acquisition of monitors and controls for systems, services, and personnel.
		L3: Evaluate operational monitoring results with respect to system and service functionality and security, and malicious content and application of countermeasures.
		L4: Lead maintenance and evolution of operational systems while preserving assured functionality and security.
		L5: Research, analyze, and recommend best practices for operational monitoring with respect to system and service functionality and security.

(continued)

Table D.1 *Continued*

KA	Unit	Knowledge/Skill/Effectiveness
		Competency Activities
System Operational Assurance	System Control	L1: Provide support for the installation and use of tools for monitoring and controlling system operation.
		L2: Support the implementation of effective responses to operational system accidents, failures, and intrusions.
		L3: Implement effective responses to operational system accidents, failures, and intrusions.
		L4: Lead and plan for effective responses to operational system accidents, failures, and intrusions, including maintenance of business survivability and continuity of operations in adverse environments.
		L5: Research, analyze, and recommend best practices for system control with respect to operational system accidents, failures, and intrusions, including business survivability and continuity of operations in adverse environments.

Appendix E

Proposed SwA Competency Mappings

When the model was developed, as part of our review process, several organizations mapped actual organizational positions to the competency model designations. This provided us with a checkpoint showing that our model designations were applicable to real organizations, and not just a theoretical exercise. These mappings are shown in Tables E.1 and E.2.

Table E.1 Proposed SwA Competency Mappings from the (ISC)[2] Applications Security Advisory Board—Initial List of Job Titles[1]

KA	Unit	Knowledge/Skill/Effectiveness — Job Titles	Behavioral Indicators
Assurance Across Lifecycles	Software Lifecycle Processes	L1: Application Security Analyst	2—Intermediate 3—Advanced
		L2: Application Security Engineer	2—Intermediate 3—Advanced
		L3: Software Architect	3—Advanced
		L4: Application Security Architect, Senior Software Architect, Information Assurance Architect	3—Advanced 4—Expert
		L5: Software Team Lead, Principal Security Architect	4—Expert
	Software Assurance Processes and Practices	L1: QA Analyst	2—Intermediate 3—Advanced
		L2: QA Engineer	2—Intermediate 3—Advanced
		L3: Senior QA Engineer	3—Advanced 4—Expert
		L4: Lead QA Engineer	3—Advanced 4—Expert
		L5: Principal QA Engineer, QA Engineer Manager	4—Expert

Risk Management			
Risk Management Concepts	L1: Information Assurance Analyst	2—Intermediate	3—Advanced
	L2: Information Assurance Analyst 2	2—Intermediate	3—Advanced
	L3: Information Assurance Engineer	2—Intermediate	3—Advanced
	L4: Information Assurance Architect	3—Advanced	
	L5: Lead Information Assurance Architect, Information Assurance Manager	3—Advanced	4—Expert
Risk Management Process	L1: Information Assurance Analyst	2—Intermediate	3—Advanced
	L2: Information Assurance Engineer	2—Intermediate	3—Advanced
	L3: Information Assurance Architect	3—Advanced	3—Advanced
	L4: Product Manager	3—Advanced	
	L5: Lead Information Assurance Architect, Information Assurance Manager	3—Advanced	4—Expert
Software Assurance Risk Management	L1: Information Assurance Analyst	2—Intermediate	3—Advanced
	L2: Information Assurance Engineer	2—Intermediate	3—Advanced
	L3: Information Assurance Architect	3—Advanced	
	L4: Product Manager	3—Advanced	
	L5: Lead Information Assurance Architect, Information Assurance Manager	3—Advanced	4—Expert

(continued)

Table E.1 *Continued*

KA	Unit	Knowledge/Skill/Effectiveness — Job Titles	Behavioral Indicators
Assurance Assessment	Assurance Assessment Concepts	L1: Information Assurance Analyst	2—Intermediate
			3—Advanced
		L2: Information Assurance Engineer	2—Intermediate
			3—Advanced
		L3: Information Assurance Architect	3—Advanced
		L4: Product Manager	3—Advanced
		L5: Lead Information Assurance Architect, Information Assurance Architect	3—Advanced
			4—Expert
	Measurement for Assessing Assurance	L1: Information Assurance Analyst	2—Intermediate
			3—Advanced
		L2: Information Assurance Engineer	2—Intermediate
			3—Advanced
		L3: Information Assurance Architect	3—Advanced
		L4: Product Manager	3—Advanced
		L5: Lead Information Assurance Architect, Information Assurance Architect	3—Advanced
			4—Expert
	Assurance Assessment Process	L1: Information Assurance Analyst	2—Intermediate
			3—Advanced
		L2: Information Assurance Engineer	2—Intermediate
			3—Advanced
		L3: Information Assurance Architect	3—Advanced
		L4: Product Manager	3—Advanced
		L5: Lead Information Assurance Architect, Information Assurance Architect	3—Advanced
			4—Expert

Making the Business Case for Assurance	L1: Information Assurance Analyst	2—Intermediate
		3—Advanced
	L2: Information Assurance Engineer	2—Intermediate
		3—Advanced
	L3: Information Assurance Architect	3—Advanced
	L4: Product Manager	3—Advanced
	L5: Lead Information Assurance Architect, Information Assurance Architect	3—Advanced
		4—Expert
Managing Assurance	L1: Information Assurance Analyst	2—Intermediate
		3—Advanced
	L2: Information Assurance Engineer	2—Intermediate
		3—Advanced
	L3: Information Assurance Architect	3—Advanced
	L4: Product Manager	3—Advanced
	L5: Lead Information Assurance Architect, Information Assurance Architect	3—Advanced
		4—Expert
Compliance Considerations for Assurance	L1: Information Assurance Analyst, Information Security Analyst	2—Intermediate
		3—Advanced
	L2: Information Assurance Engineer, Information Security Engineer	2—Intermediate
		3—Advanced
	L3: Information Assurance Architect, Information Security Architect	3—Advanced
	L4: Product Manager	3—Advanced
	L5: Lead Information Assurance Architect, Information Assurance Architect, Lead Information Security Architect	3—Advanced
		4—Expert

(continued)

Table E.1 *Continued*

KA	Unit	Knowledge/Skill/Effectiveness — Job Titles	Behavioral Indicators
System Security Assurance	For Newly Developed and Acquired Software for Diverse Applications	L1: Software Developer, Software Programmer, QA Analyst, Software Implementer	2—Intermediate 3—Advanced
		L2: QA Engineer, Software Engineer, Requirements Engineer, Programmer 1	1—Basic 2—Intermediate 3—Advanced
		L3: Programmer 2, Programmer 3, QA Lead, QA Engineer 2	2—Intermediate 3—Advanced
		L4: Senior Software Developer, Senior Software Engineer, Senior Software Architect	3—Advanced 4—Expert
		L5: Lead Software Engineer, Lead Software Developer	3—Advanced 4—Expert
	For Diverse Operational (Existing) Systems	L1: Software Developer, Software Programmer, QA Analyst, Software Implementer	2—Intermediate 3—Advanced
		L2: QA Engineer, Software Engineer, Requirements Engineer, Programmer 1	1—Basic 2—Intermediate 3—Advanced
		L3: Programmer 2, Programmer 3, QA Lead, QA Engineer 2	2—Intermediate 3—Advanced
		L4: Senior Software Developer, Senior Software Engineer, Senior Software Architect	3—Advanced 4—Expert
		L5: Lead Software Engineer, Lead Software Developer	3—Advanced 4—Expert

Category	Role	Level
Ethics and Integrity in Creation, Acquisition, and Operation of Software Systems	L1: Information Assurance Analyst	2—Intermediate
		3—Advanced
	L2: Information Assurance Engineer	2—Intermediate
		3—Advanced
	L3: Information Assurance Architect	3—Advanced
	L4: Product Manager	3—Advanced
	L5: Lead Information Assurance Architect, Information Assurance Architect	3—Advanced
		4—Expert
Assurance Technology	L1: QA Analyst	2—Intermediate
		3—Advanced
	L2: QA Engineer QA Analyst 2	2—Intermediate
		3—Advanced
	L3: Senior QA Engineer QA Engineer 2, QA Analyst 3	3—Advanced
	L4: Lead QA Engineer	3—Advanced
	L5: Principal QA Engineer	4—Expert
Assured Software Development	L1: Software Developer, Software Programmer, QA Analyst, Software Implementer	2—Intermediate
		3—Advanced
	L2: QA Engineer, Software Engineer, Requirements Engineer, Programmer 1	2—Intermediate
		3—Advanced

(continued)

Table E.1 *Continued*

| KA | Unit | Knowledge/Skill/Effectiveness | Behavioral |
		Job Titles	Indicators
System Functionality Assurance		L3: Programmer 2, Programmer 3, QA Lead, QA Engineer 2	2—Intermediate 3—Advanced
		L4: Senior Software Developer, Senior Software Engineer, Senior Software Architect	3—Advanced
		L5: Lead Software Engineer, Lead Software Developer	3—Advanced 4—Expert
	Assured Software Analytics	L1: Software Developer, Software Programmer, QA Analyst, Software Implementer	2—Intermediate 3—Advanced
		L2: QA Engineer, Software Engineer, Requirements Engineer, Programmer 1	2—Intermediate 3—Advanced
		L3: Programmer 2, Programmer 3, QA Lead, QA Engineer 2	2—Intermediate 3—Advanced
		L4: Senior Software Developer, Senior Software Engineer, Senior Software Architect	3—Advanced
		L5: Lead Software Engineer, Lead Software Developer	3—Advanced
	Assurance in Acquisition	L1: Software Developer, Software Programmer, QA Analyst, Software Implementer	2—Intermediate 3—Advanced
		L2: QA Engineer, Software Engineer, Requirements Engineer, Programmer 1	2—Intermediate 3—Advanced
		L3: Programmer 2, Programmer 3, QA Lead, QA Engineer 2	2—Intermediate 3—Advanced

System Operational Assurance		Role	Proficiency
		L4: Senior Software Developer, Senior Software Engineer, Senior Software Architect	3—Advanced
		L5: Lead Software Engineer, Lead Software Developer	3—Advanced
	Operational Procedures	L1: Software Developer, Software Programmer, QA Analyst, Software Implementer	2—Intermediate 3—Advanced
		L2: QA Engineer, Software Engineer, Requirements Engineer, Programmer 1	2—Intermediate 3—Advanced
		L3: Programmer 2, Programmer 3, QA Lead, QA Engineer 2	2—Intermediate 3—Advanced
		L4: Senior Software Developer, Senior Software Engineer, Senior Software Architect	3—Advanced
		L5: Lead Software Engineer, Lead Software Developer	3—Advanced
	Operational Monitoring	L1: Operations Analyst	2—Intermediate 3—Advanced
		L2: Operations Engineer	2—Intermediate 3—Advanced
		L3: Operations Engineer 2	2—Intermediate 3—Advanced
		L4: Senior Operations Engineer	3—Advanced
		L5: Lead Operations Engineer	3—Advanced

(continued)

Table E.1 *Continued*

KA	Unit	Knowledge/Skill/Effectiveness		Behavioral Indicators
		Job Titles		
System Operational Assurance	System Control	L1: Operations Analyst		2—Intermediate
				3—Advanced
		L2: Operations Engineer		2—Intermediate
				3—Advanced
		L3: Operations Engineer 2		2—Intermediate
				3—Advanced
		L4: Senior Operations Engineer		3—Advanced
		L5: Lead Operations Engineer		3—Advanced

[1] From *Software Assurance Competency Model* [Hilburn 2013a].

Table E.2 *Proposed SwA Competency Mappings from (ISC)² Application Security Advisory Board Reviewers—Comprehensive List of Job Titles*

KA	Unit	Knowledge/Skill/Effectiveness — Job Titles	Behavioral Indicators
Assurance Across Lifecycles	Software Lifecycle Processes	L1: Acceptance Tester, Junior Information Assurance Engineer, Programmer 1	1—Basic 2—Intermediate
		L2: Application Security Analyst, Application Security Engineer, Information Assurance Analyst, Information Assurance Engineer, Maintenance Engineer, Programmer 2, QA Engineer, Release Engineer, Software Developer, Software Implementer, Support Engineer, Integration Engineer, Test Engineer	2—Intermediate 3—Advanced
		L3: Consultant Architect, Consulting Engineer, Information Assurance Architect, Programmer 3, Requirements Engineer, Software Architect, Software Manager, Software Team Lead, Senior Information Assurance Engineer, Senior Programmer, Senior Software Analyst, Senior Software Developer, Senior Software Engineer, Application Security Architect, Security Control Assessor	3—Advanced
		L4: Information Assurance Manager, Lead Software Engineer, Principal Information Assurance Engineer, Principal Software Engineer, Product Manager, Project Manager, Senior Software Architect	3—Advanced 4—Expert
		L5: Chief Information Assurance Engineer, Chief Software Engineer	4—Expert

(continued)

Table E.2 *Continued*

KA	Unit	Knowledge/Skill/Effectiveness	Behavioral Indicators
		Job Titles	
Assurance Across Lifecycles	Software Assurance Processes and Practices	L1: Acceptance Tester, Junior Information Assurance Engineer, Programmer 1	1—Basic 2—Intermediate
		L2: Application Security Analyst, Application Security Engineer, Information Assurance Analyst, Information Assurance Engineer, Maintenance Engineer, Programmer 2, QA Engineer, Release Engineer, Software Developer, Software Implementer, Support Engineer, Integration Engineer, Test Engineer	2—Intermediate 3—Advanced
		L3: Consultant Architect, Consulting Engineer, Information Assurance Architect, Programmer 3, Requirements Engineer, Software Architect, Software Manager, Software Team Lead, Senior Information Assurance Engineer, Senior Programmer, Senior Software Analyst, Senior Software Developer, Senior Software Engineer, Application Security Architect, Security Control Assessor	3—Advanced
		L4: Information Assurance Manager, Lead Software Engineer, Principal Information Assurance Engineer, Principal Software Engineer, Product Manager, Project Manager, Senior Software Architect	3—Advanced 4—Expert
		L5: Chief Information Assurance Engineer, Chief Software Engineer	4—Expert

Risk Management		
Risk Management Concepts	L1: Acceptance Tester, Junior Information Assurance Engineer, Programmer 1	1—Basic 2—Intermediate
	L2: Application Security Analyst, Application Security Engineer, Information Assurance Analyst, Information Assurance Engineer, Maintenance Engineer, Programmer 2, QA Engineer, Release Engineer, Software Developer, Software Implementer, Support Engineer, Integration Engineer, Test Engineer	2—Intermediate 3—Advanced
	L3: Consultant Architect, Consulting Engineer, Information Assurance Architect, Programmer 3, Requirements Engineer, Software Architect, Software Manager, Software Team Lead, Senior Information Assurance Engineer, Senior Programmer, Senior Software Analyst, Senior Software Developer, Senior Software Engineer, Application Security Architect, Security Control Assessor	3—Advanced
	L4: Information Assurance Manager, Lead Software Engineer, Principal Information Assurance Engineer, Principal Software Engineer, Product Manager, Project Manager, Senior Software Architect	3—Advanced 4—Expert
	L5: Chief Information Assurance Engineer, Chief Software Engineer	4—Expert

(continued)

Table E.2 *Continued*

KA	Unit	Knowledge/Skill/Effectiveness		Behavioral Indicators
		Job Titles		
Risk Management	Risk Management Process	L1: Acceptance Tester, Junior Information Assurance Engineer, Programmer 1		1—Basic 2—Intermediate
		L2: Application Security Analyst, Application Security Engineer, Information Assurance Analyst, Information Assurance Engineer, Maintenance Engineer, Programmer 2, QA Engineer, Release Engineer, Software Developer, Software Implementer, Support Engineer, Integration Engineer, Test Engineer		2—Intermediate 3—Advanced
		L3: Consultant Architect, Consulting Engineer, Information Assurance Architect, Programmer 3, Requirements Engineer, Software Architect, Software Manager, Software Team Lead, Senior Information Assurance Engineer, Senior Programmer, Senior Software Analyst, Senior Software Developer, Senior Software Engineer, Application Security Architect, Security Control Assessor		3—Advanced
		L4: Information Assurance Manager, Lead Software Engineer, Principal Information Assurance Engineer, Principal Software Engineer, Product Manager, Project Manager, Senior Software Architect		3—Advanced 4—Expert
		L5: Chief Information Assurance Engineer, Chief Software Engineer		4—Expert

Software Assurance Risk Management	L1: Acceptance Tester, Junior Information Assurance Engineer, Programmer 1	1—Basic 2—Intermediate
	L2: Information Assurance Analyst, Information Assurance Engineer, Maintenance Engineer, Programmer 2, QA Engineer, Release Engineer, Software Developer, Software Implementer, Support Engineer, Integration Engineer, Test Engineer	2—Intermediate 3—Advanced
	L3: Application Security Analyst, Application Security Engineer, Consultant, Consulting Architect, Consulting Engineer, Information Assurance Architect, Programmer 3, Requirements Engineer, Software Architect, Software Manager, Software Team Lead, Senior Information Assurance Engineer, Senior Programmer, Senior Software Analyst, Senior Software Developer, Senior Software Engineer, Application Security Architect, Security Control Assessor	3—Advanced
	L4: Information Assurance Manager, Lead Software Engineer, Principal Information Assurance Engineer, Principal Software Engineer, Product Manager, Project Manager, Senior Software Architect	3—Advanced 4—Expert
	L5: Chief Information Assurance Engineer, Chief Software Engineer	4—Expert

(continued)

Table E.2 *Continued*

KA	Unit	Knowledge/Skill/Effectiveness	Behavioral Indicators
		Job Titles	
Assurance Assessment	Assurance Assessment Concepts	L1: Acceptance Tester, Junior Information Assurance Engineer, Programmer 1	1—Basic 2—Intermediate
		L2: Information Assurance Analyst, Information Assurance Engineer, Maintenance Engineer, Programmer 2, QA Engineer, Release Engineer, Software Developer, Software Implementer, Support Engineer, Integration Engineer, Test Engineer	2—Intermediate 3—Advanced
		L3: Application Security Analyst, Application Security Engineer, Consultant, Consulting Architect, Consulting Engineer, Information Assurance Architect, Programmer 3, Requirements Engineer, Software Architect, Software Manager, Software Team Lead, Senior Information Assurance Engineer, Senior Programmer, Senior Software Analyst, Senior Software Developer, Senior Software Engineer, Application Security Architect, Security Control Assessor	3—Advanced
		L4: Information Assurance Manager, Lead Software Engineer, Principal Information Assurance Engineer, Principal Software Engineer, Product Manager, Project Manager, Senior Software Architect	3—Advanced 4—Expert
		L5: Chief Information Assurance Engineer, Chief Software Engineer	4—Expert

Measurement for Assessing Assurance	L1: Acceptance Tester, Junior Information Assurance Engineer, Programmer 1	1—Basic
		2—Intermediate
	L2: Information Assurance Analyst, Information Assurance Engineer, Maintenance Engineer, Programmer 2, QA Engineer, Release Engineer, Software Developer, Software Implementer, Support Engineer, Integration Engineer, Test Engineer	2—Intermediate
		3—Advanced
	L3: Application Security Analyst, Application Security Engineer, Consultant, Consultant Architect, Consulting Engineer, Information Assurance Architect, Programmer 3, Requirements Engineer, Software Architect, Software Manager, Software Team Lead, Senior Information Assurance Engineer, Senior Programmer, Senior Software Analyst, Senior Software Developer, Senior Software Engineer, Application Security Architect, Security Control Assessor	3—Advanced
	L4: Information Assurance Manager, Lead Software Engineer, Principal Information Assurance Engineer, Principal Software Engineer, Product Manager, Project Manager, Senior Software Architect	3—Advanced
		4—Expert
	L5: Chief Information Assurance Engineer, Chief Software Engineer	4—Expert

(continued)

Table E.2 *Continued*

KA	Unit	Knowledge/Skill/Effectiveness		Behavioral Indicators
		Job Titles		
Assurance Assessment	Assurance Assessment Process	L1: Acceptance Tester, Junior Information Assurance Engineer, Programmer 1		1—Basic 2—Intermediate
		L2: Information Assurance Analyst, Information Assurance Engineer, Maintenance Engineer, Programmer 2, QA Engineer, Release Engineer, Software Developer, Software Implementer, Support Engineer, Integration Engineer, Test Engineer		2—Intermediate 3—Advanced
		L3: Application Security Analyst, Application Security Engineer, Consultant, Consultant Architect, Consulting Engineer, Information Assurance Architect, Programmer 3, Requirements Engineer, Software Architect, Software Manager, Software Team Lead, Senior Information Assurance Engineer, Senior Programmer, Senior Software Analyst, Senior Software Developer, Senior Software Engineer, Application Security Architect, Security Control Assessor		3—Advanced
		L4: Information Assurance Manager, Lead Software Engineer, Principal Information Assurance Engineer, Principal Software Engineer, Product Manager, Project Manager, Senior Software Architect		3—Advanced 4—Expert
		L5: Chief Information Assurance Engineer, Chief Software Engineer		4—Expert

Assurance Management			
Making the Business Case for Assurance	L1: Junior Information Assurance Engineer	1—Basic	2—Intermediate
	L2: Information Assurance Analyst, Information Assurance Engineer	2—Intermediate	3—Advanced
	L3: Application Security Analyst, Application Security Engineer, Consultant, Consultant Architect, Consulting Engineer, Information Assurance Architect, Requirements Engineer, Software Architect, Senior Information Assurance Engineer, Senior Programmer, Senior Software Analyst, Senior Software Developer, Application Security Architect	3—Advanced	
	L4: Information Assurance Manager, Principal Information Assurance Engineer, Principal Software Engineer, Product Manager, Project Manager, Senior Software Architect	3—Advanced	4—Expert
	L5: Chief Information Assurance Engineer, Chief Software Engineer	4—Expert	
Managing Assurance	L1: Acceptance Tester, Junior Information Assurance Engineer	1—Basic	2—Intermediate
	L2: Application Security Analyst, Application Security Engineer, Information Assurance Analyst, Information Assurance Engineer, Maintenance Engineer, QA Engineer, Release Engineer, Software Implementer	2—Intermediate	3—Advanced

(continued)

Table E.2 *Continued*

KA	Unit	Knowledge/Skill/Effectiveness — Job Titles	Behavioral Indicators
Assurance Management		L3: Consultant Architect, Consulting Engineer, Information Assurance Architect, Programmer 3, Requirements Engineer, Software Architect, Software Manager, Software Team Lead, Senior Information Assurance Engineer, Senior Programmer, Senior Software Analyst, Senior Software Developer, Senior Software Engineer, Application Security Architect	3—Advanced
		L4: Information Assurance Manager, Lead Software Engineer, Principal Information Assurance Engineer, Principal Software Engineer, Product Manager, Project Manager, Senior Software Architect	3⁻—Advanced; 4—Expert
		L5: Chief Information Assurance Engineer, Chief Software Engineer	4—Expert
	Compliance Considerations for Assurance	L1: Junior Information Assurance Engineer	1—Basic; 2—Intermediate
		L2: Application Security Analyst, Application Security Engineer, Information Assurance Analyst, Information Assurance Engineer	2—Intermediate; 3—Advanced
		L3: Consultant Architect, Consulting Engineer, Information Assurance Architect, Programmer 3, Requirements Engineer, Software Architect, Software Manager, Software Team Lead, Senior Information Assurance Engineer, Senior Programmer, Senior Software Analyst, Senior Software Developer, Senior Software Engineer, Application Security Architect	3⁻—Advanced

System Security Assurance		L4: Information Assurance Manager, Lead Software Engineer, Principal Information Assurance Engineer, Principal Software Engineer, Product Manager, Project Manager, Senior Software Architect	3—Advanced 4—Expert
		L5: Chief Information Assurance Engineer, Chief Software Engineer	4—Expert
	For Newly Developed and Acquired Software for Diverse Applications	L1: Acceptance Tester, Junior Information Assurance Engineer, Programmer 1	1—Basic 2—Intermediate
		L2: Application Security Analyst, Application Security Engineer, Information Assurance Analyst, Information Assurance Engineer, Maintenance Engineer, Programmer 2, QA Engineer, Release Engineer, Software Developer, Software Implementer, Support Engineer, Integration Engineer, Test Engineer	2—Intermediate 3—Advanced
		L3: Consultant Architect, Consulting Engineer, Information Assurance Architect, Programmer 3, Requirements Engineer, Software Architect, Software Manager, Software Team Lead, Senior Information Assurance Engineer, Senior Programmer, Senior Software Analyst, Senior Software Developer, Senior Software Engineer, Application Security Architect, Security Control Assessor	3—Advanced

(continued)

Table E.2 *Continued*

KA	Unit	Knowledge/Skill/Effectiveness		Behavioral Indicators
		Job Titles		
		L4: Information Assurance Manager, Lead Software Engineer, Principal Information Assurance Engineer, Principal Software Engineer, Product Manager, Project Manager, Senior Software Architect		3—Advanced 4—Expert
		L5: Chief Information Assurance Engineer, Chief Software Engineer		4—Expert
System Security Assurance	For Diverse Operational (Existing) Systems	L1: Acceptance Tester, Junior Information Assurance Engineer, Programmer 1		1—Basic 2—Intermediate
		L2: Application Security Analyst, Application Security Engineer, Information Assurance Analyst, Information Assurance Engineer, Maintenance Engineer, Programmer 2, QA Engineer, Release Engineer, Software Developer, Software Implementer, Support Engineer, Integration Engineer, Test Engineer		2—Intermediate 3—Advanced
		L3: Consultant Architect, Consulting Engineer, Information Assurance Architect, Programmer 3, Requirements Engineer, Software Architect, Software Manager, Software Team Lead, Senior Information Assurance Engineer, Senior Programmer, Senior Software Analyst, Senior Software Developer, Senior Software Engineer, Application Security Architect, Security Control Assessor		3—Advanced

Knowledge Area	Level	Roles	Proficiency
	L4	Information Assurance Manager, Lead Software Engineer, Principal Information Assurance Engineer, Principal Software Engineer, Product Manager, Project Manager, Senior Software Architect	3—Advanced 4—Expert
	L5	Chief Information Assurance Engineer, Chief Software Engineer	4—Expert
Ethics and Integrity in Creation, Acquisition, and Operation of Software Systems	L1	Acceptance Tester, Junior Information Assurance Engineer, Programmer 1	1—Basic 2—Intermediate
	L2	Application Security Analyst, Application Security Engineer, Information Assurance Analyst, Information Assurance Engineer, Maintenance Engineer, Programmer 2, QA Engineer, Release Engineer, Software Developer, Software Implementer, Support Engineer, Integration Engineer, Test Engineer	2—Intermediate 3—Advanced
	L3	Consultant Architect, Consulting Engineer, Information Assurance Architect, Programmer 3, Requirements Engineer, Software Architect, Software Manager, Software Team Lead, Senior Information Assurance Engineer, Senior Programmer, Senior Software Analyst, Senior Software Developer, Senior Software Engineer, Application Security Architect, Security Control Assessor	3—Advanced
	L4	Information Assurance Manager, Lead Software Engineer, Principal Information Assurance Engineer, Principal Software Engineer, Product Manager, Project Manager, Senior Software Architect	3—Advanced 4—Expert
	L5	Chief Information Assurance Engineer, Chief Software Engineer	4—Expert

(continued)

Table E.2 *Continued*

KA	Unit	Knowledge/Skill/Effectiveness Job Titles	Behavioral Indicators
	Assurance Technology	L1: Acceptance Tester, Junior Information Assurance Engineer, Programmer 1	1—Basic 2—Intermediate
		L2: Application Security Analyst, Application Security Engineer, Consultant, Information Assurance Analyst, Information Assurance Engineer, Maintenance Engineer, Programmer 2, QA Engineer, Release Engineer, Software Developer, Software Implementer, Support Engineer, Integration Engineer, Test Engineer	2—Intermediate 3—Advanced
		L3: Consultant Architect, Consulting Engineer, Information Assurance Architect, Programmer 3, Requirements Engineer, Software Architect, Software Manager, Software Team Lead, Senior Information Assurance Engineer, Senior Programmer, Senior Software Analyst, Senior Software Developer, Senior Software Engineer, Application Security Architect, Security Control Assessor	3—Advanced
		L4: Information Assurance Manager, Lead Software Engineer, Principal Information Assurance Engineer, Principal Software Engineer, Product Manager, Project Manager, Senior Software Architect	3—Advanced 4—Expert
		L5: Chief Information Assurance Engineer, Chief Software Engineer	4—Expert

System Functionality Assurance

	Roles	Level
Assured Software Development	L1: Acceptance Tester, Junior Information Assurance Engineer, Programmer 1	1—Basic 2—Intermediate
	L2: Application Security Analyst, Application Security Engineer, Consultant, Information Assurance Analyst, Information Assurance Engineer, Maintenance Engineer, Programmer 2, QA Engineer, Release Engineer, Software Developer, Software Implementer, Support Engineer, Integration Engineer, Test Engineer	2—Intermediate 3—Advanced
	L3: Consultant Architect, Consulting Engineer, Information Assurance Architect, Programmer 3, Requirements Engineer, Software Architect, Software Manager, Software Team Lead, Senior Information Assurance Engineer, Senior Programmer, Senior Software Analyst, Senior Software Developer, Senior Software Engineer, Application Security Architect, Security Control Assessor	3—Advanced
	L4: Information Assurance Manager, Lead Software Engineer, Principal Information Assurance Engineer, Principal Software Engineer, Product Manager, Project Manager, Senior Software Architect	3—Advanced 4—Expert
	L5: Chief Information Assurance Engineer, Chief Software Engineer	4—Expert

(continued)

Table E.2 *Continued*

KA	Unit	Knowledge/Skill/Effectiveness		Behavioral Indicators
		Job Titles		
System Functionality Assurance	Assurance Technology	L1: Acceptance Tester, Junior Information Assurance Engineer, Programmer 1		1—Basic 2—Intermediate
		L2: Application Security Analyst, Application Security Engineer, Information Assurance Analyst, Information Assurance Engineer, Maintenance Engineer, Programmer 2, QA Engineer, Release Engineer, Software Developer, Software Implementer, Support Engineer, Integration Engineer, Test Engineer		2—Intermediate 3—Advanced
		L3: Consultant Architect, Consulting Engineer, Information Assurance Architect, Programmer 3, Requirements Engineer, Software Architect, Software Manager, Software Team Lead, Senior Information Assurance Engineer, Senior Programmer, Senior Software Analyst, Senior Software Developer, Senior Software Engineer, Application Security Architect		3—Advanced
		L4: Information Assurance Manager, Lead Software Engineer, Principal Information Assurance Engineer, Principal Software Engineer, Product Manager, Project Manager, Senior Software Architect		3—Advanced 4—Expert
		L5: Chief Information Assurance Engineer, Chief Software Engineer		4—Expert

Assurance in Acquisition	L1: Acceptance Tester, Junior Information Assurance Engineer, Programmer 1	1—Basic 2—Intermediate
	L2: Information Assurance Analyst, Information Assurance Engineer, Maintenance Engineer, Programmer 2, QA Engineer, Release Engineer, Software Developer, Software Implementer, Support Engineer, Integration Engineer, Test Engineer	2—Intermediate 3—Advanced
	L3: Application Security Analyst, Application Security Engineer, Consultant, Consultant Architect, Consulting Engineer, Information Assurance Architect, Programmer 3, Requirements Engineer, Software Architect, Software Manager, Software Team Lead, Senior Information Assurance Engineer, Senior Programmer, Senior Software Analyst, Senior Software Developer, Senior Software Engineer, Application Security Architect	3—Advanced
	L4: Information Assurance Manager, Lead Software Engineer, Principal Information Assurance Engineer, Principal Software Engineer, Product Manager, Project Manager, Senior Software Architect	3—Advanced 4—Expert
	L5: Chief Information Assurance Engineer, Chief Software Engineer	4—Expert

Table E.2 *Continued*

KA	Unit	Knowledge/Skill/Effectiveness — Job Titles	Behavioral Indicators
System Operational Assurance	Operational Procedures	L1: Junior Information Assurance Engineer	1—Basic 2—Intermediate
		L2: Information Assurance Analyst, Information Assurance Engineer, Maintenance Engineer, QA Engineer, Release Engineer, Support Engineer	2—Intermediate 3—Advanced
		L3: Application Security Analyst, Application Security Engineer, Consulting Engineer, Software Manager, Software Team Lead, Senior Information Assurance Engineer	3—Advanced
		L4: Information Assurance Manager, Principal Information Assurance Engineer, Principal Software Engineer, Product Manager, Project Manager	3—Advanced 4—Expert
		L5: Chief Information Assurance Engineer, Chief Software Engineer	4—Expert
	Operational Monitoring	L1: Junior Information Assurance Engineer	1—Basic 2—Intermediate
		L2: Information Assurance Analyst, Information Assurance Engineer, Maintenance Engineer, Programmer 2, QA Engineer, Release Engineer, Software Developer, Software Implementer, Support Engineer, Integration Engineer, Test Engineer	2—Intermediate 3—Advanced

Category	Level / Roles	Proficiency
	L3: Application Security Analyst, Application Security Engineer, Consultant, Consultant Architect, Consulting Engineer, Information Assurance Architect, Programmer 3, Requirements Engineer, Software Architect, Software Manager, Software Team Lead, Senior Information Assurance Engineer, Senior Programmer, Senior Software Analyst, Senior Software Developer, Senior Software Engineer, Application Security Architect	3—Advanced
	L4: Information Assurance Manager, Lead Software Engineer, Principal Information Assurance Engineer, Principal Software Engineer, Product Manager, Project Manager, Senior Software Architect	3—Advanced 4—Expert
	L5: Chief Information Assurance Engineer, Chief Software Engineer	4—Expert
System Control	L1: Junior Information Assurance Engineer	1—Basic 2—Intermediate
	L2: Information Assurance Analyst, Information Assurance Engineer, Maintenance Engineer, Support Engineer	2—Intermediate 3—Advanced
	L3: Application Security Analyst, Application Security Engineer, Consulting Engineer, Information Assurance Architect, Software Manager, Senior Information Assurance Engineer, Senior Programmer, Senior Software Analyst, Senior Software Engineer, Application Security Architect, Security Control Assessor	3—Advanced
	L4: Information Assurance Manager, Lead Software Engineer, Principal Information Assurance Engineer, Principal Software Engineer	3—Advanced 4—Expert
	L5: Chief Information Assurance Engineer, Chief Software Engineer	4—Expert

References

[Hilburn 2013]

Hilburn, Thomas B.; Ardis, Mark A.; Johnson, Glenn; Komecki, Andrew J.; & Mead, Nancy R. *Software Assurance Competency Model.* CMU/SEI-2013-TN-004. Software Engineering Institute, Carnegie Mellon University. 2013. http://resources.sei.cmu.edu/library/asset-view.cfm?assetid=47953.

Appendix F

BSIMM Assessment Final Report

April 1, 2016

Prepared for:
FakeFirm
123 Fake Street
Anytown, USA 12345

Prepared by:
Cigital, Inc.
21351 Ridgetop Circle
Suite 400
Dulles, VA 20166

Cigital, Inc.

21351 Ridgetop Circle
Suite 400
Dulles, VA 20166
Phone: + 1 (703) 404-9293

www.cigital.com

Table of Contents

List of Figures

Preface

Purpose

This document contains Cigital's final report on the FakeFirm BSIMM assessment.

Audience

This document is intended for FakeFirm employees who will lead the software security group (SSG) and related software security initiative (SSI) activities.

Contacts

The following are the primary Cigital staff to contact with questions regarding this assessment.

Contact	Title	Contact	Email Address
M. Consultant	Managing Consultant	703-555-1212	mconsultant@cigital.com
Sammy Migues	Principal	703-404-5830	smigues@cigital.com
M. Principal	Managing Principal	703-555-1212	mprincipal@cigital.com

1 Executive Summary

The Building Security In Maturity Model (BSIMM) is a unique tool built from our observation-based approach to capturing the collective activities in diverse software security initiatives (SSIs). An SSI is an executive-sponsored, proactive effort comprising all activities aimed at building, acquiring, running, and maintaining secure software. It establishes a formal ability to balance the risk and cost associated with software engineering processes to ensure the firm meets business objectives safely. In addition, an SSI ensures a firm's software routinely meets applicable regulatory, statutory, and audit requirements while also ensuring clients can meet theirs when using the firm's software.

To build BSIMM, we initiated data research and analysis in 2008 by assessing software security efforts in nine firms and using those results to create BSIMM1. As of September 2015, we've performed BSIMM assessments for 104 firms of various sizes in diverse vertical markets. In that time, we continually adjusted the model to reflect our real-world observations, adding or moving activities to reflect current reality. Over time, we also drop old data to keep the model fresh. Therefore, the BSIMM stands as the only useful and current reflection of actual practices in software security.

There are 78 firms represented in BSIMM6. As a confirmation of BSIMM's usefulness, 26 of those firms have had two BSIMM assessments and 10 have had three or more assessments. Though initiatives differ in some details, all share common ground that the BSIMM captures and describes. It therefore functions as a universal yardstick, capable of measuring any SSI and facilitating strategic planning by the SSI leadership. As a general term, we call these SSI leaders the software security group (SSG).

Figure F.1 below shows the Software Security Framework (SSF) we use as the BSIMM foundation. It includes four broad domains of Governance, Intelligence, SSDL Touchpoints, and Deployment. See Appendix A: BSIMM Background for additional detail on BSIMM history and the SSF domains.

Within the four SSF domains are 12 practices (e.g., Strategy & Metrics) that collectively contain the 112 software security activities in BSIMM6. Within each practice, we divide these activities into three levels based primarily on observation frequency across all participants. See Appendix B: BSIMM Activities for summaries of each practice, including the activities and their assigned levels. We provide comprehensive activity descriptions in the BSIMM report at http://bsimm.com. Because BSIMM is an observational model and records our research, the activity set it contains changes over time.

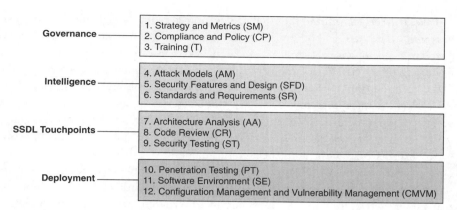

Figure F.1 *BSIMM Software Security Framework*

Any such attestation-based, time-limited engagement will prevent detailed business process analysis. However, it is important to understand that a BSIMM scorecard is neither an audit finding nor a report card. It is simply a snapshot of current software security effort through the BSIMM lens. Part of its value lies in the fact that, as of BSIMM6, we have conducted 235 assessments in the same manner, making all the results over time directly comparable to each other.

In this assessment for FakeFirm, Cigital interviewed individuals representing various software security roles. In some cases, we also reviewed artifacts that clarified a given topic. Our team then analyzed the resulting data until reaching unanimous agreement on whether we observed in FakeFirm's environment each of the 112 BSIMM6 activities. Given a final list of observations, we were able to produce the data representations provided in this report. This knowledge helps SSG owners understand where their initiative stands with respect to other real-world SSIs and clarifies possible strategic steps to mature the firm's efforts.

For this April 2016 BSIMM assessment, Cigital interviewed 11 individuals. At this time, the software security group (SSG), known in FakeFirm as the Application Security Team (AST), has been active for about two years and includes five full-time people. The AST leader has the following reporting chain to FakeFirm's CEO: Director (AST Lead) → CISO → CIO → CEO. There are currently six people in the AST's satellite, referred to as "S-SDLC Risk Managers." The AST and Risk Managers support 850 developers in creating, acquiring, and maintaining a portfolio of 250 applications. FakeFirm uses a spreadsheet to track the software portfolio and the inventory is currently incomplete.

FakeFirm has centralized the AST in a corporate group outside the various business units. The AST embodies its high-level approach to software security governance in a documented secure SDLC with two software security gates, one at beginning of the SDLC to establish testing expectations and one at the end of the SDLC to do testing. However, adherence to the gates is voluntary at this time. The AST supplements the secure SDLC with policies and standards, including some secure coding standards. It works directly with Legal, Risk, and Compliance groups to ensure the FakeFirm also meets privacy and compliance objectives related to software. It also works with IT to specify and maintain operating system, server, and device security controls. New developers, testers, and architects receive software security training via a brief in-person session during onboarding. The AST does outreach to executives and other groups, but only through informal meetings and data sharing.

The AST works directly with engineering teams to discover software security defects through architecture analysis, penetration testing, and static analysis. While the AST manages these efforts centrally, much of the labor is out-sourced. The AST usually enhances such testing by taking advantage of attack intelligence. Processes ensure most security defects receive an assigned a severity level and the AST tracks those security defects scheduled for remediation.

Other important SSI characteristics include:

- A relatively mature static source code analysis process that uses customized rules
- A mature process to capture information about attacks against FakeFirm software and create developer training
- Black-box security testing for Web applications embedded in the quality assurance process, helping to ensure security defects are caught during the development cycle
- Service-level agreement boilerplate for software security responsibilities, but limited use in vendor contracts
- Data classification that is informal and effectively equates to "everything is important"

From FakeFirm's software security efforts summarized above, Cigital observed 37 BSIMM activities in this assessment. Figure F.2 shows in dark gray (blue in eBook) the distribution of the observed activities across the 12 SSF practices, normalized to a 100% scale. For example, if we observed half of the activities in a given practice, the chart would display that as 50%. To allow for comparison, the light gray (orange in eBook) area shows the normalized averages for the entire BSIMM6 participant pool.

To aid in visualization, Figure F.3 below shows the same data, but as a bar chart.

Recall that the SSF shown in Figure F.1 above forms the BSIMM foundation. The SSF comprises 12 practices, each of which contains several BSIMM activities, for a total of 112. After a BSIMM assessment, we create a scorecard showing the number of activities observed out of 112 (37 for this assessment). To allow comparisons, Figure F.4 shows the distribution of scores for the 78 firms in the BSIMM6 data pool along with the average age of the SSIs in each group.

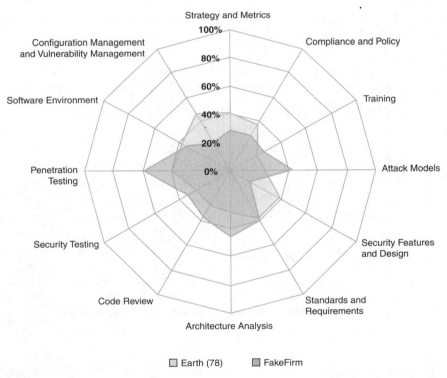

Figure F.2 *Normalized Percentage of Activities Observed in each BSIMM Practice (Spider)*

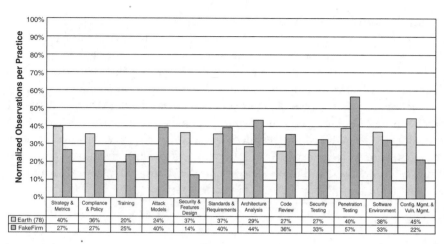

Figure F.3 *Normalized Percentage of Activities Observed in each BSIMM Practice (Bar)*

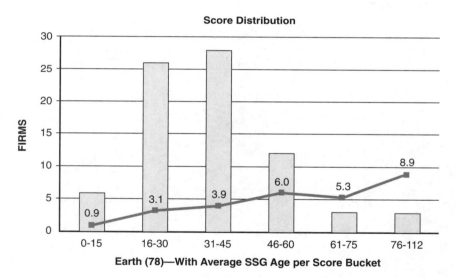

Figure F.4 *BSIMM6 Assessment Score Distribution*

From a planning perspective, our experience shows that it is better to have a well-rounded effort distributed across the SSF practices. It is also important to remember that we have never observed all 112 activities in a single firm and such a feat is probably not a reasonable goal. A firm should always base activity selection—resource allocation in the SSI—on actual need.

While a BSIMM assessment provides an unbiased inventory of the software security activities underway, this targeted review alone cannot provide a complete measurement of SSI sufficiency or effectiveness. That requires additional data and analysis.

In the following sections, Cigital provides additional representations of Fake-Firm's BSIMM assessment results. FakeFirm can use these results and accompanying recommendations to guide SSI improvements.

2 Data Gathering

A BSIMM assessment objectively creates a scorecard depicting current software security activity, thereby facilitating internal analysis, decision support, and budgeting. To gather this information, Cigital conducts interviews to get a detailed understanding of FakeFirm's approach to and execution of its SSI. Cigital may also review artifacts that explain important software security processes. Cigital then analyzes the resulting data to give credit in a BSIMM scorecard for each software security activity observed out of 112.

Typically, we conduct our primary interviews with the SSG owner and one or more of his or her direct reports. We usually follow this with interviews of others directly involved in planning, instantiating, or executing the SSI. These individuals may be in any of several roles, including SSG executive sponsor, business analysis, architecture, development, testing, operations, audit, risk, and compliance.

For this BSIMM assessment, Cigital interviewed the following individuals:

- Person, CIO
- Person, CISO and SSG Leader
- Person, SSG member
- Person, SSG member
- Person, SSG member
- Person, Security Architecture Head
- Person, Security Operations Head
- Person, Quality Assurance Head
- Person, Mobile Development Head
- Person, Web Development Head
- Person, Risk, and Compliance

3 High-Water Mark

As seen in Appendix B: BSIMM Activities, each of the 112 BSIMM6 activities is assigned a level of 1, 2, or 3. Cigital used interview data to create a scorecard and then chart the highest level activity—the "high-water mark"—observed in each of the twelve BSIMM practices. We assign the high-water mark with a very simple algorithm. If we observed a level 3 activity in a given practice, we assign a "3" without regard for whether level 2 or 1 activities were also observed. We assigned a high-water mark of 2, 1, or 0 similarly.

Figure F.5 below compares FakeFirm high-water marks with the average high-water marks for the BSIMM6 participant pool. Because the spider diagram shows only a single data point per practice, it is a very low-resolution view of software security effort. However, this view provides useful comparisons between firms, between business units, and within the same firm over time.

Figure F.5 *High-Water Mark per Practice Compared to Average of 78 BSIMM6 Firms*

The light gray line with boxes (green in eBook) depicts the average high-water marks from 0 to 3 achieved by BSIMM6 participants.
The dark gray line with diamonds (blue in eBook) depicts the high-water marks from 0 to 3 achieved by FakeFirm.

Compared to the average high-water marks of all BSIMM6 participants, FakeFirm marks appear above the average in Training, Attack Models, Architecture Analysis, Code Review, and Penetration Testing. FakeFirm marks appear near the average in Compliance & Policy, Standards & Requirements, Security Testing, Software Environment, and Configuration Management & Vulnerability Management. FakeFirm marks appear below the average in Strategy & Metrics and in Security Features & Design.

4 BSIMM Practices

Recall that the spider diagram in Figure F.5 above shows only the high-water mark level reached in each BSIMM practice. While useful for comparing groups or visualizing change over time, performing a single high-level activity in a practice—and few or no other activities—skews the spider diagram such that it may not accurately reflect true effort within a given practice.

To overcome this and facilitate additional analysis, the two diagrams below provide a higher resolution view of the 37 BSIMM6 activities observed at FakeFirm. This type of diagram makes evident the "activity density" by showing the observed activities segregated vertically into their respective practices and then horizontally into their respective levels.

Figure F.6 below facilitates analysis by practice to clarify where Cigital may have observed higher-level activities with few or no associated lower-level activities. From a vertical practice perspective, FakeFirm achieved a high-water mark of "3" in two practices: Code Review and Penetration Testing. In Penetration Testing, we also observed a majority of lower level activities, indicating practice maturity, but we did not observe such a majority of lower level activities in Code Review. Similarly, FakeFirm achieved a high-water mark of "2" in eight practices and here we observed a majority of lower level activities in four practices, with Training, Attack Models, Software Environment, and Configuration Management & Vulnerability Management being the exceptions. We observed a majority of activities in one of the two practices where FakeFirm achieved a high-water mark of "1," with Security Features & Design being the exception.

Figure F.7 below facilitates analysis by level to highlight where the current SSI does not include foundational level 1 activities. From a horizontal software security foundation perspective, we observed activities in all practices at level 1, but we did not observe a majority of level 1 activities in Training, Attack Models, Security Features & Design, Software Environment, and Configuration Management & Vulnerability Management. We observed level 2 activities in nine of 12 practices; however, we observed only a single level 2 activity in nearly every practice, with Standards & Requirements being the exception. For the two practices where we observed a level 3 activity, each has a single observation.

To facilitate an additional level of analysis, Cigital provides below the assessment scorecard containing data on each of the activities observed as well as comparable observation data from other firms.

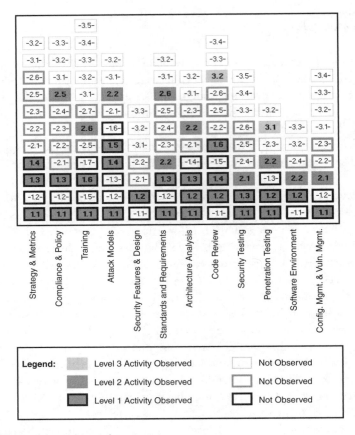

Figure F.6 *Activities Observed per Practice*

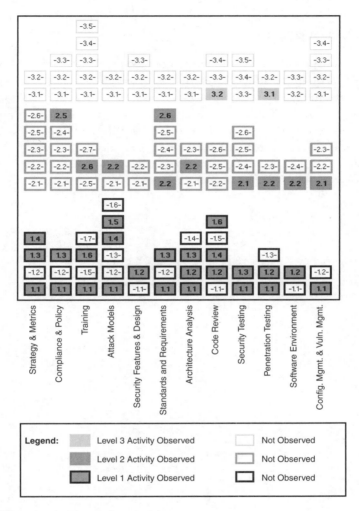

Figure F.7 *Activities Observed per Level*

5 BSIMM Scorecard

Figure F.8 below provides detailed information about FakeFirm's SSI. Primarily, it lists in the four columns marked "FakeFirm" the 37 activities Cigital observed during this assessment. In the "BSIMM6 Firms" columns, the scorecard provides the count of firms (out of 78) in which Cigital observed each activity. See the table on the following page for more explanation. In addition, see Appendix B: BSIMM Activities for the short name associated with each BSIMM activity (e.g., SM1.3 is "Educate executives").

BSIMM6 Scorecard for: FakeFirm   **Observations: 37**

GOVERNANCE			INTELLIGENCE			SSDL TOUCHPOINTS			DEPLOYMENT		
ACTIVITY	BSIMM6 FIRMS	FakeFirm	ACTIVITY	BSIMM6 FIRMS	FakeFirm	ACTIVITY	BSIMM6 FIRMS	FakeFirm	ACTIVITY	BSIMM6 FIRMS	FakeFirm
Strategy and Metrics			**Attack Models**			**Architecture Analysis**			**Penetration Testing**		
[SM1.1]	41	1	[AM1.1]	17	1	[AA1.1]	67	1	[PT1.1]	69	1
[SM1.2]	40		[AM1.2]	51		[AA1.2]	29	1	[PT1.2]	47	1
[SM1.3]	36	1	[AM1.3]	31		[AA1.3]	22	1	[PT1.3]	47	
[SM1.4]	66	1	[AM1.4]	8	1	[AA1.4]	46		[PT2.2]	20	1
[SM2.1]	36		[AM1.5]	46	1	[AA2.1]	12		[PT2.3]	17	
[SM2.2]	29		[AM1.6]	11		[AA2.2]	9	1	[PT3.1]	10	1
[SM2.3]	30		[AM2.1]	6		[AA2.3]	13		[PT3.2]	8	
[SM2.5]	17		[AM2.2]	8	1	[AA3.1]	6				
[SM2.6]	29		[AM3.1]	4		[AA3.2]	1				
[SM3.1]	15		[AM3.2]	2							
[SM3.2]	7										
Compliance and Policy			**Security Features and Design**			**Code Review**			**Software Environment**		
[CP1.1]	45	1	[SFD1.1]	61		[CR1.1]	18		[SE1.1]	37	
[CP1.2]	61		[SFD1.2]	59	1	[CR1.2]	53	1	[SE1.2]	69	1
[CP1.3]	41	1	[SFD2.1]	24		[CR1.4]	55	1	[SE2.2]	31	1
[CP2.1]	19		[SFD2.2]	39		[CR1.5]	24		[SE2.4]	25	
[CP2.2]	23		[SFD3.1]	8		[CR1.6]	27	1	[SE3.2]	10	
[CP2.3]	25		[SFD3.2]	11		[CR2.2]	7		[SE3.3]	5	
[CP2.4]	29		[SFD3.3]	2		[CR2.5]	20				
[CP2.5]	33	1				[CR2.6]	16				
[CP3.1]	18					[CR3.2]	3	1			
[CP3.2]	11					[CR3.3]	5				
[CP3.3]	6					[CR3.4]	3				
Training			**Standards and Requirements**			**Security Testing**			**Config. Mgmt. and Vuln. Mgmt.**		
[T1.1]	59	1	[SR1.1]	57	1	[ST1.1]	61	1	[CMVM1.1]	71	
[T1.5]	26		[SR1.2]	50		[ST1.3]	66	1	[CMVM1.2]	73	
[T1.6]	17	1	[SR1.3]	52	1	[ST2.1]	24	1	[CMVM2.1]	64	1
[T1.7]	36		[SR2.2]	27	1	[ST2.4]	8		[CMVM2.2]	61	
[T2.5]	10		[SR2.3]	21		[ST2.5]	10		[CMVM2.3]	31	
[T2.6]	15	1	[SR2.4]	19		[ST2.6]	11		[CMVM3.1]	4	
[T2.7]	6		[SR2.5]	20		[ST3.3]	4		[CMVM3.2]	6	
[T3.1]	3		[SR2.6]	23	1	[ST3.4]	4		[CMVM3.3]	6	
[T3.2]	3		[SR3.1]	6		[ST3.5]	5		[CMVM3.4]	3	
[T3.3]	3		[SR3.2]	11							
[T3.4]	8										
[T3.5]	4										

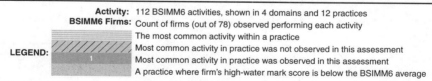

Activity: 112 BSIMM6 activities, shown in 4 domains and 12 practices
BSIMM6 Firms: Count of firms (out of 78) observed performing each activity
The most common activity within a practice
LEGEND:
Most common activity in practice was not observed in this assessment
Most common activity in practice was observed in this assessment
A practice where firm's high-water mark score is below the BSIMM6 average

Figure F.8 *BSIMM Scorecard with Earth Data*

The following is an explanation of the scorecard shown in Figure F.8 above:

Activity columns	Lists each of the 112 activities included in BSIMM6. For names of each activity, see Appendix B or see http://bsimm.com for an interactive chart of long descriptions
BSIMM6 Firms columns	Gives the count of BSIMM6 participants in which the activity was observed, providing an indication of the prevalence of an activity in the current data pool
FakeFirm columns	Indicates with a "1" each activity observed during this assessment
▨	Highlights the most common activity in each BSIMM6 practice
▨	Indicates a common activity also observed in FakeFirm. These include: • SM1.4–Identify gate locations, gather necessary artifacts • T1.1–Provide awareness training • SR1.1–Create security standards • AA1.1–Perform security feature review • CR1.4–Use automated tools along with manual review • ST1.3–Drive tests with security requirements and security features • PT1.1–Use external penetration testers to find problems • SE1.2–Ensure host and network security basics are in place
▨	Indicates a common activity not observed in FakeFirm. In this list are: • CP1.2–Identify PII obligations • AM1.2–Create a data classification scheme and inventory • SFD1.1–Build and publish security features • CMVM1.2–Identify software bugs found in operations monitoring and feed them back to development

☐ Highlights a practice where FakeFirm has not reached the same high-water mark as the average of the current participants (i.e., where FakeFirm's high-water mark is "inside" that of the data pool average in Figure F.5 above). In this list are:

- Strategy & Metrics, Compliance & Policy, Security Features & Design, and Configuration Management & Vulnerability Management

It is important to remember that this scorecard represents Cigital's observations specific to software security activity as measured by the BSIMM. Observation—or the lack of observation—of a given activity is inherently neither good nor bad. Judging sufficiency and effectiveness for the activities observed requires a deeper analysis of FakeFirm's business objectives, processes, and software. Results of such an analysis can form a cornerstone for strategic broadening and deepening of the current SSI.

6 Comparison within Vertical

Figure F.9 below summarizes the level reached by FakeFirm in each practice and compares it to the subset of BSIMM6 participants in the financial industry (FI) vertical.

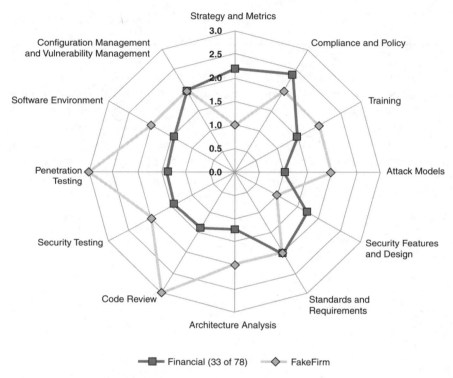

Figure F.9 *High-Water Mark per Practice Compared to Participants in a Vertical*

The dark gray line with boxes (red in eBook) depicts the average high-water marks from 0 to 3 achieved by BSIMM6 participants in a vertical.

The light gray line with triangles (blue in eBook) depicts the high-water marks from 0 to 3 achieved by FakeFirm.

Compared to the average high-water marks of all current financial industry BSIMM6 participants, FakeFirm marks appear above the average in Training, Attack Models, Architecture Analysis, Code Review, Security Testing, Penetration Testing, and Software Environment. FakeFirm marks appear near the average in Compliance & Policy, Standards & Requirements, and Configuration Management & Vulnerability Management. FakeFirm marks appear below the average in Strategy & Metrics and Security Features & Design.

Compared to the averages shown in Figure F.5 above for the entire BSIMM data pool, the most significant changes are in Strategy & Metrics, Compliance & Policy, Training, and Standards & Requirements, where the high-water mark average is higher amongst FIs than for the entire data pool (BSIMM Earth), and Software Environment, where the average is lower.

Figure F.10 below provides detailed information about FakeFirm's SSI. Primarily, it lists in the four columns marked "FakeFirm" the 37 activities Cigital observed during this assessment. In the "BSIMM6 FI" columns, the scorecard provides the count of financial firms (out of 33) in which Cigital observed each activity.

BSIMM6 Scorecard for: FakeFirm   **Observations: 37**

GOVERNANCE			INTELLIGENCE			SSDL TOUCHPOINTS			DEPLOYMENT		
ACTIVITY	BSIMM6 FIRMS	FakeFirm	ACTIVITY	BSIMM6 FIRMS	FakeFirm	ACTIVITY	BSIMM6 FIRMS	FakeFirm	ACTIVITY	BSIMM6 FIRMS	FakeFirm
Strategy and Metrics			Attack Models			Architecture Analysis			Penetration Testing		
[SM1.1]	21	1	[AM1.1]	7	1	[AA1.1]	29	1	[PT1.1]	31	1
[SM1.2]	16		[AM1.2]	27	/////	[AA1.2]	8	1	[PT1.2]	23	1
[SM1.3]	17	1	[AM1.3]	16		[AA1.3]	7	1	[PT1.3]	18	
[SM1.4]	30	1	[AM1.4]	1	1	[AA1.4]	25		[PT2.2]	3	1
[SM2.1]	19		[AM1.5]	23	1	[AA2.1]	5		[PT2.3]	6	
[SM2.2]	14		[AM1.6]	1		[AA2.2]	1	1	[PT3.1]	1	1
[SM2.3]	10		[AM2.1]	2		[AA2.3]	4		[PT3.2]	3	
[SM2.5]	12		[AM2.2]	1	1	[AA3.1]	2				
[SM2.6]	17		[AM3.1]	0		[AA3.2]	0				
[SM3.1]	10		[AM3.2]	0							
[SM3.2]	0										
Compliance and Policy			Security Features and Design			Code Review			Software Environment		
[CP1.1]	22	1	[SFD1.1]	29	/////	[CR1.1]	9		[SE1.1]	18	
[CP1.2]	25	/////	[SFD1.2]	27	1	[CR1.2]	26	1	[SE1.2]	31	1
[CP1.3]	23	1	[SFD2.1]	11		[CR1.4]	21	1	[SE2.2]	10	1
[CP2.1]	12		[SFD2.2]	15		[CR1.5]	7		[SE2.4]	5	
[CP2.2]	11		[SFD3.1]	5		[CR1.6]	13	1	[SE3.2]	0	
[CP2.3]	10		[SFD3.2]	5		[CR2.2]	2		[SE3.3]	1	
[CP2.4]	16		[SFD3.3]	0		[CR2.5]	10				
[CP2.5]	14	1				[CR2.6]	8				
[CP3.1]	16					[CR3.2]	2	1			
[CP3.2]	6					[CR3.3]	2				
[CP3.3]	3					[CR3.4]	3				
Training			Standards and Requirements			Security Testing			Config. Mgmt. and Vuln. Mgmt.		
[T1.1]	27	1	[SR1.1]	29	1	[ST1.1]	28	1	[CMVM1.1]	31	1
[T1.5]	15		[SR1.2]	23		[ST1.3]	28	1	[CMVM1.2]	31	/////
[T1.6]	6	1	[SR1.3]	21	1	[ST2.1]	13	1	[CMVM2.1]	30	1
[T1.7]	20		[SR2.2]	15	1	[ST2.4]	4		[CMVM2.2]	25	
[T2.5]	3		[SR2.3]	11		[ST2.5]	3		[CMVM2.3]	13	
[T2.6]	8	1	[SR2.4]	5		[ST2.6]	0		[CMVM3.1]	0	
[T2.7]	1		[SR2.5]	11		[ST3.3]	1		[CMVM3.2]	2	
[T3.1]	1		[SR2.6]	12	1	[ST3.4]	0		[CMVM3.3]	3	
[T3.2]	1		[SR3.1]	2		[ST3.5]	1		[CMVM3.4]	0	
[T3.3]	0		[SR3.2]	6							
[T3.4]	5										
[T3.5]	1										

Activity: 112 BSIMM6 activities, shown in 4 domains and 12 practices
BSIMM6 FIs: Count of FI firms (out of 33) observed performing each activity

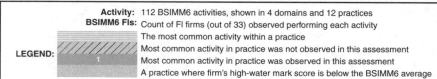

LEGEND:
The most common activity within a practice
///// Most common activity in practice was not observed in this assessment
1 Most common activity in practice was observed in this assessment
A practice where firm's high-water mark score is below the BSIMM6 average

Figure F.10 *BSIMM Scorecard with Vertical Data*

The following is an explanation of the scorecard shown in Figure F.10 above:

Activity columns	Lists each of the 112 activities included in BSIMM6. For names of each activity, see Appendix B or see http://bsimm.com for an interactive chart of long descriptions
BSIMM6 FI columns	Gives the count of BSIMM6 participants in which the activity was observed, providing an indication of the prevalence of an activity in the current data pool
FakeFirm columns	Indicates with a "1" each activity observed during this assessment
	Highlights the most common activity in each BSIMM6 practice
	Indicates a common activity also observed in FakeFirm. These include:

- SM1.4–Identify gate locations, gather necessary artifacts
- T1.1–Provide awareness training
- SR1.1–Create security standards
- AA1.1–Perform security feature review
- CR1.2–Have SSG perform ad hoc review
- ST1.3–Drive tests with security requirements and security features
- PT1.1–Use external penetration testers to find problems
- SE1.2–Ensure host and network security basics are in place

Indicates a common activity not observed in FakeFirm. In this list are:

- CP1.2–Identify PII obligations
- AM1.2–Create a data classification scheme and inventory
- SFD1.1–Build and publish security features
- CMVM1.2–Identify software bugs found in operations monitoring and feed them back to development

(continued)

	Highlights a practice where FakeFirm has not reached the same high-water mark as the average of the current participants (i.e., where FakeFirm's high-water mark is "inside" that of the data pool average in Figure F.9 above). In this list are:

- Strategy & Metrics, Compliance & Policy, Security Features & Design, Configuration Management & Vulnerability Management

7 Conclusion

FakeFirm is performing the single most important activity related to improving software security: it has a dedicated software security group that can get resources and drive organizational change.

Compared to the average high-water marks of all BSIMM6 participants, FakeFirm marks appear above the average in Training, Attack Models, Architecture Analysis, Code Review, and Penetration Testing. FakeFirm marks appear near the average in Compliance & Policy, Standards & Requirements, Security Testing, Software Environment, and Configuration Management & Vulnerability Management. FakeFirm marks appear below the average in Strategy & Metrics and in Security Features & Design.

From a vertical practice perspective, FakeFirm achieved a high-water mark of "3" in two practices: Code Review and Penetration Testing. In Penetration Testing, we also observed a majority of lower level activities, indicating true practice maturity, but we did not observe such a majority of lower level activities in Code Review. Similarly, FakeFirm achieved a high-water mark of "2" in eight practices and here we observed a majority of lower level activities in four practices, with Training, Attack Models, Software Environment, and Configuration Management & Vulnerability Management being the exceptions. We observed a majority of activities in one of the two practices where FakeFirm achieved a high-water mark of "1," with Security Features & Design being the exception.

From a horizontal software security foundation perspective, we observed activities in all practices at level 1, but we did not observe a majority of level 1 activities in Training, Attack Models, Security Features & Design, Software Environment, and Configuration Management & Vulnerability Management. We observed level 2 activities in nine of 12 practices; however, we observed only a single level 2 activity in nearly every practice, with Standards & Requirements being the exception. For the two practices where we observed a level 3 activity, each has a single observation.

Using the BSIMM assessment data, FakeFirm might choose one or more of the following to broaden and deepen its SSI:

- Determine whether it is appropriate to begin doing the remaining four activities (those marked with slashes in Figure F.8) from the 12 common activities.

- Perform a more complete risk, compliance, and needs analysis for the SSI. These results of such an analysis can drive the larger strategy for comprehensive top-down enhancements.

- Perform a software security business process analysis focusing on sufficiency, efficiency, and maturity. The results of such an analysis can drive tactical changes that increase effectiveness and reduce cost.

- Commission a detailed analysis of a set of SDLC artifacts, such as the requirements, design, code, and deployed module for one or more critical applications. Determining the root causes (e.g., lack of a given BSIMM activity) for the software security defects discovered can drive targeted bottom-up SSI enhancements.

Independent of the general choices above and based on our experience in similar environments, we recommend FakeFirm consider the following when choosing its next set of SSI improvements.

- Secure SDLC—FakeFirm has created an SDLC overlay that includes two security gates, one for "Permit to Build" and one for "Permit to Deploy." However, the SSG is not involved in all development projects. In addition, the software security gates are voluntary even in large, critical projects. Over the next 12 months, FakeFirm should institute process improvements that ensure the SSG is aware of all development and software acquisition projects worldwide. At the same time, FakeFirm should phase in mandatory compliance with various aspects of the SDLC security gates. For example, mandatory remediation of critical security defects within a given timeframe could be required immediately, while phasing in remediation of high and medium security defects over a period of months. Similarly, static analysis and penetration testing should quickly become mandatory for all critical applications, and should become mandatory for all applications over the next 12-18 months.

- Inventory—FakeFirm does not have a robust inventory of applications, PII, or open source software. Ensuring all software flows appropriately through various SDLC gates becomes complicated when the inventory is unknown. Without a data classification scheme, prioritizing projects and making a PII inventory is effectively impossible. FakeFirm should immediately begin an inventory initiative that accounts for all applications in the SSG's purview, ensures each application receives a criticality rating, and associates each application with the levels of data levels. Over the next 12 months, expand the inventory to include the open source used and the current security status for each application. In addition, begin including software security waiver information for each application.

- Training—FakeFirm has a small amount of software security training that it uses to improve awareness. However, FakeFirm provides the training only in person, only to developers, and only at onboarding time. Over the next six months, FakeFirm should begin providing on-demand, role-based software security training to all roles involved in the SDLC. This will increase global awareness and increase technical skill in the major engineering roles such as requirements analysis, architecture, development, and testing. FakeFirm should also investigate the opportunity to provide training in the developer environment using IDE-based tools.

In our experience, it is better to have a well-rounded effort distributed across the SSF practices than to focus on a small number of practices. It is also important to remember that we have never observed all 112 activities in a single firm and such a feat is probably not a reasonable goal. A firm should always base activity selection—that is, resource allocation in the SSI—on actual need.

Appendix A: BSIMM Background

Where did BSIMM come from? The Building Security In Maturity Model (BSIMM) is the result of a multi-year study of real-world software security initiatives. We present the model as built directly out of data observed in 78 software security initiatives from firms including: Adobe, Aetna, ANDA, Autodesk, Bank of America, Black Knight Financial Services, BMO Financial Group, Box, Capital One, Cisco, Citigroup, Comerica, Cryptography Research, Depository Trust and Clearing Corporation, Elavon, EMC, Epsilon, Experian, Fannie Mae, Fidelity, F-Secure, HP Fortify, HSBC, Intel Security, JPMorgan Chase & Co., Lenovo, LinkedIn, Marks & Spencer, McKesson, NetApp, NetSuite, Neustar, Nokia, NVIDIA, PayPal, Pearson Learning Technologies, Qualcomm, Rackspace, Salesforce, Siemens, Sony Mobile, Symantec, The Advisory Board, The Home Depot, Trainline, TomTom, U.S. Bank, Vanguard, Visa, VMware, Wells Fargo, and Zephyr Health.

By quantifying the practices of many different organizations, we can describe the common ground they share as well as the variation that makes each unique. Our aim is to help the wider software security community plan, carry out, and measure initiatives of their own. The BSIMM is not a "how to" guide, nor is it a one-size-fits-all prescription. Instead, the BSIMM is a reflection of the software security state of the art.

We recorded observations from these firms using our Software Security Framework (SSF, see Figure F.1) as the basis for our interviews. The SSF comprises four domains and 12 practices.

- In the governance domain, the strategy and metrics practice encompasses planning, assigning roles and responsibilities, identifying software security goals, determining budgets, and identifying metrics and gates. The compliance and policy practice focuses on identifying controls for compliance regimens such as PCI DSS and HIPAA, developing contractual controls such as service level agreements to help control COTS and out-sourced software risk, setting organizational software security policy, and auditing against that policy. Training has always played a critical role in software security because software developers and architects often start with very little security knowledge.

- The intelligence domain creates organization-wide resources. Those resources are divided into three practices. Attack models capture information used to think like an attacker: threat modeling, abuse case development and refinement, data classification, and technology-specific attack patterns. The security features and design practice is charged with creating usable security patterns for major security controls (meeting the standards defined in the next practice), building middleware frameworks for those controls, and creating and publishing other proactive security guidance. The standards and requirements practice involves eliciting explicit security requirements from the organization, determining which COTS to recommend, building standards for major security controls (such as authentication, input validation, and so on), creating security standards for technologies in use, and creating a standards review board.

- The SSDL Touchpoints domain is probably the most familiar of the four. This domain includes the essential software security best practices integrated into the SDLC. Two important software security capabilities are architecture analysis and code review. Architecture analysis encompasses capturing software architecture in concise diagrams, applying lists of risks and threats, adopting a process for review (such as STRIDE or Architectural Risk Analysis), and building an assessment and remediation plan for the organization. The code review practice includes use of code review tools, development of tailored rules, customized profiles for tool use by different roles (for example, developers versus auditors), manual analysis, and tracking/measuring results. The security testing practice is concerned with pre-release testing including integrating security into standard quality assurance processes. The practice includes use of black box security tools (including fuzz testing) as a smoke test in QA, risk-driven white box testing, application of the attack model, and code coverage analysis. Security testing focuses on vulnerabilities in construction.

- By contrast, in the deployment domain, the penetration testing practice involves more standard outside—in testing of the sort carried out by security specialists. Penetration testing focuses on vulnerabilities in final configuration, and provides direct feeds to defect management and mitigation. The software environment practice concerns itself with OS and platform patching, web application firewalls, installation and configuration documentation, application monitoring, change management, and ultimately code signing. Finally, the configuration management and vulnerability management practice concerns itself with patching and updating applications, version control, defect tracking and remediation, and incident handling.

What is the BSIMM's purpose? The BSIMM quantifies the activities carried out by real software security initiatives. Because these initiatives make use of different methodologies and different terminology, the BSIMM requires a framework that allows us to describe all of the initiatives in a uniform way. Our Software Security Framework (SSF) and activity descriptions provide a common vocabulary for explaining the salient elements of a software security initiative, thereby allowing us to compare initiatives that use different terms, operate at different scales, exist in different vertical markets, or create different work products.

We classify our work as a maturity model because improving software security almost always means changing the way an organization works—something that doesn't happen overnight. We understand that not all organizations need to achieve the same security goals, but we believe all organizations can benefit from using the same measuring stick.

We created the BSIMM in order to learn how software security initiatives work and to provide a resource for people looking to create or improve their own software security initiative. In general, every firm creates their software security initiative with some high-level goals in mind. The BSIMM is appropriate if your business goals for software security include:

- Informed risk management decisions
- Clarity on what is "the right thing to do" for everyone involved in software security
- Cost reduction through standard, repeatable processes
- Improved code quality

By clearly noting objectives and by tracking practices with metrics tailored to your own initiative, you can use the BSIMM as a measurement tool to guide your own software security initiative.

Why do you call it BSIMM6? BSIMM is an "observational" model for which we started gathering data in 2008. That is, it is a descriptive model rather than a prescriptive model. BSIMM does not tell you what you should do; rather, it tells you what the BSIMM community is doing. Put another way, BSIMM is not a set of "best practices" as defined by some committee for some generic problem. Rather, BSIMM is a set of "actual practices" being performed on a daily basis by forward-thinking firms. We update the model approximately every year and BSIMM6 is the sixth such update.

What new terminology have you introduced? Nomenclature has always been a problem in computer security, and software security is no exception. A number of BSIMM terms have particular meanings for us and here are some of the most important:

- Activity—Actions carried out or facilitated by the SSG as part of a practice. We divide activities into three levels. Each activity is directly associated with an objective.

- Domain—One of the four major groupings in the Software Security Framework. The domains are governance, intelligence, SSDL touchpoints, and deployment.

- Practice—One of the twelve categories of BSIMM activities. Each domain in the Software Security Framework has three practices. Activities in each practice are divided into three levels corresponding to maturity.

- Satellite—A group of interested and engaged developers, architects, software managers, and testers who have a natural affinity for software security and are organized and leveraged by a software security initiative.

- Secure Software Development Lifecycle (SSDL)—Any SDLC with integrated software security checkpoints and activities.

- Security Development Lifecycle (SDL)—A term used by Microsoft to describe their Secure Software Development Lifecycle.

- Software Security Framework (SSF)—The basic structure underlying the BSIMM, comprising twelve practices divided into four domains.

- Software Security Group (SSG)—The internal group charged with carrying out and facilitating software security. We have observed that step one of a software security initiative is forming an SSG.

- Software Security Initiative—An organization-wide program to instill, measure, manage, and evolve software security activities in a coordinated fashion. Also known in the literature as an Enterprise Software Security Program (see Chapter 10 of the book, *Software Security*).

How should I use the BSIMM? The BSIMM is a measuring stick for software security. The best way to use the BSIMM is to compare and contrast your own initiative with the data we present. You can then identify goals and objectives of your own and look to the BSIMM to determine which further activities make sense for you.

The BSIMM data show that high maturity initiatives are well rounded—carrying out numerous activities in all twelve of the practices described by the model. The model also describes how mature software security initiatives evolve, change, and improve over time.

Instilling software security into an organization takes careful planning and always involves broad organizational change. By using the BSIMM as a guide for your own software security initiative, you can leverage the many years of experience captured in the model. You should tailor the implementation of the activities the BSIMM describes to your own organization (carefully considering your objectives). Note that no organization carries out all of the activities described in the BSIMM.

The following are the most common uses for the BSIMM:

- As a measuring stick to facilitate apples-to-apples comparisons between firms, business units, vertical markets, and so on

- As a way to measure an initiative's improvement over time

- As a way to objectively gather data on current software security activity and use it to drive budgets and change

- As a way to understand software security maturity in vendors, business partners, acquisitions, and so on

- As a way to understand how the software security discipline is evolving worldwide

- As a way to become part of a private community that discusses issues and solutions

Who should use the BSIMM? The BSIMM is appropriate for anyone responsible for creating and executing a software security initiative. We have observed that successful software security initiatives are usually run by senior executives who report to the highest levels in an organization. These executives lead an internal group that we call the Software Security Group (SSG), charged with directly executing or facilitating the activities described in the BSIMM. We wrote the BSIMM with the SSI and SSG leadership in mind.

How do I construct a software security initiative? Of primary interest is identifying and empowering a senior executive to manage operations, garner resources, and provide political cover for a software security initiative. Grassroots approaches to software security sparked and led solely by developers and their direct managers have a poor record of accomplishment in the real world. Likewise, initiatives spearheaded by resources from an existing network security group often run into serious trouble when it comes time to interface with development groups. By identifying a senior executive and putting him or her in charge of software security directly, you address two management 101 concerns—accountability and empowerment. You also create a place in the organization where software security can take root and begin to thrive.

The second most important role in a software security initiative after the senior executive is that of the Software Security Group. Every single one of the 78 programs we describe in the BSIMM has an SSG. Successfully carrying out the activities in the BSIMM successfully without an SSG is very unlikely (and we haven't observed this in the field), so create an SSG as you start working to adopt the BSIMM activities. The best SSG members are software security people, but software security people are often impossible to find. If you must create software security types from scratch, start with developers and teach them about security.

Though no two of the 78 firms we examined had exactly the same SSG structure (suggesting that there is no one set way to structure an SSG), we did observe some commonalities that are worth mentioning. At the highest level of organization, SSGs come in three major flavors: those organized according to technical SDLC duties, those organized by operational duties, and those organized according to internal business units. Some SSGs are highly distributed across a firm, and others are very centralized and policy-oriented. If we look across all of the SSGs in our study, there are several common "subgroups" that are often observed: people dedicated to policy, strategy, and metrics; internal "services" groups that (often separately) cover tools, penetration testing, and middleware development plus shepherding; incident response groups; groups responsible for training development and delivery; externally-facing marketing and communications groups; and, vendor-control groups.

Of course, all other stakeholders also play important roles. These include:

- Builders, including developers, architects, and their managers must practice security engineering, ensuring that the systems that we build are defensible and not riddled with holes. The SSG will interact directly with builders when they carry out the activities described in the BSIMM. As an organization matures, the SSG usually attempts to empower builders so that they can carry out most of the BSIMM activities themselves with the SSG helping in special cases and providing oversight. In this version of the BSIMM, we often don't explicitly point out whether a given activity is to be carried out by the SSG or by developers or by testers, although in some cases we do attempt to clarify responsibilities in the goals associated with activity levels within practices. You should come up with an approach that makes sense for your organization and takes into account workload and your software lifecycle.

- Testers concerned with routine testing and verification should do what they can to keep a weather eye out for security problems. Some of the BSIMM activities in the Security Testing practice can be carried out directly by QA.

- Operations people must continue to design reasonable networks, defend them, and keep them up. As you will see in the Deployment domain of the SSF, software security does not end when software is shipped, deployed, or otherwise made available to clients and partners.

- Administrators must understand the distributed nature of modern systems and begin to practice the principle of least privilege, especially when it comes to applications they host or attach to as services in the cloud.

- Executives and middle management, including Line of Business owners and Product Managers, must understand how early investment in security design and security analysis affects the degree to which users will trust their products. Business requirements should explicitly address security needs. Any sizeable business today depends on software to work. Software security is a business necessity.

- Vendors, including those who supply COTS, custom software, and software-as-a-service, are increasingly subjected to SLAs and reviews (such as vBSIMM) that help ensure products are the result of a secure SDLC.

Am I now part of a BSIMM group? The firms participating in the BSIMM Project make up the BSIMM Community. A moderated private mailing list allows participating SSG leaders to discuss solutions with those who face the same issues, discuss strategy with someone who has already addressed an issue, seek out mentors from those are farther along a career path, and band together to solve hard problems.

The BSIMM Community also hosts annual private conferences where representatives from each firm gather in an off-the-record forum to discuss software security initiatives.

The BSIMM website (http://bsimm.com) includes a credentialed BSIMM Community section where we post some information from the conferences, working groups, and mailing list-initiated studies.

Appendix B: BSIMM Activities

This appendix contains a summary table of activities for each of the 12 BSIMM practices.

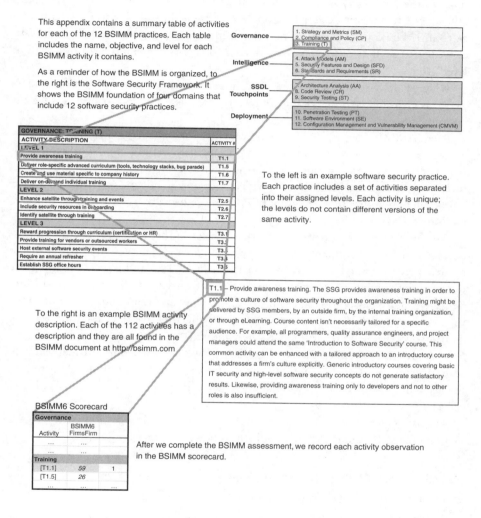

This appendix contains a summary table of activities for each of the 12 BSIMM practices. Each table includes the name, objective, and level for each BSIMM activity it contains.

As a reminder of how the BSIMM is organized, to the right is the Software Security Framework. It shows the BSIMM foundation of four domains that include 12 software security practices.

Governance
- 1. Strategy and Metrics (SM)
- 2. Compliance and Policy (CP)
- 3. Training (T)

Intelligence
- 4. Attack Models (AM)
- 5. Security Features and Design (SFD)
- 6. Standards and Requirements (SR)

SSDL Touchpoints
- 7. Architecture Analysis (AA)
- 8. Code Review (CR)
- 9. Security Testing (ST)

Deployment
- 10. Penetration Testing (PT)
- 11. Software Environment (SE)
- 12. Configuration Management and Vulnerability Management (CMVM)

GOVERNANCE: TRAINING (T)

ACTIVITY DESCRIPTION	ACTIVITY #
LEVEL 1	
Provide awareness training	T1.1
Deliver role-specific advanced curriculum (tools, technology stacks, bug parade)	T1.5
Create and use material specific to company history	T1.6
Deliver on-demand individual training	T1.7
LEVEL 2	
Enhance satellite through training and events	T2.5
Include security resources in onboarding	T2.6
Identify satellite through training	T2.7
LEVEL 3	
Reward progression through curriculum (certification or HR)	T3.1
Provide training for vendors or outsourced workers	T3.2
Host external software security events	T3.3
Require an annual refresher	T3.4
Establish SSG office hours	T3.5

To the left is an example software security practice. Each practice includes a set of activities separated into their assigned levels. Each activity is unique; the levels do not contain different versions of the same activity.

T1.1 – Provide awareness training. The SSG provides awareness training in order to promote a culture of software security throughout the organization. Training might be delivered by SSG members, by an outside firm, by the internal training organization, or through eLearning. Course content isn't necessarily tailored for a specific audience. For example, all programmers, quality assurance engineers, and project managers could attend the same 'Introduction to Software Security' course. This common activity can be enhanced with a tailored approach to an introductory course that addresses a firm's culture explicitly. Generic introductory courses covering basic IT security and high-level software security concepts do not generate satisfactory results. Likewise, providing awareness training only to developers and not to other roles is also insufficient.

To the right is an example BSIMM activity description. Each of the 112 activities has a description and they are all found in the BSIMM document at http://bsimm.com

BSIMM6 Scorecard

Governance		
Activity	BSIMM6 FirmsFirm	
...	...	
...	...	
Training		
[T1.1]	59	1
[T1.5]	26	
...	...	...

After we complete the BSIMM assessment, we record each activity observation in the BSIMM scorecard.

The assigned levels are also embedded in the activity numeric identifiers (e.g., SM"2".1 is a Strategy & Metrics activity at level 2). For more detail on each activity, read the BSIMM document at https://www.bsimm.com/download/ (registration not required). Level assignment for each activity stems from its frequency of occurrence in the BSIMM data pool. The most frequently observed activities are generally in level 1, while those activities observed infrequently are in level 3. Changes in the BSIMM data pool over time may result in promoting or demoting activities to other levels, such as promoting from level 2 to level 3 or demoting from level 2 to level 1.

When an activity moves to a new level, it receives a new numeric identifier and its previous identifier is retired. For example, if XX2.2 is promoted to level 3, XX2.2 is not reused later.

Each BSIMM activity is unique. There are no cases where, for example, one activity requires the SSG to do something to 80% of the portfolio and another activity requires the SSG to do the same thing to a larger percentage of the portfolio. Therefore, regardless of the total effort expended, focusing on only one or two activities in a practice will not improve the total BSIMM score because we aren't observing any additional activities.

As we observe new software security activities in the field, they become candidates for inclusion in the model. If we observe a candidate activity not yet in the model, we determine based on previously captured data and BSIMM mailing list queries how many firms probably carry out that activity. If the answer is multiple firms, we take a closer look at the proposed activity and figure out how it fits with the existing model. If the answer is only one firm, we table the candidate activity as too specialized. Furthermore, if the candidate activity replicates an existing activity or simply refines an existing activity, we drop it from consideration. If several firms carry out the activity today and the activity is not simply a refinement of an existing activity, we will consider it for inclusion in the next BSIMM release.

The list below provides all changes to the BSIMM model since inception:
From BSIMM to BSIMM2, we made the following changes:

- T2.3 Require annual refresher became T3.4

- CR1.3 was removed from the model

- CR2.1 Use automated tools along with manual review became CR1.4

- SE2.1 Use code protection became SE3.2

- SE3.1 Use code signing became SE2.4

From BSIMM2 to BSIMM3, we made the following changes:

- SM1.5 Identify metrics and drive initiative budgets with them became SM2.5
- SM2.4 Require security sign-off became SM1.6
- AM2.3 Gather attack intelligence became AM1.5
- ST2.2 Allow declarative security/security features to drive tests became ST1.3
- PT2.1 Use pen testing tools internally became PT1.3

From BSIMM3 to BSIMM4, we made the following changes:

- T2.1 Role-based curriculum became T1.5
- T2.2 Company history in training became T1.6
- T2.4 On-demand CBT became T1.7
- T1.2 Security resources in onboarding became T2.6
- T1.4 Identify satellite with training became T2.7
- T1.3 Office hours became T3.5
- AM2.4 Build internal forum to discuss attacks became AM1.6
- CR2.3 Make code review mandatory became CR1.5
- CR2.4 Use centralized reporting became CR1.6
- ST1.2 Share security results with QA became ST2.4
- SE2.3 Use application behavior monitoring and diagnostics became SE3.3
- CR3.4 Automate malicious code detection added to model
- CMVM3.3 Simulate software crisis added to model

From BSIMM4 to BSIMM-V, we made the following changes:

- SFD2.3 Find and publish mature design patterns from the organization became SFD3.3
- SR2.1 Communicate standards to vendors became SR3.2
- CR3.1 Use automated tools with tailored rules became CR2.6
- ST2.3 Begin to build and apply adversarial security tests (abuse cases) became ST3.5
- CMVM3.4 Operate a bug bounty program added to model

From BSIMM-V to BSIMM6, we made the following changes:

- SM1.6 Require security sign-off became SM2.6
- SR1.4 Create secure coding standards became SR2.6
- ST3.1 Include security tests in QA automation became ST2.5
- ST3.2 Perform fuzz testing customized to application APIs became ST2.6

On the following pages are tables showing the activities included in each BSIMM6 practice.

a

GOVERNANCE: STRATEGY AND METRICS (SM)			
ACTIVITY DESCRIPTION	ACTIVITY #	OBSERVATIONS	PARTICIPANT %
LEVEL 1			
Publish process (roles, responsibilities, plan), evolve as necessary	SM1.1	41	53%
Create evangelism role and perform internal marketing	SM1.2	40	51%
Educate executives	SM1.3	36	46%
Identify gate locations, gather necessary artifacts	SM1.4	66	85%
LEVEL 2			
Publish data about software security internally	SM2.1	36	46%
Enforce gates with measurements and track exceptions	SM2.2	29	37%
Create or grow a satellite	SM2.3	30	38%
Identify metrics and use them to drive budgets	SM2.5	17	22%
Require security sign-off	SM2.6	29	37%
LEVEL 3			
Use an internal tracking application with portfolio view	SM3.1	15	19%
Run an external marketing program	SM3.2	7	9%

b

GOVERNANCE: COMPLIANCE AND POLICY (CP)			
ACTIVITY DESCRIPTION	ACTIVITY #	OBSERVATIONS	PARTICIPANT %
LEVEL 1			
Unify regulatory pressures	CP1.1	45	58%
Identify PII obligations	CP1.2	61	78%
Create Policy	CP1.3	41	53%
LEVEL 2			
Identify PII data inventory	CP2.1	19	24%
Require security sign-off for compliance-related risk	CP2.2	23	29%
Implement and track controls for compliance	CP2.3	25	32%
Paper all vendor contracts with software security SLAs	CP2.4	29	37%
Ensure executive awareness of compliance and privacy obligations	CP2.5	33	42%
LEVEL 3			
Create regulator eye-candy	CP3.1	18	23%
Impose policy on vendors	CP3.2	11	14%
Drive feedback from SSDL data back to policy	CP3.3	6	8%

c

GOVERNANCE: TRAINING (T)			
ACTIVITY DESCRIPTION	ACTIVITY #	OBSERVATIONS	PARTICIPANT %
LEVEL 1			
Provide awareness training	T1.1	59	76%
Deliver role-specific advanced curriculum (tools, technology stacks, bug parade)	T1.5	26	33%
Create and use material specific to company history	T1.6	17	22%
Deliver on-demand individual training	T1.7	36	46%
LEVEL 2			
Enhance satellite through training and events	T2.5	10	13%
Include security resources in onboarding	T2.6	15	19%
Identify satellite through training	T2.7	6	8%
LEVEL 3			
Reward progression through curriculum (certification or HR)	T3.1	3	4%
Provide training for vendors or outsourced workers	T3.2	3	4%
Host external software security events	T3.3	3	4%
Require an annual refresher	T3.4	8	10%
Establish SSG office hours	T3.5	4	5%

d

INTELLIGENCE: ATTACK MODELS (AM)			
ACTIVITY DESCRIPTION	ACTIVITY #	OBSERVATIONS	PARTICIPANT %
LEVEL 1			
Build and maintain a top N possible attacks list	AM1.1	17	22%
Create a data classification scheme and inventory	AM1.2	51	65%
Identify potential attackers	AM1.3	31	40%
Collect and publish attack stories	AM1.4	8	10%
Gather and use attack intelligence	AM1.5	46	59%
Build an internal forum to discuss attacks	AM1.6	11	14%
LEVEL 2			
Build attacks patterns and abuse cases tied to potential attackers	AM2.1	6	8%
Create technology-specific attack patterns	AM2.2	8	10%
LEVEL 3			
Have a science team that develops new attack methods	AM3.1	4	5%
Create and use automation to do what attackers will do	AM3.2	2	3%

e

INTELLIGENCE: SECURITY FEATURES AND DESIGN (SFD)			
ACTIVITY DESCRIPTION	ACTIVITY #	OBSERVATIONS	PARTICIPANT %
LEVEL 1			
Build and publish security features	SFD1.1	61	78%
Engage SSG with architecture	SFD1.2	59	76%
LEVEL 2			
Build secure-by-design middleware frameworks and common libraries	SFD2.1	24	31%
Create SSG capability to solve difficult design problems	SFD2.2	39	50%
LEVEL 3			
Form a review board or central committee to approve and maintain secure design patterns	SFD3.1	8	10%
Require use of approved security features and frameworks	SFD3.2	11	14%
Find and publish mature design patterns from the organization	SFD3.3	2	3%

f

INTELLIGENCE: STANDARDS AND REQUIREMENTS (SR)			
ACTIVITY DESCRIPTION	ACTIVITY #	OBSERVATIONS	PARTICIPANT %
LEVEL 1			
Create security standards	SR1.1	57	73%
Create a security portal	SR1.2	50	64%
Translate compliance constraints to requirements	SR1.3	52	67%
LEVEL 2			
Create a standards review board	SR2.2	27	35%
Create standards for technology stacks	SR2.3	21	27%
Identify open source	SR2.4	19	24%
Create SLA boilerplate	SR2.5	20	26%
User secure coding standards	SR2.6	23	29%
LEVEL 3			
Control open source risk	SR3.1	6	8%
Communicate standards to vendors	SR3.2	11	14%

g

SSDL TOUCHPOINTS: ARCHITECTURE ANALYSIS (AA)			
ACTIVITY DESCRIPTION	ACTIVITY #	OBSERVATIONS	PARTICIPANT %
LEVEL 1			
Perform security feature review	AA1.1	67	86%
Perform design review for high-risk applications	AA1.2	29	37%
Have SSG lead design review efforts	AA1.3	22	28%
Use a risk questionnaire to rank applications	AA1.4	46	59%
LEVEL 2			
Define and use AA process	AA2.1	12	15%
Standardize architectural descriptions (including data flow)	AA2.2	9	12%
Make SSG available as AA resource or mentor	AA2.3	13	17%
LEVEL 3			
Have software architects lead design review efforts	AA3.1	6	8%
Drive analysis results into standard architecture patterns	AA3.2	1	1%

h

SSDL TOUCHPOINTS: CODE REVIEW (CR)			
ACTIVITY DESCRIPTION	ACTIVITY #	OBSERVATIONS	PARTICIPANT %
LEVEL 1			
Use a top N bugs list (real data preferred)	CR1.1	18	23%
Have SSG perform ad hoc review	CR1.2	53	68%
Use automated tools along with manual review	CR1.4	55	71%
Make code review mandatory for all projects	CR1.5	24	31%
Use centralized reporting to close the knowledge loop and drive training	CR1.6	27	35%
LEVEL 2			
Enforce coding standards	CR2.2	7	9%
Assign tool mentors	CR2.5	20	26%
Use automated tools with tailored rules	CR2.6	16	21%
LEVEL 3			
Build a factory	CR3.2	3	4%
Build a capability for eradicating specific bugs from the entire codebase	CR3.3	5	6%
Automate malicious code detection	CR3.4	3	4%

i

SSDL TOUCHPOINTS: SECURITY TESTING (ST)			
ACTIVITY DESCRIPTION	ACTIVITY #	OBSERVATIONS	PARTICIPANT %
LEVEL 1			
Ensure QA supports edge/boundary value condition testing	ST1.1	61	78%
Drive tests with security requirements and security features	ST1.3	66	85%
LEVEL 2			
Integrate black box security tools into the QA process	ST2.1	24	31%
Share security results with QA	ST2.4	8	10%
Include security tests in QA automation	ST2.5	10	13%
Perform fuzz testing customized to application APIs	ST2.6	11	14%
LEVEL 3			
Drive tests with risk analysis results	ST3.3	4	5%
Leverage coverage analysis	ST3.4	4	5%
Begin to build and apply adversarial security tests (abuse cases)	ST3.5	5	6%

j

DEPLOYMENT: PENETRATION TESTING (PT)			
ACTIVITY DESCRIPTION	ACTIVITY #	OBSERVATIONS	PARTICIPANT %
LEVEL 1			
Use external penetration testers to find problems	PT1.1	69	88%
Feed results to the defect management and mitigation system	PT1.2	47	60%
Use penetration testing tools internally	PT1.3	47	60%
LEVEL 2			
Provide penetration testers with all available information	PT2.2	20	26%
Schedule periodic penetration tests for application coverage	PT2.3	17	22%
LEVEL 3			
Use external penetration testers to perform deep-dive analysis	PT3.1	10	13%
Have the SSG customize penetration testing tools and scripts	PT3.2	8	10%

k

DEPLOYMENT: SOFTWARE ENVIRONMENT (SE)			
ACTIVITY DESCRIPTION	ACTIVITY #	OBSERVATIONS	PARTICIPANT %
LEVEL 1			
Use application intput monitoring	SE1.1	37	47%
Ensure host and network security basics are in place	SE1.2	69	88%
LEVEL 2			
Publish installation guides	SE2.2	31	40%
Use code signing	SE2.4	25	32%
LEVEL 3			
Use code protection	SE3.2	10	13%
Use application behavior monitoring and diagnostics	SE3.3	5	6%

DEPLOYMENT: CONFIGURATION MANAGEMENT & VULNERABILITY MANAGEMENT (CMVM)			
ACTIVITY DESCRIPTION	ACTIVITY #	OBSERVATIONS	PARTICIPANT %
LEVEL 1			
Create or interface with incident response	CMVM1.1	71	91%
Identify software defects found in operations monitoring and feed them back to dev.	CMVM1.2	73	94%
LEVEL 2			
Have emergency codebase response	CMVM2.1	64	82%
Track software bugs found in operations through the fix process	CMVM2.2	61	78%
Develop an operations inventory of applications	CMVM2.3	31	40%
LEVEL 3			
Fix all occurrences of software bugs found in operations	CMVM3.1	4	5%
Enhance the SSDL to prevent software bugs found in operations	CMVM3.2	6	8%
Simulate software crisis	CMVM3.3	6	8%
Operate a bug bounty program	CMVM3.4	3	4%

About Cigital

Cigital is one of the world's largest application security firms. We go beyond traditional testing services to help organizations find, fix, and prevent vulnerabilities in the applications that power their business. Our holistic approach to application security offers a balance of managed services, professional services, and products tailored to fit your specific needs. We don't stop when the test is over. Our experts also provide remediation guidance, program design services, and training that empower you to build and maintain secure applications.

Our proactive methods helps clients reduce costs, speed time to market, improve agility to respond to changing business pressures and threats, and focus resources where they are needed most. Cigital's managed services maximize client flexibility, while reducing operational friction and cost. Cigital gives organizations of any size access to the scale, security expertise, and practices needed to build a successful software security initiative.

Cigital is headquartered near Washington, D.C. with regional offices in the U.S., London, and India.

For more information, visit us at www.Cigital.com

Appendix G

Measures from Lifecycle Activities, Security Resources, and Software Assurance Principles

Measures are selected to provide justification that the steps performed to build a software system or product sufficiently address software assurance. Sampling from each lifecycle phase is one approach to determine that expectations are being met. Table G.1 provides examples for these measurements. Interviews with resources responsible for addressing security can provide evidence and example questions to solicit useful data are listed in Table G.2.

Confirmation that the principles for software assurance are appropriately addressed through security activities in the lifecycle can be verified using Table G.3. In addition, the principles can indicate measures that could be collected to provide evidence that a lifecycle is appropriately addressing software assurance (Table G.4).

Table G.1 *Examples of Lifecycle-Phase Measures*

Lifecycle Phase	Examples of Software Security Measures
Requirements Engineering	• Percentage of relevant software security principles reflected in requirements-specific actions (assuming that security principles essential for a given development project have been selected) • Percentage of security requirements that have been subject to analysis (risk, feasibility, cost–benefit, performance tradeoffs) prior to being included in the specification • Percentage of security requirements covered by attack patterns, misuse/abuse cases, and other specified means of threat modeling and analysis
Architecture and Design	• Percentage of architectural/design components subject to attack-surface analysis and measurement • Percentage of architectural/design components subject to architectural risk analysis • Percentage of high-value security controls covered by a security design pattern
Coding	• Percentage of software components subject to static and dynamic code analysis against known vulnerabilities and weaknesses • Percentage of defects discovered during coding where the defects were injected in architecture and design or injected in requirements specification • Percentage of software components subject to code integrity and handling procedures, such as chain-of-custody verification, anti-tampering, and code signing
Testing	• Percentage of defects discovered during testing where the defects were injected in coding, in architecture and design, or in requirements specification • Percentage of software components with demonstrated satisfaction of security requirements as represented by a range of testing approaches (functional, risk-based, fuzz, penetration, black box, white box, code coverage, etc.) • Percentage of software components that demonstrated required levels of attack resistance and resilience when subject to attack patterns, misuse/abuse cases, and other specified means of threat modeling and analysis

Table G.2 *Prototype Set of Questions for Software Security*[1]

	Security Risk Focus Area	Principles
1	Program Security Objectives	Are the program's security objectives realistic and achievable?
2	Security Plan	Does the plan for developing and deploying the system sufficiently address security?
3	Contracts	Do contract mechanisms with partners, collaborators, subcontractors, and suppliers sufficiently address security?
4	Security Process	Does the process being used to develop and deploy the system sufficiently incorporate security?
5	Security Task Execution	Are security-related tasks and activities performed effectively and efficiently?
6	Security Coordination	Are security activities within the program coordinated appropriately?
7	External Interfaces	Do work products from partners, collaborators, subcontractors, or suppliers meet security requirements?
8	Organizational and External Conditions	Are organizational and external conditions facilitating completion of security tasks and activities?
9	Event Management	Is the program able to identify and manage potential events and changing circumstances that affect its ability to meet its software security objectives?
10	Security Requirements	Do requirements sufficiently address security?
11	Security Architecture and Design	Do the architecture and design sufficiently address security?
12	Code Security	Is the code sufficiently secure?
13	Integrated System Security	Does the integrated system sufficiently address security?
14	Adoption Barriers	Have barriers to customer/user adoption of the system's security features been managed appropriately?
15	Operational Security Compliance	Does the system design comply with expected security policies, laws, and regulations?

(continued)

Table G.2 *Continued*

Security Risk Focus Area		Principles
16	Operational Security Preparedness	Are people prepared to maintain the system's security over time?
17	Product Security Risk Management	Is the approach for managing product security risk sufficient?

[1] From *Integrated Measurement and Analysis Framework for Software Security* [Alberts 2010].

Table G.3 *Mapping Between Security Risk Focus Areas and Principles for Software Security*[2]

Security Risk Focus Area		Principles	
1	Program Security Objectives	6	Well planned and dynamic; also influenced by principles 1 and 4
2	Security Plan	6	Well planned and dynamic; also influenced by principle 1
3	Contracts	2	Interactions; also influenced by principles 1 and 3
4	Security Process	6	Well planned and dynamic; also influenced by principles 1 and 3
5	Security Task Execution	3, 5, 7	Trusted dependencies, coordination, and education (assignment of authority), and measurable; also influenced by principles 1 and 2
6	Security Coordination	3, 5	Trusted dependencies, coordination, and education (assignment of authority); also influenced by principles 1 and 2
7	External Interfaces	2	Interactions; also influenced by principles 1 and 3
8	Organizational and External Conditions	1, 5	Risk; coordination and education; also influenced by principles 6 and 7
9	Event Management	4, 6	Attacker; well planned and dynamic; also influenced by principle 7
10	Security Requirements	1, 6, 7	Risk; well planned and dynamic; measurable; also influenced by principles 2 and 4

11	Security Architecture and Design	1, 6, 7	Risk; well planned and dynamic; measurable; also influenced by principles 2 and 4
12	Code Security	1, 6, 7	Risk; well planned and dynamic; measurable; also influenced by principles 2 and 4
13	Integrated System Security	1, 6, 7	Risk; well planned and dynamic; measurable; also influenced by principles 2 and 4
14	Adoption Barriers	5	Coordination and education
15	Operational Security Compliance	1, 6, 7	Risk; well planned and dynamic; measurable; also influenced by principles 2 and 4
16	Operational Security Preparedness	5	Coordination and education
17	Product Security Risk Management	1	Risk; also influenced by principle 7

[2] From "Principles and Measurement Models for Software Assurance" [Mead 2013b].

Table G.4 *The Seven Principles of Evidence*[3]

Principle	Description
Risk	• Number of active and latent threats, categorized • Incidents reported by category of threat • Likelihood of occurrence for each threat category • Financial and/or human safety estimate of impact for each threat category
Interactions (note that this category indicates a level of complexity that increases the risk of assurance problems)	• Component count • Interactions with other components per component • Interactions with other technologies per technology component • Human–computer interactions per individual interface

(continued)

Table G.4 *Continued*

Principle	Description
Trusted Dependencies	• Number of levels of subcontracting in the supply chain (in other words, have the subcontractors, in turn, execute subcontracts, and what is the depth of this activity) • Number of suppliers by level • Hierarchical and peer dependencies between suppliers by level • Number of (vetted) trusted suppliers in the supply chain by level
Measure of Attacker Interest	• Number of successful and attempted attacks by type/category • Number of attacks by degree of potential harm (usually expressed in dollars) • Number of attacks per component • Number of threats that could cause an immediate harmful outcome, such as taking down a company's website • Number of defects per function point (FP)
Coordination	• Number of vulnerabilities that have been categorized and prioritized as important by stakeholder • Number of mitigations assigned per owner • Number of interfaces in the product, by component as an indicator of complexity • Number of product threats versus mitigations deployed
Well Planned and Dynamic	• Number of vulnerabilities placed under operational assurance management • Number of identified application vulnerabilities where a solution has been assigned and implemented • Percent defect removal rate for operational threats monitored • Defect density for a standard time period, by component

Principle	Description
Measurable	• Count of measures used to help operational assurance management control • Count of measures used to support technical work • Defect removal efficiency for component/software product/system
	Count of measures and types used per lifecycle phase

[3] From *Common Weakness Enumeration: A Community-Developed Dictionary of Software Weakness Types* [MITRE 2014].

References

[Alberts 2010]

Alberts, Christopher J.; Allen, Julia H.; & Stoddard, Robert W. *Integrated Measurement and Analysis Framework for Software Security*. CMU/SEI-2010-TN-025. Software Engineering Institute, Carnegie Mellon University. 2010. http://resources.sei.cmu.edu/library/asset-view.cfm?AssetID=9369

[Mead 2013]

Mead, Nancy R.; Shoemaker, Dan; & Woody, Carol. Principles and Measurement Models for Software Assurance. *International Journal of Secure Software Engineering*. Volume 4. Number 1. April 2013.

[MITRE 2014]

MITRE. *Common Weakness Enumeration: A community-developed dictionary of software weakness types*. June 9, 2016 [accessed]. http://cwe.mitre.org/.

Index

A

access paths, 31

ACM (Association for Computing Machinery), 12

acquirers, 57

acquisition. *See* software acquisition

acquisition cases

    acquisition of COTS software, 151–158

    acquisition organization that specifies requirements as RFP, 151

    acquisition organization with typical client role, 151–156

activities (BSIMM), 310, 315–318

ADM (Asset Definition and Management) process area, 66

Alberts, Christopher, 13

alert originators (AOs), 14

alerts, emergency

    definition of, 14

    WEA (Wireless Emergency Alerts) case study

        description, 13–14

        mission thread example, 217–219

        preparation for mission thread analysis, 213–215

        security analysis, 219–224

        systems of systems, 213–215

alignment of risk, 8

Allspaw, John, 160

analysis. *See* gap analysis; malware analysis; risk analysis

analytics, Software Assurance Competency Model, 246

Android operating system, 175

AOs (alert originators), 14

Applications Security Advisory Board, proposed SwA competency mappings

    comprehensive list of job titles, 259–277

    initial list of job titles, 249–258

architecture, security measures for, 40, 326

Assessment Final Report (BSIMM)

    audience, 283

    comparison within vertical, 300–304

    conclusion, 305–307

    contacts, 283

    copyright page, 279–280

    data gathering, 290

    executive summary, 284–289

    high-water mark, 291–292

    list of figures, 282

    overview, 108–113

    practices, 293

    purpose, 283

    scorecard, 293

    table of contents, 281

assessment of risk, 21

Asset Definition and Management (ADM) process area, 66

Association for Computing Machinery (ACM), 12

assurance. *See* software assurance (SwA)

assurance cases, 10–13

assurance models, 121

assured systems, 40–42

attacks

    attacker interest, measures of, 330

    expecting, 8–9

audience (BSIMM Assessment Final Report), 283

audits, 9

automation of information security standards

J-K

L

M

W-X-Y-Z